GREENE & GREENE

Architecture as a Fine Art
Furniture and Related Designs

RANDELL L. MAKINSON

with photographs by Marvin Rand

GIBBS·SMITH PUBLISHER

Salt Lake City

Published by
Gibbs Smith, Publisher
P.O. Box 667
Layton, Utah 84041

Orders: (800) 748-5439
www.gibbs-smith.com

Printed and bound in the United States of America

Library of Congress Cataloging-in-Publication Data

Makinson, Randell L., 1932-
  Greene & Greene: architecture as a fine art : furniture and related designs /
Randell L. Makinson.--Combination ed.
      p. cm.
Includes bibliographical references and index.
  ISBN 0-58685-105-5
  1. Greene & Greene. 2. Architecture--United States--20th century. 3. Arts and
crafts movement--United States. 4. Furniture design--United States--History--
20th century. 5. Decorative arts--United States--History--20th century. I. Title.
NA737. G73 A4 2001
728'.37'0922--dc21
                              2001004581

Main stairway, Duncan/Irwin House, 1905. Photo by Thomas A. Heinz, © 2001 RLM Associates.

Preface

Randell L. Makinson, May 2001

The architectural principles, grace of composition, and quest for master craftsmanship that lay at the soul of the work of American architects Greene & Greene during the first three decades of the last century continue to inspire our society today. Not only has the study of their work and that of such contemporaries as William Morris, Charles Rennie Mackintosh, H. H. Richardson, Gustav Stickley, Louis Sullivan, and Frank Lloyd Wright focused attention on historic architecture, but it has also broadened our interests in preservation, handcrafted furniture, the decorative arts, and landscape—concepts at the core of the international Arts & Crafts movement. Now these ideas are a part of our lives, seen frequently on television, in interpretive or careful reproductions of their furnishings advertised widely in magazines, and seen in our architecture.

The current products of these influences vary considerably in quality, but there is little question that the principles espoused by this handful of progressive designers stand as valid in our contemporary world as when first practiced. The materials, technology, and labor force have changed, the resulting designs are a new language, yet the finest works in architectural design today are based on the very fundamental principles embraced by Charles and Henry Greene as well as the followers of William Morris in England, Western Europe, and the United States.

In terms of compositional grace and master craftsmanship, Greene & Greene remain unsurpassed. International interest in their lives and works continues to increase, offering challenges to scholars, collectors, and Arts & Crafts enthusiasts, and intriguing each new generation. New researchers, writers, and craftsmen in all mediums share their knowledge and enthusiasm through a growing number of conferences, lectures, books, and products. And one by one, new owners are carefully researching their Greene & Greene houses, and meticulously restoring them to their original integrity.

While the two seminal books herein continue to be the foundation of a Greene & Greene library, a fascination with the multifaceted aspects of the men and their work is unending and has been complemented by my more recent publications, *Greene & Greene: The Passion and the Legacy* (1998) and *Greene & Greene: The Blacker House* (2000) (done with Thomas A. Heinz and Brad Pitt), both issued by Gibbs Smith, Publisher. Currently, in collaboration with Thomas A. Heinz, the following studies are forthcoming: *Greene & Greene: Creating a Style; Greene & Greene: The Decorative Arts; Greene & Greene: The Furniture; Greene & Greene in Stone*, and *Greene & Greene: The Bungalows.*

Studying the spectrum of architects Charles and Henry Greene's work is important to a comprehensive understanding of American architecture and offers a wide range of opportunities for research. A growing number of scholars are bringing forth important analysis and new information. At the same time, the knowledge gained from the study of the Greenes' works in serious restoration is bringing about a new and better understanding of an architectural vocabulary that we now identify as a distinct Greene & Greene Style.

Charles W. Hollister House, 1898; restored in 2000.
Photo by Thomas A. Heinz, © 2001 RLM Associates.

East terrace, Robert R. Blacker House, 1907. Photo by Thomas A. Heinz, © 2001 RLM Associates.

GREENE & GREENE

Architecture as a Fine Art

RANDELL L. MAKINSON

with new photographs by Marvin Rand
and an Introduction by Reyner Banham

GIBBS·SMITH PUBLISHER

Salt Lake City

To my family

Copyright © 1977 by Gibbs Smith, Publisher
Library of Congress Card Catalog number: 76-57792
ISBN: 0-87905-126-4

Manufactured in the United States of America
01 00 99 98   15 14 13 12

Contents

Preface

Ralph Adams Cram could not have been more correct when he wrote in 1913 of the work of Charles and Henry Greene and their California contemporaries: "One must see the real and revolutionary thing in its native haunts of Berkeley and Pasadena to appreciate it in all its varied charm and striking beauty." My own real introduction to the work of Greene and Greene was such an unusual and intimate occasion that the enthusiasm and appreciation thus generated has decisively influenced my life for over twenty years. It began in 1954 while I was a student in the School of Architecture at the University of Southern California. I was standing behind the camera and tripod in the street in front of the Gamble house in Pasadena when Cecil Gamble came out to see what I was doing. When I explained my interest in the works of Greene and Greene, he and Mrs. Gamble graciously invited me to see the entire house and garden. This chance meeting was the beginning of my long association with Greene and Greene, the Gamble family and the Gamble house.

The finest illustrations are just no substitute for that first step into the living room of the Gamble house, the touch of the restored interiors of the Bentz house, the view of the autumn leaves against the shingles and clinker brick of the Thorsen house, the smell of fresh wood seventy years later when sand blasting has removed pink latex from the rough sawn timber ceiling of the van Rossem-Neill house, the curious way the upstairs bedroom of the Pratt house conveys the charms of an alpine ski-lodge and yet feels quite appropiate in the arid Ojai valley, and the symphony of one of the Greenes' magnificent structures in silhouette against the late California sunset.

After the excitement of my first day in the Gamble house, it was indeed frustrating to find only a few scattered but inspiring magazine articles about the work of Greene and Greene. As a result, the copies of the blueprints which the Gambles loaned to me became the initial documents of the research files from which my studies have developed and from which this book, a manuscript on the Greenes' furniture, my previous articles, and my work at The Gamble House have been derived. From those initial blueprints, my files have developed continually over the years, and have been made available to students, architects, home owners and scholars, many of whom have contributed to the public awareness of the Greenes' work through their own papers, theses and books. Portions of these files, along with documents graciously given by the Greene families, comprised the nucleus of the Greene and Greene Library.

Equally significant has been the placement of the Gamble home in the public domain. This has given thousands of visitors a personal contact with the Greenes' work in its original context and has also provided the opportunity over the last decade for some of us to explore previously unknown elements of the Greenes' art which time, association and restoration have unfolded.

Through the years the initial interest in the Greenes' masterpieces has broadened to include a closer look at their earlier work, thus dispelling some popular misconceptions such as the supposed similarity in their work. While this idea stems from their repetitive use of similar materials and certain details, a serious review of each of their works exhibits considerable diversity because in each design the Greenes attempted with an almost religious zeal to meet the challenge of each new site and to adapt their plans to the attitudes and lifestyles of each client.

Furthermore, we have placed too much emphasis on the larger and more costly structures and given too little credit to the extremely important early years when the quickly evolving expression of the Greenes was emerging in the form of modest dwellings possessing extraordinary livability, grace and character. We have tended to pay too much attention to the Greenes' interest in the Orient, have allowed the photogeneity of the larger works to dominate short essays on the Greenes, have overlooked the diversity of site and floor planning among the various designs, and thus have not emphasized the extremely flexible nature of the Greenes' architectural vocabulary. Moreover, we have continually attempted to bracket the Greenes and their work into neatly bound eras, styles, titles or periods which, on closer examination, seem somewhat artifical or even misleading. At the same time, we have paid too little attention to Charles Sumner Greene and Henry Mather Greene as individual artists whose ability to complement and stimulate each other allowed the level of genius to blossom which endures as part of the architectural heritage we treasure today.

There has also been a tendency to identify Greene and Greene only with the shingle bungalow. While this period of their work separated them from most of their contemporaries and established their international acclaim, it represents but a short span of time in their architectural careers. Although the glamour of their extraordinary masterpieces of the years 1907 through 1909 has attracted the greatest attention of writers and photographers, it is in the work of 1903 and 1904 where Greene and Greene developed the architectural vocabulary which made the later refinements of the grand bungalows possible. It was during these two years that the Greenes finally became completely at ease and began building with simple materials and strong basic convictions an architectural style which quickly influenced and changed American home design.

Although in the two decades of my involvement with the Greene and Greene legacy there have been changes in some of these attitudes, the initial intent of this book remains the same—to present a biographical look at Charles and Henry Greene and the events, attitudes and experiences behind the individual development of their art; to provide a visual demonstration of their changing artistic expression through a chronological sequence of illustrations; and to organize the material as an easy reference to the individual examples of their work. Unfortunately, space does not permit an elaboration of much of the detailed research on each project nor the inclusion of all the fine photographs developed by Marvin Rand.

Information and documentation comprising much of the research has been obtained from the Greene family, from the Environmental Design Library, University of California at Berkeley, and from the Avery Architectural Library, Columbia University.

I am particularly indebted to O'Neill Ford who first introduced me to the work of Greene and Greene; to Professor Robert Judson Clark, Professor Robert W. Winter, and Esther McCoy with each of whom I have been closely associated at various periods of my study; to Professor Reyner Banham for his timely and fresh look at the Arts and Crafts Movement in his introduction; to Marvin Rand whose photography of over two decades sensitively captures the Greenes' work; to the American Institute of Architects which granted me a Rehmann Fellowship for the early research; to the National Endowment for the Humanities for the grant which allowed for the study of the Greenes' furniture and related designs; to Margaret Nixon for her confidence, interest and careful evaluation, whose editing has enriched this manuscript; to Adrian and Joyce Wilson for the book design, to publishers Gibbs and Catherine Smith for their interest in this book, and to Richard Firmage for additional editing.

This entire study has been associated with my work at the University of Southern California and I wish to express my appreciation to my colleagues for their encouragement; and particularly to Dean A. Quincy Jones, Arthur B. Gallion, Sam T. Hurst, and Ralph Knowles, former deans of the School of Architecture and Fine Arts, Professors Emmet L. Wemple, Calvin C. Straub (now at Arizona State University), Dr. Frank C. Baxter; and to Philip Enquist and Peter Wohlfahrtstaetter; and to Donald Woodruff.

Additionally for their periodic council, time and cooperation: Professors David Gebhard, William H. Jordy, Adolph Placzek, Kenneth H. Cardwell, and Stephen Tobriner; and especially to those gifted writers of the late 1940s and early 1950s whose articles re-introduced and inspired a new appreciation of Greene and Greene—L. Morgan Yost and Jean Murray Bangs.

Very grateful thanks go to those special persons who have made this subject come alive through their time, association, experiences and personal contact with the work itself—the gracious members of the Greene families—particularly Nathaniel and Genevieve Greene, Isabelle and Alan McElwain, William and Harriott Greene, Henry D. and Ruth Greene, and Gordon and Betty Greene; those present owners of the structures who have the good fortune to be a part of our living heritage; those of my associates in the Docent Council of The Gamble House who have through special projects been of very personal assistance, and to many others, each of whom contributed in varying degrees over the years of my research.

For providing the opportunity for all to be enriched by a continuing and close relationship with the work of Greene and Greene my personal appreciation to James N. and Harriet Gamble and to the Gamble family heirs of Cecil and Louise Gamble for sharing the Gamble home with ongoing generations; and to Nancy Ullrich, Doris Gertmenian, Jane Unruh and Irene Wright without whose personal concern and help this book would not have been completed; to my father and my late mother; and to Ronald R. Chitwood and Paula and Harold Stewart whose continued encouragement, understanding, help and presence made my work possible.

Randell L. Makinson
Pasadena, 1976

Introduction

The works in architecture of Charles and Henry Greene look so totally at home in Southern California — and especially so in Pasadena—that it is often difficult to conceive of them as part of any nation-wide, let alone world-wide, movement...they seem so specific to that "Arroyo Culture" of which they are the chief ornaments and the true treasure-houses. Yet within two blocks of where I have begun to write these introductory words in Buffalo, New York, there is a house—that of Charles Rohlfs, woodcarver and furniture maker—whose white-stuccoed asymmetrical gable and spare craftsmanly woodwork would not have looked at all out of place had he built it in that same year, but on the tree-knotted slopes of the Arroyo Seco, in the landscape where the Greenes were building.

It is not appearance that creates the affinity between these widely spaced works, but rather the Arts and Crafts philosophy that inspired so many architects and designers around the world in those years. I have met it too in the very different woodlands of the suburbs of Berlin in the house of Hermann Muthesius, stern founder of modern design in Germany, but also an Arts and Crafts architect of real merit in those same years before the First World War. Behind all these men and their common stock of ideas and attitudes there lay, ultimately, the writings of that most eminent Victorian, John Ruskin, whose *Seven Lamps of Architecture* and, above all, *The Lamp of Truth*, had summoned artists, architects and craftsmen back to a doctrine of honesty in purpose, materials and manufacture.

Yet it is one thing to utter ringing phrases, and quite another thing to deliver the physical goods that make those phrases persuasive to the hand and eye. The man who said "Have nothing in your house that you do not know to be useful or believe to be beautiful," and then went on to make such things of use and beauty to stock his own house was William Morris, father of the Arts and Crafts Movement in England and inspirer of such parallel activities as Gustav Stickley's *Craftsman* magazine, Elbert Hubbard's "Roycrofters" and a whole tribe of others around the world. Morris was the physical begetter of the global movement whose spiritual father was Ruskin; he was also a late-Victorian upper-middle-class house-owner whose deeply-held socialist principles did not prevent him from being a tolerably successful businessman when he put his mind to it, a manufacturer of artistic and craftsmanly furnishings for sale.

For sale to whom? "To the filthy rich, God blast them!" stormed Morris one time, kicking a half-completed table in its craftsmanly slats. For if it was the doom of the Arts and Crafts to do little, in the long run, to improve the domestic and aesthetic conditions of the labouring poor in spite of its socialistic leanings, its triumph was in being taken up by the one stratum of society that could both understand it and afford its usually expensive handworked quality. The International Arts and Crafts Villa Movement —to which the works of the brothers Greene irresistibly belong—was to be the last, brief and almost perfect flowering of that striving bourgeois ethic of plain living and high thinking that had contributed so much to the life of the Victorian epoch, whose members had now discovered how to live high as well as think high by the neat compromise of buying luxurious comfort that could be excused as art. What's more—socially responsible art!

That may sound cynical; yet the world has since under-written the wisdom and morality of that comfortable compromise with approving enthusiasm—the reputation of Frank Lloyd Wright is proof of it. Wright's fame was first founded, and still chiefly rests, upon those houses of craftsmanly inspiration that he was building around Chicago in precisely those same years before the Great War. The affinity between "Wright and his California Contemporaries" was first authoritatively noted by Henry-Russell Hitchcock in 1958; and it already seems inconceivable that it should have been so little noticed before, but for it to be noticed and felt in the way that it is now noticed and felt—with or without cynicism!—has required some important adjustments in our historical perspective. If the work of the brothers Greene is now a matter of consuming international interest, then it is because we have a clearer view of them as a highly individual design team working almost idiosyncratically in a very particular place in an unrepeatable age, and at the same time as part of a world-wide community of men of craftsmanly inspiration who were often known to one another personally and visited one another like medieval monks on pilgrimages in order to compare notes and experiences.

To see them under either of these lights, we have to remove from that whole generation the historical illumination under which they have been almost exclusively presented to us so far—that of *Pioneers of the Modern Movement*. This noble category, which gives the title to Nikolaus Pevsner's truly world-changing book of 1936, gave the Greenes' contemporaries a place in history only as links in a chain, and their importance seems to have been conditional on the importance of the links on either side of them. Thus Hermann Muthesius is accorded great importance as the true link between Pevsner's two great heroes, William Morris and Walter Gropius, but only as a theorist; his work as an architect is not noted.

However, the categorisation of *pioneer* could be worse injustice than this. The English architect of that generation nearest in spirit to the Greenes was almost certainly that Quaker maniac for simplicity, C. F. A. Voysey. Grouped among the pioneers largely because he had the approval of Muthesius, Voysey later found himself honored as a father of Modern Architecture in a London exhibition of 1937. Angry and sickened, the old man thumped the floor with his cane, demanding "Why have they made *me* responsible for all that?" If Voysey felt himself responsible for anything at all, it would be for what Muthesius' English mentor, W. R. Lethaby, had called "our English free building," the natural succession to William Morris.

Now that Pioneership of the Modern Movement is seen by most radical younger historians as nothing to be proud of, it becomes easier—almost mandatory—to see and to emphasize their individualities, to turn once again to those really difficult cases like the Greenes who have always resisted categorisation and to treasure them for being unique, unclassifiable. It is already noticeable that even American historians are less eager to tidy them away under provincial variants of nationwide labels like *Late* Shingle Style or *Western* Stick Style. The Greenes in Pasadena are most worth studying as the Greenes in Pasadena—like Mackintosh in Glasgow or Wright in Oak Park — their historical importance is in their particularity, not their generality.

Yet what was their true generality; how can one speak of these men as a nation-wide or world-wide movement, over and above the fact that so many of them were acquainted, could travel to meet one another and saw one another's work in the newly risen international art magazines like the *Studio*? There was the community of theoretical background and moral commitment to honesty, it is true, but it usually takes more, something more concrete and tangible, to unite a body of architects or craftsmen. In the case of those Masters of the Modern Movement who succeeded the supposed pioneers for instance, it was their ability to make symbolic renderings of the Machine Age out of a few simple geometrical solids with flush white surfaces. By these forms they recognised one another from afar, even before they had time to compare theories and allegiances.

What seemed to unite the Craftsman generation more immediately than anything else must have been the recognition of aesthetic value enshrined in objects of material worth—whether that worth resided in the substance of the object, or in what had been wrought upon that substance by the craftsman's hand. It was an intensely Victorian attitude, of course, first properly elaborated by the pre-Raphaelite painters, in whose work spiritual worth seems to be guaranteed by the sheer labour that had been wrought upon the paint. The pre-Raphaelites had been Morris's first inspiration and contact with the world of art, and it must have been from them that he got that maxim about furnishing the house which was quoted above, and which Morris-mockers twist to read "Have nothing in your house that you do not believe to be rare or know to be expensive." At all events it is an attitude in which the house becomes a shrine for objects of well-wrought functional art, and the inhabitants the devoted worshippers. And it is an attitude that differs from that of the highly caricaturable vulgar Victorian collector of awful works of expensive 'fine' art, precisely in that word *functional*. These were objects of art to be sat upon, eaten off of, to hang clothes in, to arrange flowers in...and ultimately to inhabit. It was an attitude more fully embodied by the Greenes than by anyone else when—so legend insists—they incorporated pieces of jade from Mrs. Pratt's own collection in the light fittings of the Pratt house in Ojai...that indeed must have been a Lamp of Architecture that even John Ruskin would have to look up to!

This pre-occupation with highly valued hand-crafted objects of functional art seems also to have been what united these architects not only among themselves, but also with their clients and patrons. Typically—and from James McNeill Whistler onwards—the clients had been collectors of exotic ceramics, threw peasant shawls and Navaho rugs over their grand pianos, had their architects design them hand-forged fire-irons and door-furniture, and arranged their flowers exquisitely under lamps that were not always by Tiffany...because they might be the family jade!

By their deeds shall ye know them; their words can sometimes confuse the issue by transmuting the material into the purely aesthetic, the merely visual, as when Gustav Stickley characterized his Craftsman interiors thus: "Soft, rich, restful color based on the mellow radiance of wood tones...sparkling into the jewelled highlights given forth by copper, brass or embroideries." Come now, Old Craftsman, these things were surely not valued solely for the dabs of color or points of light they brought into brown wooden spaces? They were worth money, they could be possessed, they could be inherited, they were moveable and could be bought and sold.

In all too many cases, they were sold, not inherited. They have gone from their appointed places on shelf and plinth. These villas of art and craftsmanship—whether they were called villas, cottages, bungalows, *wohnhäuser* or Houses Beautiful does not matter here—were built during that last "Long Weekend" of middle-class affluence before the First World War, and very few of them stayed affluent for long after that war. The doom that waited upon that generation of patrons and clients will be touched on later, its immediate economic effect was to strip most of these houses of their moveable furnishings almost before the change in fashion that rendered most of them unsaleable and fit only for the junk-yard.

We cannot now know how much we have lost, but we can often see how totally we have lost it, and where we have lost it. The reputation of so many houses of this persuasion for being uninhabitably dark derives, as often as not, from the fact that the once-mellow radiance of wood tones has now lost the jewelled highlights of copper, brass and embroidery, and looks cavernously gloomy without the original points of focus for the view, delight for the eye, astonishment for the connoisseur. It was, in any case, a generation that used light marvellously—in that sense Stickley's purely visual description rings true—and what was dark was meant to be dark in order to give more point to what was meant to glow, gleam or glitter, or to add more depth of space because of the illumination beyond.

But rare now is the Frank Lloyd Wright interior that still has all its priceless objects of art and craft each ensconced as designed on pedestal, shelf, sill or mantel, shedding a refulgence of culture and *vertu* over its appointed space—and the nakedness without them is painful. By contrast, the completeness of an interior like that of the "winter cottage" the Greenes built for David Gamble in Pasadena is an eye-opener—the lights still shine in their appointed distribution in the broad spaces of the living room, silver gleams against a background of stained glass on the dining room sideboard, an embroidered panel takes the eye at the first landing of the staircase. It is an eye-opener into a backward view that is gentle and welcoming at first, but ultimately jolting and unsettling, as one is forced to realize how irrecoverable now is that lost world of artistic furnishing, tennis and touring cars.

Nostalgia stalks. It is all too easy to sentimentalize and romanticize that lost world. Americans cram unsuitable rooms with overbright galaxies of lovingly restored Tiffany lamps; a whole movement in Italy in the late fifties tried to regain the *tempi felici*—the happy days—of the early century by reviving the 'Liberty' style—the Italian version of the Arts and Crafts, give or take a curlicue, and named after the shop in London that had purveyed objects of craftsmanly value to most of Europe in those Golden Years before the War. The resultant Neo-Liberty style was at once dour and febrile, the designs as built and furnished never re-awoke to life, however subtle the sociological, historical and political analyses of the last high-bourgeois epoch that were trotted out to justify them.

You can't go back. Neo-Liberty produced some detailed scholarly studies of buildings by architects as diverse as Otto Wagner in Vienna and Raimondo d'Aronco in Turin —for which we must all be grateful—but in the end that wave of revivalism was a deception; too much has happened since, and irreversibly, for any of us to get back to that state of supposed innocence that white-haired Americans remember as "before the income tax came in," that Germans recall as "the days before the inflation," and for the inhabitants of Voysey's white-rendered houses is just "when we were still on the Gold Standard!"

Yet the temptation for any close historian of the period to appear, or become, a lamenter of past times is very powerful. The subject matter itself demands close and detailed study, and tends to resist the kind of large-scale generalization that preserves the longer historical perspective and prevents provincialism. So one must be wary of damning those devoted historians who are patiently restoring the period to clearer view, as men of old-fashioned and parochial vision. Julius Posener, who studies and attempts to preserve the villas of Muthesius around Berlin has no

grounds to be sentimental about a Germany that drove him to exile in Israel and the Far East. We may once have preferred the way an historian like Tom Howarth set out to prove Charles Rennie Mackintosh a pioneer of modern architecture, but we now tend to give our gratitude instead to those successive Principals of the Glasgow Art School that Mackintosh designed, for their persistence in haunting the sale-rooms of Scotland modestly buying in every stray piece of Mackintosh's work that came to the surface. And for scholarly studies of Arts and Crafts designers we would nowadays rather have a book like James Kornwulf's on Baillie Scott (which flies the word *pioneer* in its sub-title out of deference to a worn-out academic convention, but sees its subject in the world-wide context of his Arts and Crafts contemporaries).

But even that, in present circumstances, seems a geographically over-stretched view, because these designers and their works were so specific to their place that it remains difficult not to take a very short focus on them. Rare is the writer like Jean Murray Bangs who could still discuss the work of the Greenes with illuminating clarity even "from afar." More common, and commonly more useful at present is someone like Willbert Hasbrouck who has now devoted most of a lifetime as architect, scholar and editor-publisher to the *very* close study of the minutiae of the work of the Prairie School in the middle west or, to come closer indeed to the present subject, someone like Randell Makinson who for most of his active professional life has devoted himself to the study of the work of Greene and Greene—for the last decade literally from within!

Posener, Hasbrouck, Makinson are (or started as) practical architects. It is a characteristic of the designers of the Arts and Crafts that they tend to attract scholars who know, and care, how buildings are put together, how plumbed and wired and drained and ventilated. Frank Lloyd Wright, indeed, has suffered because his international fame and proneness to word-spinning have attracted to him the kind of word-smitten, iconography-hunting scholars who care for its visual impressions, and thus demean Wright merely to the status of an artist, rather than that most noble of craftsmen who from brute materials can create complete environments for the lives of men.

The glory and triumph of the architects of the Arts and Crafts persuasion was that the completeness of their environmental creations extended down to responsibility for even the smallest details of the physical matter that surrounded the lives lived within their houses. Given their beliefs and the tradition that supported those beliefs they could not simply make drawings of generalized forms and leave "intelligent sub-contractors" to work out the details. Few may have had such remarkably close relations with their craftsmen as the Greenes enjoyed with Peter Hall and his workshop in Pasadena, but all were concerned and involved in some way with the crafting of the smaller parts. If it is true in general that one will never get to understand architecture without "standing close to the brickwork," as the saying goes, to understand the architecture of the Arts and Crafts one must stand close enough to identify the wood with which the smallest joint is pegged. That is a kind of historiography that began to go out of style about the same time as the Arts and Crafts began to fade, but it must come back—is coming back—now that these men and their works are no longer accorded the rather provisional status of *pioneers*. Only a thorough brick-by-brick and stick-by-stick re-appraisal of every individual building in the setting of its own particular plot of ground and year (nay, month) of design can lay any secure foundation on which to erect a new general view to replace that discarded category of Pioneers of the Modern Movement.

Of course, when that new general view is finally offered, it will still have to include the concept of pioneership of modern architecture; the historical location of the whole generation, their associations with theorists and writers, their own teachings make it unavoidable, but it should now only be a minor sub-heading among their other works—an almost invisible one in the case of the Greenes—rather than their main historical label. In any case, it may ultimately appear that the label most truly belongs to their clients and patrons, not to the architects themselves.

James Marston Fitch once characterized the Greenes' clients thus:

...usually wealthy midwesterners of liberal Protestant or Quaker background. They belonged to that segment of opinion which supported national parks, woman's suffrage, progressive education, factory reform. They were involved in new theories of love and marriage, of birth control and child care, of diet and hygiene...

If we eliminate the specifically geographical or sectarian references from this passage we have a thumbnail sketch not just of the Greenes' patrons, but of those of the whole movement. More properly, perhaps, we should say that it is their patronesses who are described here, for the Arts and Crafts villa in all its precise local variants was, above all, the domain, the showcase, the stage set and perhaps the prison of those formidable gentlewomen who were, typically, Bernard Shaw's heroines, the "New Women." It was, I think, no accident that both in fiction (the *Forsyte Saga*) and in fact (Wright and Mamah Cheney) architects of this time got involved with clients' wives, because the wives were, more than at any previous time in the history of Western architecture, the true clients of the design process, and were now sufficiently educated and liberated to impose themselves in that role.

These ladies and their supporting (or long suffering) consorts certainly tended to see themselves as the wave of the future, and it was a future that extended well beyond the social concerns outlined by Fitch above, for it was a future which included the reform of the city as well. From the founding of Norman Shaw's Bedford Park in London's western suburbs in 1875, and similar settlements outside American cities of the same period, these liberal patrons had tended to cluster in suburbs of reforming intent, salubrious, moral or otherwise. Indeed Pasadena, where the Greenes practiced, can be seen as such a suburb, not of Los Angeles, but of the whole of industrialized North America. In these earnest enclaves, the new women and their clans admired the latest art movements, purchased the latest mechanical aids to elegant living (typically, these suburbs were where electric light and the telephone were first properly domesticated) and discussed in their various ways how the virtues of their suburban life-style and physical environment could be brought to all citizens.

Such simple and energetic futures were doomed even

while they were being conceived—when Frederick C. Robie commissioned a house with a three-car garage from Frank Lloyd Wright in 1908 he was proclaiming the death of the bicycle suburb in which he had an important stake since he was himself a manufacturer of bicycles! Such suicidal tendencies are typical of what must appear in retrospect to be a strikingly autodestructive culture, and the passage from Fitch quoted above gives a sequence of clues as to its self-destroying psychology. However conclusively the First World War may have ended the "Long Weekend," the very reforming zeal of these good liberal souls in their craftsmanly suburbs could only finish by undermining the state of leisured privilege in which they were able to cultivate their chosen arts and crafts. No matter how these proposed reforms were to be implemented, whether by direction, concensus or spontaneous popular action, they all implied major re-distributions of wealth and resources among the strata of society. One had, in fact, to be quite comfortably-off to enjoy the kind of life these splendidly simple houses could offer. No less than the luxury of wealth, the luxury of taste took money, and any major distribution of cash among the populace would threaten these enclaves of the simple life as much as more traditional strongholds of wealth.

Looking over the whole bundle of life-attitudes and expressed opinions that informed the world of the Arts and Crafts one finds that something like socialism was always part of the deal. It might be the hard-nosed Bismarckian welfare-statism to which Muthesius's hawkish patrons subscribed, it might be the tweedy, ale-quaffing egalitarianism of the William Morris connection in England, or it might be the mawkish idealization of such fetish figures as Pueblo Indians and Belgian peasants that runs through so many of the alleged works of art that blot the pages of the *Craftsman* magazine—but something like it seems always to be there.

We seem to be confronted with the extraordinary spectacle of a whole class of remarkably nice people determined, world-wide, to promote policies that would destroy their own way of life. What is equally striking is that when—as appears very clearly from H. Allen Brooks' study of *The Prairie School*—these nice people decided to retrench and survive, their chosen styles of architecture turned illiberal and conservative too. The villas designed by Muthesius become increasingly classicist as the nineteen-hundreds become the nineteen-teens, the Prairie School lost out to Neo-Colonial as its patronesses deserted it, and in Southern California the constituencies of all progressive liberal styles were usurped by the Spanish Colonial Churrigueresque introduced at the Pan-Pacific Exposition of 1915 in San Diego. The middle-classes decided to do their best to survive, and to dump the mood of expansive liberalism that had served the world well, even if it almost destroyed the class that invented it. The Arts and Crafts villa, especially in its Californian manifestation as the Bungalow, modestly relaxed and experimental, is a very fit and moving monument to a particular moment in the liberal tradition.

In its American manifestation, however, the architectural aspect of that tradition contains a component that is absent, or present only in pale reflection, elsewhere—even in Australia where, in Melbourne, the style of the Greenes took a brief hold among a landscape and a people not unlike California in many ways. Perhaps this short hold was kept brief by the fact that precisely this essentially American component was missing among a people of Anglo-Saxon origin who had not, however, experienced the subjugation of the North American continent.

For that missing component—which is a body of practice as well as a set of expressed attitudes and mental habits—is intimately derived from the process of making sense of the landscape of America, something which may be clearly felt, but is rarely easy to define or name. Clarification, if not revelation, came in my own case from the writing of the architectural historian Robert Winter, who himself lives in a craftsman house in the Arroyo in Pasadena. I am indebted to him in any case for the phrase "the Arroyo culture," but at one point in his essay in the catalogue of the exhibition *California Design 1910*, he associates with that culture the concept of "the Middle Landscape."

That concept has become well-known over the last decade through its use in Leo Marx's sensitive, one-sided but (appropriately) new-ground-breaking study of American culture, *The Machine in the Garden*. The book addresses itself to the early but perennial problem of all observers, prophets and critics of America: how to understand the American landscape. Is it a paradise given by God, or is it a wilderness to be tamed by man? The Middle Landscape is, and was, neither; it was what the Americans had done to America in taming the Wilderness just enough to make it enjoyable, and in stretching their given European sensibilities enough to perceive that part-tamed Wilderness as a Paradise Gained. The Middle Landscape, it might be argued, is what makes America American, and sets it apart, culturally, from all the other nations and territories of the world.

But the Middle Landscape is also the ordained abode (since they, one way and another, are its true creators) of those whom James Marston Fitch, in another book and another context, named as America's "Domesticated Utopians," those equally devoted women in the mould of Catherine Beecher who raised back-porch crafts and basic horticultural skills to the status of moral disciplines, never mind domestic arts. Out of this combination of pioneering homesteading and Good Housekeeping (sealed with moral approval) there finally came a kind of suburbia that does not exist anywhere else in the world.

The point is of critical importance, because it means that American Arts and Crafts architects built in a physical and cultural landscape that was denied their contemporaries elsewhere. There is a deep-seated sense in which European suburbs are a pollution committed upon the country by the town, but contrariwise there is a kind of mirror-image, grass-roots conviction that the American suburb is an attempt to call the country in to save the city. This was divined as early as the nineties by Ebenezer Howard, father of the Garden City movement, after his none-too profitable American trip. His Garden City — a phrase he certainly picked up in the United States—was a deliberate attempt to create townships of the Middle Landscape as a 'peaceful path to reform' for the ills and evils of metropolitan London. He created three such cities:Letchworth, Welwyn and Hampstead Garden suburb — this last most nearly, like, but still radically unlike, its probable American prototypes. Later, that great and perennial survivor of the Arts and Crafts, Frank Lloyd Wright, was to

offer his Middle Landscape Broadacre City to depression-stunned America as his own peaceful path to reform.

And in modern, nineteen-seventies, tract-house America, that Middle Landscape is where everybody believes they live. However cheapened, tawdry, plasticized, barn-boarded, homogenized and wood-grain aluminum-sided it may have become, this is still what foreigners find most alien, most enviable about the American way of life. Furthermore, it is still in essence, and in many of its practices, the kind of life first envisioned in Catherine Beecher's *American Woman's Home*, and later given its most desirable and authoritative form by the generation of Charles and Henry Greene. Is it too far-fetched to propose that the conspicuous craftsmanship of interiors like those by the Greenes was in some way the male equivalent of the womanly virtues of raising, picking, bottling and cooking your own produce—a domestic parity of esteem reflecting the advanced and equal role supposedly enjoyed by women in the frontier homestead. It may be far-fetched, but it is worth remembering that the place where you will most frequently read the word "craftsman" nowadays in America is as the brand-name for the do-it-yourself tools of a famous mail-order house. There is some matter in here somewhere; the word "craftsman" has a different ring, a whole peal of different rings, than what it has in Europe.

That could be argued—what seems beyond argument is that probably the most desirable embodiment of the half-tamed Middle Landscape that one might ever hope to inhabit is the picturesquely tumbled land on the sides of the Arroyo Seco in Pasadena. Its claims to special status among such Middle Landscapes were recognized as long ago as the mid-eighties of the last century, more than a decade before the brothers Greene began to build there. Those claims look even stronger now that the hand of man has wrought (for the most part) gently but decisively upon it, and has multiplied its flora with exotic growths like the olive, the eucalypt and the palm, to produce something that can be, at the right time and in the right light, uncannily like those first true and American visions of the Paradisal Wilderness, the "Peaceable Kingdom" depicted in the not-so-naive visions of the painter-preacher Edward Hicks.

Or, to phrase the whole matter more crudely but very much to our present point, American suburban houses, like those by the Greenes in Pasadena, have open-lawned front gardens, while their European contemporaries always have walled or hedged gardens. For the whole of the European tradition, and its near-Eastern forebears, Paradise had a wall set about it like the Garden of Eden after the Fall, and the entrance was gated and guarded. So the gardens of Muthesius's villas in Nicholassee have walls round them, as do the gardens of the houses by Mackintosh around Glasgow, and those of Voysey around London have walls or hedges. But none of the Craftsman period houses I have lived in or visited in America has a walled or hedged front lawn. These houses stand in Nature—or pretend to—like a farm house in its fields, more freely and more openly even than did Adam's house in Paradise. To have established such a relationship between the domestic scene at home and the natural scene beyond remains an extraordinary achievement, and one that gives every craftsman house in America (even the Rohlfs house in Buffalo which stands on a densely built street) a setting that makes it look bold and free, and its European contemporaries constrained and timid.

"But surely," the cultured European will cynically enquire, "none of the people who lived in these bold, free houses were, in fact, farmers and bottlers of home produce?" The answer is, frankly, "Almost entirely not," but the qualifying *almost* is an important one. Wright, as is well known, kept his contacts with the home farming community, and as many a student was later to find to his back-breaking cost, a Taliesin apprenticeship could involve an awful lot of gardening. More to the point, there actually were Craftsman Farms, duly recorded in the *Craftsman* magazine, and there were the Roycrofters and there were other and more tenuous connections that kept many American Arts and Crafts householders more nearly in touch with the arts of agriculture and horticulture than their European counterparts. It is difficult for a European like myself to know, ultimately, how much to make of these connections—were they simply a folk-memory of the unforgiving toil of Prairie farms that lent a decent humility to attitudes toward the world and nature, or were they self-consciously cultivated attitudes little different from those self-consciously cultivated by European liberals about "the peasantry" or "the labouring poor." Every genuine lover of the wilderness seems to have contained some elements of an opportunist Teddy Roosevelt politician; there was a gamut of attitudes to be run, and they ran it.

But it would be callow indeed to pretend that the great patrons of Craftsman architecture in the United States were anything but Big Bourgeoisie, in the original sense of "burghers" or "Townfolk." Wright's prime clients were in manufacturing, mail-ordering, and other unmistakably urban businesses. Two of the Greenes' four most conspicuous domestic clients were retired lumbermen, appropriately enough, but the other two were in oil and soap respectively. The first qualification for commissioning and enjoying this kind of architecture was to have the money to pay for it, and the second was to have the cultivation to desire it. Any Craftsman-period architect worth the name could, in fact, produce less expensive houses, and most of them occasionally went to some trouble to do so for clients whom they liked or believed in, but the works on which their reputations depend, like all the works on which architects' reputations depend, were made for "the filthy rich, God blast them!"

This is as true of the Greenes as of any of the others. Much as one may admire the cluster of more modest homes they built, for themselves and others, along Arroyo Terrace —and would that other towns could boast a cluster of more modest houses as good as these—it is the great houses for the Gambles and the Blackers in Pasadena, for the Pratts in Ojai and the Thorsens in Berkeley that made their names and still shed lustre on their reputations today. They are, by anybody's standards, a very remarkable body of work, and their long neglect by historians—because they could not be forced into the category of Pioneers of the Modern Movement—means that they still come fresh to the eyes of most of us who are not long-standing Pasadenans.

For myself I have no shame in admitting that it was my first encounters with the Greenes' work a decade or more ago that forced me to start thinking again about the whole nature of modern architecture, that sent me back to look at

Wright and Voysey and even William Morris for the first time with eyes that were not Pevsner's or Hitchcock's. For me, what was new and exciting about the Greenes' work was what was also oldest about it; to wit, its connection with the wood-building traditions of Northern Europe, with which I was at the same time becoming acquainted in Norway. It struck me forcibly then that there was in both something which in one sense was *not architecture*. As normally conceived and discussed in books by historians and critics—even, remarkably enough, in Vincent Scully's *Shingle Style*—architecture is something ultimately of Mediterranean extraction and done in massive masonry. Even in modern architecture the admiration of le Corbusier and others for smooth simplified geometrical forms "assembled in light" pays tribute to that Mediterranean tradition. True wooden architecture does not; I suppose that any simple wooden shed could tell us that, but something as big and as grand as the Blacker house punches the lesson home with greater effect by being on the scale of the kind of structure one normally discusses when talking about "Architecture with a capital A."

Many worthy and perceptive writers have handled this oddity about the Greenes' wooden architecture by making much of the Japanese connection and the known reverence in which Charles Greene in particular held Japanese art. The evidence for this is massive and well-documented and well-represented in the detail of the houses themselves, and there can be little doubt that this Orientalism was a powerful bond between them and their cultured collecting patrons, but — at the expense of flying in the face of all informed opinion about Greene and Greene—I beg to submit that the Japanese influence on the Greenes has been made too much of, and has begun to obscure the real traditions behind their work.

I am emboldened to take this line by the response of Professor Ettlinger, formerly of London University, now of Berkeley, and a man well-versed in the arts of the turn of the century. Looking up under the gables and balconies of the north end of the Gamble House he declared it "Like a Tyrolean barn," and on enquiry I find that others from Germanic and Nordic Europe where they build in wood have remarked on its likeness to their own native traditions before they found it Japanese. It may be suspected that not only the Greenes but others found in Japan primarily a way of revaluing or even rediscovering their own wood building traditions.

In any case, Japan and Europe, with Russia in between, are parts of a great belt of Northern timber-building territory, carpenter country, into which North America was incorporated after the European settlers arrived. It should also be remembered that the first timber building influence on California from the Far East was brought by the Russians, in structures such as Fort Ross, north of Bodega Bay, and that the great wooden girdle around the Northern hemisphere was thereby completed. But what this argument says in essence is that the Greenes' work in timber truly represents a European tradition refined and modified by its migration along with the European settlers across the whole agrarian width of North America from East to West, and that this is what most truly relates these houses to the homesteading tradition that created the Middle Landscape, not the domestic habits of those who have happened to inhabit them. The work of Charles and Henry Greene is alien to the inmost traditions of the European art of architecture, partly by being in wood, and partly by being a true product of the American experience. And maybe that gives their houses a subtlety in the relation of form and content that no cultured European architecture-loving mind will ever quite comprehend.

To acquire such comprehension requires, I suspect, a great deal of exposure to rather fundamental Americana—to New England farms and mid-western railroads, to old-time religion and singing the blues, to the Mason jar and hominy grits, to Sears Roebuck and Howard Johnson — and on a more than visiting-hours acquaintance with the Greenes' houses. On all the former topics I am now probably too old ever to catch up, but I have lived in the Gamble house, on and off, in fair weather and in foul, for longer and shorter periods over the last eight years. If I had not, I would not have the nerve to try and write this introduction—a nerve slightly reinforced by a brief period living in a Frank Lloyd Wright house, so that I have some standards of comparison.

Live in it you must, however. Such intensely residential

architecture is not truly to be known otherwise. That indeed, is the most compelling lesson I have learned from the Gamble house. Simply that you have to be there at all hours and in all weathers to know what the house has to offer. To know how and where it creaks when the weather changes or as it cools after dark in summer, and how it rattles in the rain, as the water cascades round the numerous sharp bends in the square-section downpipes that conduct it away from the seemingly innumerable roofs. To know how it smells in the morning, and to see one stupendous architectural vision that is only available to the early riser around six-thirty of a winter dawn, an hour when even the most assiduous visitor of national monuments is unlikely ever to be in the house.

At that hour, on certain favoured mornings, the early prowler will find the sun striking almost horizontally through the upstairs landing from front to back. That in itself is a rewarding sight, but if one then directs one's bare bedroom feet down the warm carpeted stairs to the entrance hall one will there find that same low sunlight, already dappled by its passage through the trees across the road opposite, blazing through that fantastic Tiffany glass in the entrance doors and filling the house from front to back with a luminance not to be found anywhere else. It is true that one may find it in small samples in Tiffany lamps, but they only serve as highlights, as Gustav Stickley said, among the mellow radiance of wood tones, while in that entrance hall at sun-up the wood itself is bathed in Tiffany tones from the broad swathes of gold and greenish light that pour through those doors and fall directly upon the panelling or are reflected on it from the floor. That rather formal central space of the house is transformed, for maybe an hour, into something so perfectly "cliché"—Aladdin's cave or a sacred grove—that you know it must be a great work of art because it is so obviously right and complete.

It is not one of those allegedly great architectural experiences of light, like the windows of Amiens or the pool of sunlight that falls through the oculus of the dome of the Pantheon in Rome. It lacks the celestial remoteness of the former, and the boring solemnity of the latter, but is more immediately effective than both because it is a close domestic experience, and remains in the mind with equal clarity because it is so perfect of its kind.

If I was asked to sum up the house as a whole it would be in those same two terms; it is a compelling close domestic experience, and it is about perfect of its kind. It is close and domestic in spite of its large horizontal dimensions—the living room is over thirty feet long but never looks it, largely because the embrasure of the fireplace, full of seats and cupboards and other fitments to which the parts of the human body conventionally relate, is *over sixteen feet across*, or more than half the length of the room! This is not to be rated optical contrivance—all those seats and cupboards have good functional reasons for being there; the performance of the room remains informally domestic in spite of its dimensions and its formal, almost bi-axially symmetrical plan.

Also, one finds, the lighting of the room, both by day and by night, tends to keep its visual dimensions within bounds. Particularly by night, the artificial lighting works to reduce the room to smaller functional components, and one attends to those areas of light where one has business or pleasure and not to the volume of the room as a whole. Furthermore, and to a greater extent than in even any Wright interiors I know, the lighting is distributed and switched in such a way that one can emphasize or discount the various subdivisions of the room at choice, but without ever destroying or even compromising its over-all form—though it takes ten mother-of-pearl inlaid wall switches and two independently switched art lamps to achieve this desirable effect.

Throughout the house also, modest vertical dimensions help to preserve a domestic air amongst all this grandeur. At six-foot-one I have a couple of inches clearance in all the doorways, though no more, and the ceiling heights are nowhere as ridiculously modest as they are in some of Wright's houses — whereas I have barely hair clearance under the gallery of the living room of his house for Isabel Roberts, there is no ceiling in the Greenes' Gamble House that I can quite reach at full stretch of my raised arm. Indeed, if the ceilings were any lower they would destroy the sense of reasonable domestic space by exaggerating the horizontals.

The one apparent exception to this rule of reasonable heights is in the large room—billiard room it could never have been, however the Greenes labelled it on the plans!—at the very top of the house. There the tie beams that span the bottoms of the master trusses that apparently hold the roof in shape (as a structure this roof has always caused purists to foam at the mouth) are well within reach of almost anybody's raised hand. The exposed underside of the roof timbers pitches up another two feet higher to the underside of the ridge beam, and the whole is a crafty balance between overhead space that is high enough to be of use, and the illusion of being an attic or loft squeezed under the summit of the house.

It is in any case one of the best rooms the Greenes ever designed, to my eye at least. In many ways it is more like the cabin of a wooden ship than a chamber in a great house. It has an almost continous strip of low windows along each of its main sides, but the windows under the end gables have progressively raised sills toward the center of the wall to avoid the rising line of the lower roof immediately beyond, very much as if one were looking fore and aft over the raised coaming of a yacht.

The ship-like effect has now been unintentionally enhanced by a large amount of ducting and air-conditioning plant that has recently been installed under the northerly coaming and is reached by a panel door in the end wall like the access to a ship's companion-way (air-conditioning to this upper room and two others on the east side of the house represent the only modification needed to bring its offices up to nineteen-seventies standards) and the whole effect is that of an almost secret space set apart from the rest of the life of the house.

"What a marvelous room," one might say, "for the endlessly elaborated games of make-believe by those tribes of secretive children who skirmish through the great Edwardian novels of..." and then realize that one has fallen into the ever-immanent nostalgia that the period can breed even in those like myself who were not born until the Long Weekend had been over for almost a decade. Concentrate instead on what one can know in the here and now, the physical substance of the building. It is difficult to do anything else for most of the time; wherever one looks, there is wood, elegantly hand-wrought, polished, and obsessively jointed. The interior of the Gamble House is not so much craftsmanship run riot as a kind of controlled frenzy, in which nothing has been wrought totally out of reasonable shape, yet nothing has been left alone or left plain.

It is in this rounding and shaping of the woodwork that the Japanese influence is most commonly thought to be seen, but what is interesting is that it is not Japanese carpentry that is imitated (or none that I have ever seen) but something more like the rounding and polishing of jade in *Netsuke*, or the conventions for light clouds and mist in the prints of Hokusai and Hiroshige. And since those prints were made by cutting wood there may be some devious Craftsmanly logic behind all this.

But not in the obsessive jointing. In an age when carpentry was sophisticated enough to make a clean, secret and invisible joint between any two pieces of wood meeting at any angle for any structural or functional purpose, the Greenes and their workmen made a major production number, it seems, out of practically every joint in the house. Simple mortise joints are pinned with woods of other hues, there are wedges and dovetails and ties of metal and leather, pegs everywhere and a few metal bolt heads and a whole lot of wedging blocks between horizontal timbers of the staircase structure to stop them sliding one upon the other, and even a few examples of that most pointless-looking of joints, described, I think, as the reversed-bevel block-wedged scarf. It doesn't look as if it can resist any load at all, nor can it unless it is very accurately made indeed. These must have been, or they would have pulled apart before the frame of the house was properly up. No wonder that, at fifty-five thousand dollars, the house cost twice as much as a moderate-size school that was being built in Pasadena at the same time.

Three-quarters of a century later, near enough, what are we to make of such work, and the output of the brothers Greene as a whole? A culture that thinks it can afford to send non-returnable vehicles into space wrapped in gold leaf, or is prepared to spend more on the equipment, furnishing and painting of a motor-van to be used only in the surfing season, than on the building of a modest house for all seasons, can scarcely afford to accuse the Craftsman period of having gotten its priorities wrong. They were the priorities of at least the ruling classes of that epoch, and if we are to judge the Gamble or Blacker houses by the accuracy with which they expressed and made eloquent those priorities, then these are great works of building art.

They are that by the standards of the times by which they were built; they can also measure up, I believe, to the best of their own contemporaries like Wright and Mackintosh and Voysey—indeed one must rate them better than Voysey's houses because he could be so inept and graceless a planner. But how do they measure up in the company of the most admired and prized exemplars of Western domestic architecture—the villas of Andrea Palladio in Italy, the country houses of William Kent or the Adam brothers in England, or those late extensions of the Palladian tradition in the Plantation states of America?

That comparison, I think, brings out what is unique in them. The houses of the Palladian tradition, from the beginning to end, were classical expressions of a standard, a norm, for the educated country gentleman and his world, and wherever that world spread the Palladian house, in some variant or another, went with it confirming and underwriting the normative standards of that world and its culture. All Palladian houses are comparable from age to age and place to place for more than three centuries. Craftsman houses, to say it again, are comparable as architecture only among themselves, only in their own time, and hardly at all between one location and another. As works of high art they are unshakably particular, especially as to place.

If we move down the scale of architectural pretension, however, and look at what might be described as post-Craftsman vernaculars, we see that in statistical terms (if no others) C. F. A. Voysey and Charles and Henry Greene have been the most influential architects of the Twentieth Century so far, in their own countries for certain, but also to some extent beyond their native shores. By the simple test of counting addresses at which buildings influenced by certain named architects can be found, Palladio is practically nowhere, and the Greenes seem to be practically everywhere. Insofar as the California Bungalow is the product of their work, then they did indeed create a kind of normative building type, not at the Palladian level of the self-conscious regulation of a culture and its standards, but at the level of what normal (common, regular, ordinary) folks want to live in. There is a world of difference between the conscious and pondered art of sophisticated men like the brothers Greene and the housing put up by commercial opportunists in what they see as the fashion of the hour, but there was not, in this case, any absolute gulf fixed between the two—all round Pasadena one may see California Bungalows of every conceivable intermediate gradation of architectural consciousness and commercial carelessness. The lines of communication between the Greenes and their unknown, even unwitting, followers must have been good, for one can honestly say that half a century of small houses in the Western United States would not have been the same had the Greenes never produced their few exquisitely wrought houses for a tiny cultural elite, and one will never properly understand the meaning of all those myriad common-or-garden houses for common-or-garden folk without first understanding the rare and idiosyncratic architectural works of Charles and Henry Greene.

Reyner Banham

GREENE & GREENE

I

The Forming Years 1868-1893

Charles Sumner Greene was born on October 12, 1868 in the small town of Brighton just outside Cincinnati, Ohio. His brother, Henry Mather Greene, was born fifteen months later on January 23, 1870.

Little is known of their early years beyond the fact that their father was a bookkeeper, that both parents were descended from distinguished New England families,[1] and that they moved to St. Louis in 1874. In 1876, however, their father, Thomas Greene, enrolled in the Medical College of the University of Cincinnati, and Mrs. Greene took her two sons back to the Mather farm in Wyandotte, West Virginia where they lived during the four years of her husband's medical training.

Charles and Henry, like most young boys, were fascinated by life on the farm. According to relatives, Henry was the more active and outgoing. He was constantly tagging along after the farmhands, running through the stubble or exploring the countryside. Charles, although he shared Henry's eager curiosity, was more quiet, less robust, and somewhat introspective. Both boys developed a keen interest in nature—an interest which was to remain with them throughout their lives and was continually expressed in their drawings, photographs and architecture.

1. Thomas Sumner Greene was descended from colonists John Greene and Sir George Sumner. Among members of this family were General Nathanael Greene and Christopher Greene of the Continental Army and Governor Increase Sumner and reconstructionist Senator Charles Sumner of Massachusetts. Mrs. Greene was the former Lelia Ariana Mather of Virginia whose family dated back to John Cotton and the Reverend Richard Mather. Other prominent family members included Increase, Cotton, Samuel and Nathanael Mather.

In 1880 Thomas Greene completed his medical training and the family was reunited in St. Louis where they lived in an area of multi-storied row housing. Theirs was the end unit of the block of houses three-stories high with full basements but little outdoor yard. An early photograph of the building shows it surrounded by larger brick structures of five and six stories with enormous smokestacks towering above. The interior spaces were restricted. Only their unit had the advantage of natural light from a bay window which opened to a narrow space between their building and the neighboring structure. The other rooms opened either to the front or the rear of the building—an unhealthy arrangement, their father continually pointed out.

Dr. Greene specialized in the treatment of catarrh. Consequently, his professional experience as well as his interest in architecture convinced him of the benefits of free cross-circulation of fresh air and abundant light. He was determined that his sons appreciate the importance of air circulation and lighting for he had already decided that they should become architects like their great-great-grandfather, Thomas Waldron Sumner, of early nineteenth century Boston. His sharp criticism of the house made a lasting impression on Charles and Henry which was to be reflected in their California designs.

While the boys were attending public school, Dr. Greene made the acquaintance of Calvin Milton Woodward, Professor of Civil Engineering and founder and director of the Manual Training School of Washington University, the first of its kind in America.[2] His program provided fundamentals which helped formulate a basis for the Greenes' own architectural practice. His school first opened in 1880 and, in addition to the normal high school academic curriculum, each student was required to spend two hours a day at manual training—the first year at woodworking and carpentry with an emphasis on an understanding of the inherent characteristics of wood, the second year at metalworking, and the third at toolmaking. Woodward, who was widely acclaimed as the father of manual training, was strongly influenced by the philosophies of John Ruskin and William Morris. In his teaching, he stressed the dignity of craftsmanship and is credited with introducing handcrafts into American secondary education. Dr. Greene was enthusiastic about Woodward's educational theories and believed that such training would provide an effective background for an architectural career. Accordingly, Charles was enrolled in 1883; Henry followed a year later. They responded eagerly to Woodward's program. They were introduced to the thought of Ruskin and Morris and, in addition, were taught that design determinants stemmed from function and from the appropriate analysis of materials handled in a direct manner. This was essentially a craftsman approach where form results from the nature of materials and the tools employed. Because of this high school background, the Greenes developed a real appreciation of the opportunities of the craftsman, an appreciation which is reflected in the detail of their own original work. As a result they brought a creative freshness to the American architectural scene. In later years they were quick to acknowledge the influence of Woodward and his innovative program, and they were always devoted to the school's motto: The Cultured Mind — The Skillful Hand.

In 1888 Henry graduated with honors from the Manual Training School. He was interested in engineering and eager to continue with his academic studies. But Charles, who had graduated a year earlier, rebelled at the prospect of a university education. He was interested in painting,

2. A plaque placed in 1939 by the St. Louis Chamber of Commerce marks the location of the school and reads: "Organized and erected in 1879 under the leadership of Calvin Milton Woodward. On this site stood the first Manual Training school in the United States. Incorporated under the charter of Washington University the Manual Training School functioned successfully until its discontinuance in 1917."

Row house rented by Dr. Thomas Greene in 1880 at 2017 Olive Street, St. Louis, Missouri.
Photograph courtesy of Greene and Greene Library, The Gamble House.

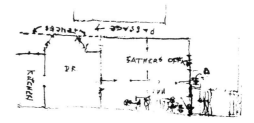

Henry M. Greene floor plan sketch on back of photograph of Olive Street house. Courtesy of Greene and Greene Library.

Dr. Greene impressed upon Charles and Henry the inadequacies of light and ventilation in row house design, and these concerns were later interpreted in their own creative designs.

photography and poetry and was reluctant to commit himself to an architectural career. In the end the family reached a compromise; Charles and Henry both agreed to a shortened program in architecture offered by MIT whereby they would be awarded a "Certificate of Partial Course" at the end of two years, after which they would have the option of continuing on toward a Bachelor's degree or beginning an apprenticeship under a licensed architect in preparation for registration.

Records of their course work indicate that they were average students, each excelled in certain subjects and was capable in others. After their Manual Training School experience, however, the courses given in Design, Orders of Architecture and History of Ornament were a new experience for Charles and Henry. Much of the material was steeped in the classic traditions which dictated not only the approach to design but also the standards of taste and, furthermore, emphasized the importance of historic styles rather than of basic principles. The young Greenes felt that at MIT the architect was regarded more as an "artisan" than as an artist and that the atmosphere stifled opportunity for creative and artistic endeavor. An expression of their feelings about the formal training at MIT was later set forth in an unpublished novel by Charles Greene in which he asked the questions:

> Why is it we are taught that it is impossible to invent anything worth while in architectural art? ... Isn't invention the life of science? Don't men of science do it every day? And science has not had the last word yet. Why not art? ...
>
> The great trouble is that the schools ignore principles and teach too much detail. One gets a mass of disjointed facts. No Inspiration, no insight ...
>
> Our students go over to Paris and learn a jumble intended for educated Frenchmen. When they come home they look upon everything American as hopelessly illiterate.... So they put Louis Quinze's interpretation of a Greek temple into the first story of an office building. A thing that the Greeks used as a sacred thing, a place of divine worship.... It's true we worship there too.. worship the dollar. Oh, it's damnable![3]

In spite of this sense of frustration, however, the History of Architecture did arouse their interest. They probably found its lessons in social history and the derivation of historical styles more important than the styles themselves and may have looked upon them only as valuable lessons rather than as criteria for future designs.

Certainly they must have found the cultural atmosphere of Boston invigorating. They attended the opera, were active in the Shakespeare Club, continued their music lessons, and visited relatives. Archive letters reveal that they also spent many of their leisure hours in local libraries and museums and expanded their classroom work with reading on a variety of subjects.[4] Charles in particular spent a great deal of time delving into Greek history, studying basic principles which would influence him throughout his life.

The Greenes spent their summer vacations in Nantucket. The contrast to the densely populated row housing of St. Louis must have impressed them and perhaps stirred memories of their early life on the Mather farm in Virginia. Their feeling for Nantucket was revealed in various pencil and watercolor drawings found in their personal sketchbooks in which the simple beauty of the sketches suggests that the quiet rolling landscape appealed to their artistic sense as much as did the structures portrayed.[5] This appreciation of the natural landscape carried over into the Greenes' own landscaping in later years.

In the spring of 1890 illness prevented both Charles and Henry from completing their work in two courses and their records (dated June 14, 1890) indicate that they were "Awarded Certificate for completion of Partial Course subject to explaining D (incomplete) in Heating and Ventilation." However, this certificate enabled them to go ahead with apprenticeships in local architectural offices with the provision that they return to part-time study in the fall to satisfy the requirement in these subjects. As apprentices they were working without pay. Their father continued to furnish them each with an allowance of $12 per month to

3. Charles Sumner Greene, *Thais Thayer*, manuscript of an unpublished novel, Documents Collection, Greene and Greene Library, The Gamble House.

4. Archive letters, Documents Collection, Greene and Greene Library, The Gamble House.

5. Documents Collection, Greene and Greene Library, The Gamble House.

Henry Mather Greene, 1888.
Photograph courtesy of Greene and Greene Library.

Charles Sumner Greene, 1888.
Photograph courtesy of Greene and Greene Library.

Henry M. Greene watercolor sketch of Nantucket countryside,
1892. Courtesy of Greene and Greene Library.

cover their necessities, but before long he began urging them to look around for other openings as he felt they should be earning as much as $100 a month for their services.

Henry was interested in the work he was doing, however. Apparently at this time he was apprenticed to architects Shepley, Rutan and Coolidge who had taken over the Henry Hobson Richardson office in 1886. Here, according to members of the Greene family, he worked on drawings for the Quad at Stanford University.

Charles was not so happy. He complained about the mundane work assigned to him and after about six months moved to a second office where he worked for only a few weeks. As early as July of 1890 he began expressing doubts about the need to return to MIT to complete the work for the certificate. Although letters from his father repeatedly stressed the importance of the certificate to his "future professional status," Charles was not easily convinced. He even went so far as to question the necessity for professional registration. Yet he had a real thirst for knowledge in the subjects in which he was interested. He spent every spare cent on books and began building a considerable library. He enrolled in an evening art class and spent the rest of his spare time in reading, photography and writing poetry. He was too busy for much of a social life or outdoor activities and this alarmed his parents who were concerned about his health. In his letters, Dr. Greene also expressed anxiety about Charles' characteristic ability to lose all sense of time when engrossed in some project and often lectured him on being more practical with his time and money. "While ideals and art are fascinating," he wrote, "you must deal first with the necessary items of bread and butter."[6] He urged both sons to associate with that level of society which could open the doors to cultural endeavors and, indeed, to prospective clients.

Dr. Greene was less worried about Henry who was leading a more balanced life, interspersing his work and study with visits to friends and attendance at musical gatherings or evening discussions.

Toward the end of the year Dr. Greene's medical practice began to dwindle and the boys were urged to economize wherever possible. In the early months of 1891 they completed the last of their work for the Heating and Ventilating class and their final Certificate was granted them on March 4, 1891.

Within the following week Charles was offered a job with the prestigious firm of H. Langford Warren which he immediately accepted.[7] Henry later moved to the firm of Chamberlin and Austin.[8] By the fall of 1891 Henry was earning $10 a week and Charles, who had by then moved over to the firm of Winslow and Wetherell, $12 a week.

The brothers found the time and incentive to work together in formulating plans to submit in the architectural competition of November, 1891 for the design of a new 10,000 sq. ft. City Hall for Brockton, Massachusetts. The program and specifications were rigidly laid out and the stipulations on materials and the plan of the structure called essentially for a facade design and an arrangement of incidental interior space. Little was left to the imagination of young architects. Charles and Henry entered the competition with great confidence. When the results were announced, the depth of their disappointment was expressed by Charles in a letter to their parents dated November 24, 1891:

> I suppose Hal has told you how hard we worked on the competition and how fruitless it was materially. In reality we gained much experience by it, though little encouragement. In fact, I am about sick of it all and disgusted with architecture generally. I thought I could learn to like it, but it is hard work...at least so far...
>
> We had worked hard day and night for two weeks and had not finished our competition drawings, and I was going down to the office, on the day they were due at Brockton. I met Mr. Wetherell and he sent me back to our room for the drawings. When I arrived at the office with them, he gave them out to the draughtsmen and had them finished; so I took the train for Brockton with the drawings in my

6. Letter dated November 24, 1891; Documents Collection, Greene and Greene Library, The Gamble House.

7. Warren, who had secured a position, at age 24, in the office of H. H. Richardson had served as Richardson's assistant in design for five years at the peak of Richardson's career.

8. Chamberlin had earlier worked both for Sturgis and Brigham and later for McKim, Mead and White.

hand. I arrived there and walked up to the mayor who introduced me to the committee of about 20 aldermen and asked me to show and explain my plans to them. He assisted me to pin...

Unfortunately the balance of the letter is missing and thus there is no record describing either the design or the way in which it was received.

Over the next few months Charles grew more and more independent in his thinking. He developed a strong interest in Impressionist painting, continued his studies of poetry, philosophy and history and found himself more and more in conflict over the prospect of an architectural career. Meanwhile Dr. and Mrs. Greene, both of whom were ailing, moved to the "little country town" of Pasadena, California, where they rented a house on Colorado Street. Faced with continuing poor health, financial problems and loneliness, they wrote to their sons at the end of the year and proposed that they, too, come to California.

For Charles and Henry the decision to leave Boston was not an easy one. They changed their minds several times. Finally, for reasons unknown, Charles lost his job. This may have been a significant factor in making their decision, for in mid-August, 1893, they left for Pasadena.

On the way west they stopped in Chicago to attend the World's Columbian Exposition. Here they were introduced for the first time to Japanese architecture. They were both deeply moved by the Ho-o-den, the official exhibit of the Japanese government. This was a half-scale replica of the Ho-o-do of Byodo-in Temple at Uji, near Kyoto, and had been brought from Japan in pieces and assembled in Chicago by Japanese workmen. With its elegant proportions, it was an excellent example of Buddhist temples of the Fujiwara period (895-1185).[9] The structures, built primarily of unpainted wood, straw, plaster and paper intrigued the Greenes by their composition and use of heavy timbers, their exposed joinery, and the subtle way in which they were sited in the landscape. They were so impressed by such bold and direct uses of structure that they made special arrangements the following year to attend the Mid-Winter Exposition in San Francisco in order to visit the Japanese hill and water gardens. Here again they found an architectural expression which to them was a beautiful marriage between the sensitive craftsman's respect for natural materials and the care with which he fitted his work into the environment. However, the Japanese influence, significant as it was, did not appear in the Greenes' work until several years later when they came to recognize the similarity between Japanese asceticism and their own craftsman background.

9. Okakura Kakudzo, *The Ho-o-den, an Illustrated Description*, Chicago, 1893, p. 21.

Charles Greene photograph.
Courtesy of Greene and Greene Library.

Charles' interest in nature and photography is evidenced in
this photograph which he took opposite his own home on
Arroyo View Drive.

II

The Early Work – A Decade in Search   1893-1903

When young Charles and Henry Greene stepped off the train in Pasadena they had no thought of establishing permanent residence in California. They assumed from their parents' letters that the area was a country town with none of the cultural advantages of the big cities of the East, and certainly no opportunity for prospective young architects. Opportunities existed, however.

In 1893 Pasadena was a rapidly growing city not quite twenty years old with a population of "solid, mature, well educated business and professional men with families, seeking a healthy, moderate climate and cultural satisfaction."[1] It had gone through one of the greatest building and land speculation booms in American history and had emerged as a wealthy, cultural, and intellectually stimulating center which attracted more and more winter visitors to its many resort hotels. The citizenry was interested in building fine public buildings and business houses; and luxurious, magnificently landscaped homes, costly churches, school buildings, and elaborate gardens appeared along the avenues. Land values spiraled. Publications of the day extolled Pasadena's ideal location (some five miles from the center of Los Angeles) and the healthful quality of its mild climate. From the rolling flower-covered hills, the visitor could look out upon over sixty miles of undulating land covered with vast vineyards, orange and olive groves, orchards, and fields of wheat, corn and vegetables that made up the San Gabriel Valley. To the west and southwest, some twenty-five miles distant, the Pacific Ocean continually licked at the winding California coastline. To the north stood Mount Wilson and the resort areas of Mount Lowe, and to the east the snow covered peaks of

Mounts San Antonio, San Jacinto and Baldy. And throughout Southern California were the incomparable Franciscan missions.

The Greenes were deeply impressed with the missions. Some years later Charles Greene wrote:

> The old art of California—that of the mission fathers—is old enough to be romantic and mysterious too. Study it and you will find a deeper meaning than books tell or sun-dried bricks and plaster show. Then, too, those old monks came from a climate not unlike this. They built after their own fashion and their knowledge of climate and habits of life, were bred in the bone. Therefore, giving heed to these necessary and effective qualities there is good and just reason why we should study their works. The same spirit that made it possible for this little band of men to accomplish so much may again produce something as good.[2]

The brothers were fascinated by this new country, but before long they were faced with the necessity of making important decisions about their future. They had almost decided to return to Boston or Chicago to seek work in architectural offices there when John Breiner, a friend of their father, casually mentioned that he intended to build a small cottage. Dr. Greene promptly suggested that his sons be given the project, and shortly thereafter the brothers were dealing with their first client.[3]

1. Paul G. Bryan, *Pasadena Pioneer Pictorial*, Mountain View Mausoleum Association, Altadena, California, 1954, p.1.

2. Charles Sumner Greene, "California Home Making," Tournament of Roses Edition, *Pasadena Daily News*, January 2, 1905, pp. 26, 27.

3. Interview by the author with Henry Greene's daughter, Mrs. Alan R. McElwain, 1956.

   It is possible that the Breiner house was the first structure for the Greenes but not the first job. In a letter to Charles dated October 6, 1938 Henry wrote: "Reminds me of our first job of designing those concrete boxes for old Mr. Hutchenson, the candy man. Do you remember?" College of Environmental Design Library, Documents Collection, University of California, Berkeley.

For office space, Charles and Henry rented a room where they drew up the design and prepared working drawings. No record of these plans remain. The small cottage for John Breiner assumes importance only as the deciding factor in their decision to remain and set up practice in Pasadena. Late in 1894 the family moved into a larger two-story cottage at 848 East Colorado Street where Dr. and Mrs. Greene were to reside for nearly a decade. Before long, however, Charles and Henry were financially able to establish their own separate residences.

Throughout the 1890s the brothers kept up a considerable correspondence with their many friends and relatives in the East. Charles often forwarded his own paintings and photographs of nearby arroyos and missions to his close friends and, with a typical concern for his work, included detailed instructions on the framing of these gifts. His letters, particularly those to his lady friends, were often filled with poetry, which he produced profusely, as well as with constant references to the works of Emerson. In one letter of February 24, 1895 Charles expressed distress at not having the time to spend at his music, poetry, painting and photography. In another he wrote:

> There is more responsibility in building a barn well when one has to carry it through one's self, than in building a state house when others fight the outside battles. It isn't very hard to make a tolerable speech but it *is hard* to make people listen. I can't always leave my cares at the office as I used to, and so you see the action things push aside the passion ones. But I seldom lie down at night without thinking of the things that give me most pleasure. (I try to put the others away.)[4]

4. Letter to his cousin in Boston written in late 1895; Documents Collection, Greene and Greene Library, The Gamble House.

Vista over "Grace Hill," Pasadena, c. 1895.
Photograph courtesy of Pasadena Historical Society.

Several of the fine homes of the period are shown against the background of the nearby hills.

Cottage, Pasadena.
Photograph courtesy of Greene and Greene Library.

This typical Pasadena cottage at 848 East Colorado Street was rented by Dr. and Mrs. Greene.

Below:
Colorado Street at Fair Oaks Avenue, Pasadena.
Photograph courtesy of Pasadena Historical Society.

The crossroads of Pasadena's thriving business district in the early 1890s.

For Charles the mid-nineties was a period of searching for his inner self and the real meaning of life. In the same letter he confessed:

> No, no I haven't grown callous yet. I know you think that I'm not very affectionate and I think so myself sometimes, but I always come back to the feeling that I am only differently from others. I'm sorry I'm different, but its pretty much the same case as poor Jacob Faith feels "What's done can't be helped."

In other letters he related his current interest in studying passages from the Bible. Although Charles followed no particular faith he had strong religious and philosophical interests which in later life led him into a profound study of Buddhism. His search for meaning found varying expression. For several years letters to a young lady friend in St. Louis took the form of a serialized diary of a fictional character named Sir Jacob Grubnuddle, in which Charles expounded his own views of love, of moonlit walks by the seashore, and solitary hours of meditation.[5]

The responsibilities of conducting the business may have frustrated Charles' desire for more intellectual pursuits, but Henry seemed to thrive on the day to day contacts and duties connected with the office. In addition he became active in various civic affairs, and in the Americus Marching Club, where he was a Corporal in Company B. He joined a society of young actors and singers, a group that put on musical shows in the popular Lowe's Opera House. His particular favorites were the Gilbert and Sullivan productions that the small group presented. He also belonged to a singing group, the Amphion Quartet.

For the Greenes the period 1893 to 1903 were years of experimentation, of searching for the forms, methods and materials appropriate to the life and culture of California. They were caught up in a constant battle between the fundamentals they had learned at the Manual Training School and the popular styles of the day. Their own work clearly reflected their dilemma and their first years of practice produced a variety of styles. But in time their designs showed a simplification, a gradual reduction in the use of applied or excess ornament. Strong forms began to emerge and a trend away from the traditional became increasingly apparent.

During the course of their work on the Breiner cottage, a second client appeared with a commission for the design of a tombstone, hardly a subject to stimulate ambitious young architects, but one which was accepted and carried out.[6]

5. The series of known letters to Bess Hulbert began in November 1897 and continued until August 1899. Documents Collection, Greene and Greene Library, The Gamble House.

6. Interviews conducted by the author with members of the Henry Greene family.

Henry Greene at his drawing table.
Courtesy of Greene and Greene Library.

In the autumn of 1894 they were approached with several commissions by the Pasadena Security Investment Company for whom they designed at least three different residences.[7] Although the plans and designs for these houses were typical of the times there were certain features identifying their work. On the larger house the incised pattern of the top of the chimney is almost a signature; the inverted California poppy form roof over the bay window of the second floor and the cobblestone foundation often appeared in their work during these early years.

7. Addresses for these houses are not known and it is not certain that they were actually constructed. However, drawings indicate that one of the designs was identified as house No. 3.

HOUSE FOR THE
PASADENA SECURITY INVESTMENT Co
PASADENA, CAL.

FRONT ELEVATION

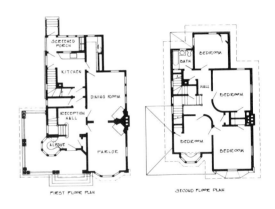

FIRST FLOOR PLAN   SECOND FLOOR PLAN

FRONT ELEVATION

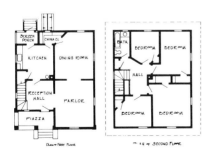

PLAN OF FIRST FLOOR   PLAN OF SECOND FLOOR

Pasadena Security Investment Company houses, 1894. Courtesy of Avery Architectural Library.

Although the houses were typical of the period, the recessed detail of the top of the chimney is an early signature of the Greenes, and the inverted poppy roof form appeared often in their early work.

By 1896 more elaborate and sizeable plans were on the boards. One such design possessed an outrageous mixture of elements which suggests either the dilemma of the Greenes or the input of a dominant client. Identified only as Job No. 11, it is highly possible that the plan was never constructed. However, its combination of disparate elements suggests the architectural conflict in which the Greenes were caught at this time. Formally organized about a central court, the partial one and two-story plaster structure echoed mission forms except for the stone basement with arched windowed foundation wall, reminiscent of the work of H. H. Richardson, the carved gargoyle knee braces on the front and side piazzas, the Greene touch to the chimney cap and, appearing for the first time, the curling butterfly wrought iron brackets for the roof drains.

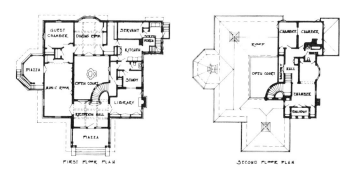

Unidentified Job No. 11, address and construction unknown, 1896. Courtesy of Avery Architectural Library.

This design reflects the Mission Style except for the stone basement (which is more reminiscent of H. H. Richardson), the carved gargoyle knee braces of the piazzas and the Greene touch to the chimney cap.

Robert S. Allen house,
325 S. Euclid Avenue,
Pasadena, 1895.
(Demolished)

In contrast, the Robert S. Allen house (1896) was an uninspired design in which the strong horizontals of the wood siding and roof lines dominated the simple rectangular two-story structure. The cobblestones, already utilized in foundations, now appeared in the porch piers, an early prediction of the boulder and clinker brick piers which became a trademark of the Greenes.

Kinney-Kendall Building, 65 E. Colorado Street, Pasadena, 1896. *Pasadena Illustrated Souvenir Book*, 1903.

Like many of the creative architects of the period who would become entwined in the Arts and Crafts Movement, the Greenes were at their best with residential structures. The lone large commercial structure executed by the firm was the Kinney-Kendall Block (1896) built in the center of Pasadena.[8] The design possessed a sense of simplicity which set it apart from surrounding buildings. Strong horizontal bands of windows lighted the second and third levels. Ornamentation was concentrated in the spandrels and cornices and was expressed as a textural relief contrasting dramatically with the columns and window walls. Constructed of iron and glass, it was one of the largest structures in town at the time. Much attention was focused on the young architects who moved their offices into it upon its completion in December of 1897.

8. Major alterations over the years have left little of the original strong design character of the building.

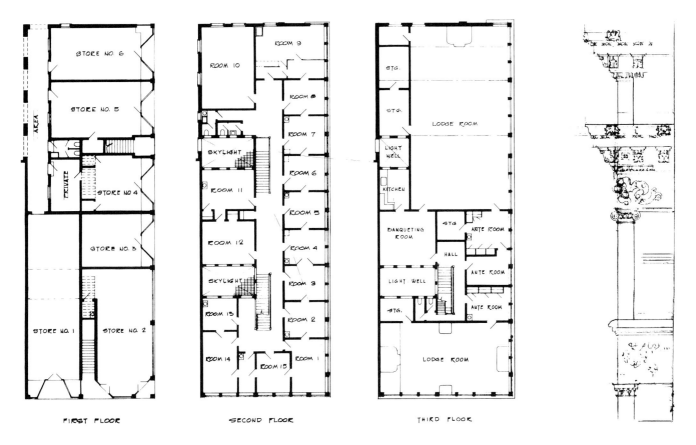

FIRST FLOOR   SECOND FLOOR   THIRD FLOOR

The largest of the few commercial structures built by Greene and Greene, the bold Kinney-Kendall Building was distinguished in Pasadena by its extensive use of windows for light and ventilation. Its decorative features were concentrated in the spandrel and cornice, giving added horizontality to the clean design.

Kinney-Kendall Building, sketch of cornice from the Greenes' scrapbook. Courtesy of Greene and Greene Library.

It is uncertain whether the Greenes were acquainted with Orson Squire Fowler's book on the octagonal house, but their fascination with octagonal geometry as a planning and building form is quite clear.[9] It appeared frequently in their early work and was carried along into their Craftsman period after the turn of the century. The flatly angled geometry of the bay window was, of course, not original but, like Frank Lloyd Wright, they used the angular form to break up the square or rectangle in an effort to extend the spatial quality of interiors. As used in the larger house for the Pasadena Security Investment Company (1894) the octagon is of minor effect as an entry alcove and verges on the quaint. However, the bay window of the upstairs bedroom substantially alters both the character of the space and the frontal elevation. The octagon and related geometry of the bay window were more fully expressed in the Theodore P. Gordon house (1897). Here the form was carried through the first floor plan into the second and was accentuated with the inverted poppy roof form. The strength of this corner tower is lessened by the strange combination of classical columns, cobblestone foundations, baroque decoration, diamond-paned windows and horizontal wood siding.

9. Orson S. Fowler, *A Home For All—The Octagon House*, 1853.

Theodore P. Gordon house, 820 N. Los Robles Avenue, Pasadena, 1897 (Demolished).
Courtesy of Avery Architectural Library.

The Greenes' use of the octagon was more effective here than in earlier designs and more directly changed the quality of the interior spaces.

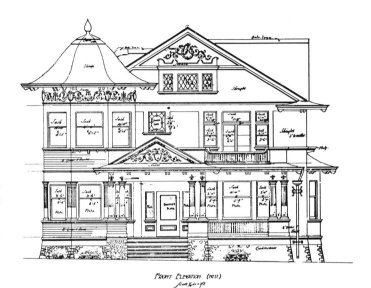

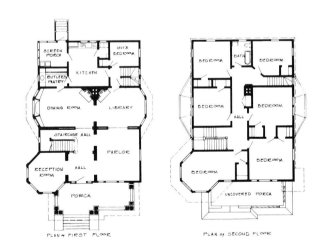

Historical influences were more simply handled in the classic front elevation of the house for Dr. George S. Hull (1897).[10] Behind the facade the plan breaks from tradition and is elongated to follow the narrow linear property lines. On the adjoining property they built a small office for Dr. Hull but did not carry over the classic design of the main house. Here, as in the Gordon house, they softened the harsh line of the front gable by letting the corner of the eave creep slightly around and be expressed horizontally on the front elevation—a detail they often employed.

10. Subsequently, the house and office were demolished for the construction of the major structure, of Chinese influence, built by its second owner, Mrs. Grace Nicholson, to house her residence and antique and gift shop.

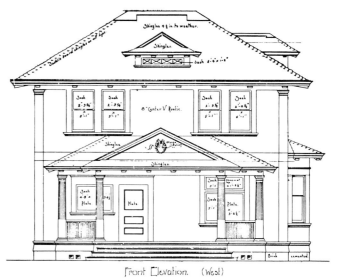

Front Elevation. (West)

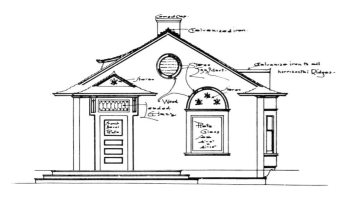

Dr. George S. Hull office, 36 N. Los Robles Avenue, Pasadena, 1897 (Demolished). Courtesy of Avery Architectural Library.

Dr. George S. Hull house, 46 N. Los Robles Avenue, Pasadena, 1897 (Demolished). Courtesy of Avery Architectural Library.

Behind the facade, the classical design gives way to an elongated plan brought about by the narrow lot lines.

The stylistic confusion which was a part of the 1890s and apparent in the Greenes' search for appropriate directions was seen in the design for a house for Edward B. Hosmer in 1896 and in the series of plans done in 1897 for Howard Longley. The first complete set of drawings wrap a fairly traditional box plan in complex elevations of a mixture of historic detail with a mission parapet over the attic dormer. An alternative scheme was a dramatic departure. This plan exhibited a real attempt to experiment with the octagonal form. A simple shingle style design finally met the combined interests of architects and clients. The interior plan finally built, while less imaginative, did open up the living room into a large free space and eliminated the dated parlor concept.[11]

11. The Longley house is the earliest example of a Greene and Greene design standing today. It is dangerously close to the freeway right of way and its future is not certain. While the exterior is now painted, the structure is in nearly original form with the exceptions of the Greene addition in 1912 and an addition to the west at a later date.

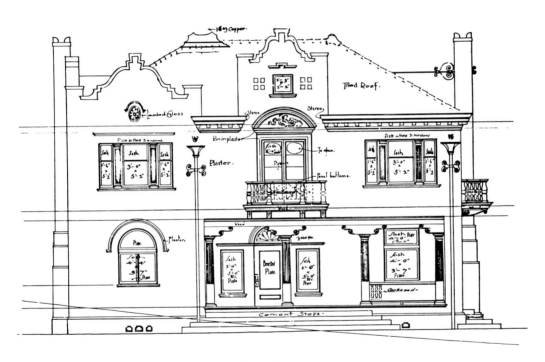

Edward B. Hosmer house, 229 S. Orange Grove Avenue, Pasadena, 1896 (Demolished).
Courtesy of Avery Architectural Library.

Here the Mission decor is mixed with late Georgian Revival windows, doors and balustrade, all wrapped about a tight formal plan.

The changing character of the various schemes for the Longley house indicates the Greenes' quest for appropriate forms. The pencil sketch from the Greenes' scrapbook shows an early elevation study for the Longley house utilizing a sweeping porch roof. Courtesy of Greene and Greene Library.

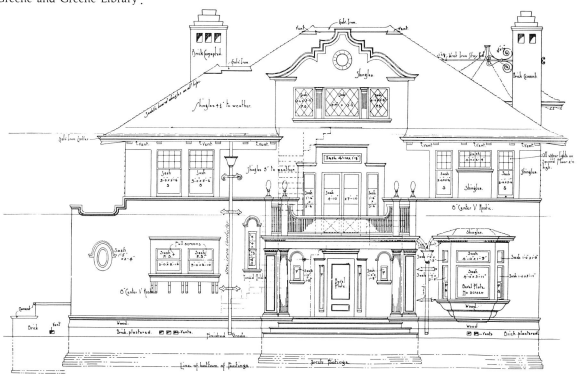

Scheme No. 1 for the Howard Longley house, 1897. Courtesy of Avery Architectural Library.

Howard Longley house, 1005 Buena Vista Street, South Pasadena, 1897. Marvin Rand photograph.

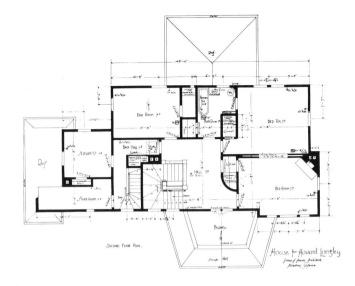

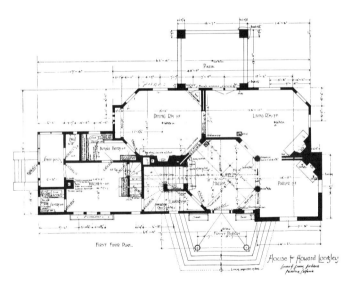

Intermediate plan for the Howard Longley house, 1897. Courtesy of Avery Architectural Library.

Although a real effort to explore octagonal geometry in the plan, the form failed to be expressed convincingly on the exterior. The plan as built lost the uniqueness of the experimental scheme.

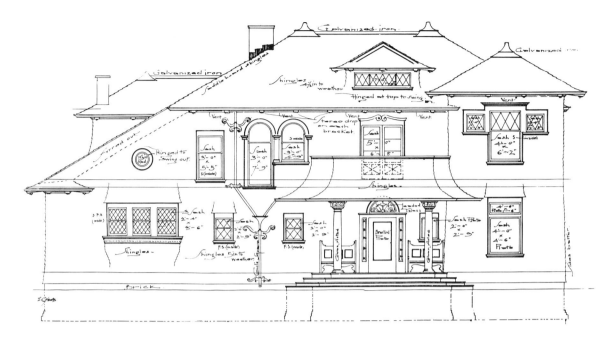

Howard Longley house, front elevation for the octagonal
scheme and also for the final design.
Courtesy of Avery Architectural Library.

Downspout.

Gargoyle on rear elevation.
Marvin Rand photographs.

In 1898 the brothers designed three residences which successively provide a clear picture of the exploration and changing directions in their early work. The first of these was the home for Winthrop B. Fay. The exterior of simple clapboard siding provided a quiet contrast to the elaborate forms and decoration in the design which was a mixture of late Queen Anne and Colonial Revival styles. Two-story semi-circular windows balanced the tower on the left. The central formal entry portico supported a terrace with an eighteenth century balustrade which continued across the front elevation, wrapping around the octagonal tower. At the third level the Greenes used a Palladian window with french doors in the center opening onto a narrow balcony with a heavy broad solid balustrade. The overall composition of disparate elements was fortunately brought together under the strong symmetrical roof line of the front gable.

Winthrop B. Fay house, 71 S. Euclid Avenue, Pasadena, 1898.
Pasadena Illustrated Souvenir Book, 1903. (Demolished)

The first of three residences built in 1898 which reflect the experimentation and changing directions in the Greenes' early work.

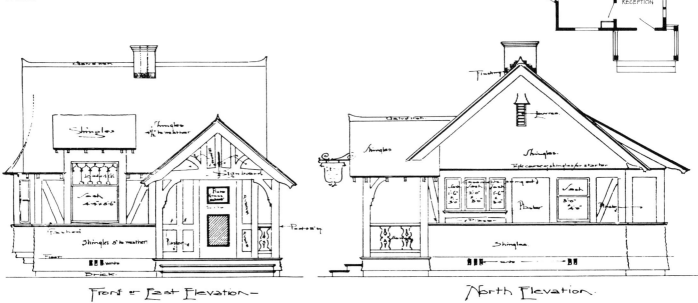

Dr. W. H. Roberts office, 29 N. Euclid Avenue, Pasadena, 1898. (Demolished) Courtesy of Avery Architectural Library.

The second residence was the William B. Tomkins house built on the barren flatlands of San Rafael Heights. This design, a dramatic contrast to the Fay house, represented a transition from the Shingle Style into the Craftsman Style. The shingle-clad upper level with strong horizontal lines accentuated by the solid shingled balustrade of the front terrace extends beyond each end of the structure. Craftsman ideas are expressed in the dashed stucco-covered brick and exposed stone forms of the first level. The stonework, with the stones carefully arranged by size, was left exposed while the brick was stuccoed. This gave even greater mass to the ground level by providing a visual transition at the corners between the structure and the barren, flat site.

William B. Tomkins house, San Rafael Avenue near Nithsdale Road, Pasadena, 1898 (Demolished).
Pasadena, California—The City Beautiful, 1902.

In contrast to the late Queen Anne and Colonial Revival styles of the Fay house, the Tomkins house exhibits a transition from the Shingle Style into elements of the Craftsman Style.

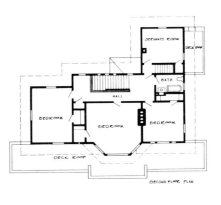

William B. Tomkins house, living room.
Pasadena, California—The City Beautiful, 1902.

The living room was representative of the Aesthetic Movement and was in striking contrast to the Shingle Style exterior.

Living room of the rented home of Charles Greene about 1901.
Pasadena, California—The City Beautiful, 1902.

This photograph and those of the interiors of the homes of Henry Greene and of Frank Lloyd Wright suggest that they were all formerly a part of the Aesthetic Movement.

In striking contrast to the exterior, the interior of the living room seems to explode into a "Moorish" fantasy of curving vault-like ceiling forms which spring from various columns exposed within the space and along the walls. The walls themselves were kept simple and the single example of structural ornament is the elaborate "Syrian" design of the capitals which are dramatic transitions between the plastered walls and the undulating ceiling. Great swags of fabric swoop between the capitals. But most interesting were the interior furnishings. The floor was covered with various sized oriental rugs. Victorian furniture was randomly placed and a large pillow sat in the middle of the floor. About the room were various paintings, examples of what appear to be Indian pottery, and a hurricane lamp. Through the columns in the library area were several cabinets stuffed with books and presumably somewhere there would be displayed the fashionable peacock feather.

One might deduce that this agglomeration of artifacts solely represented the tastes of the owner except that in the same publication illustrating the Tomkins house there is an equally cluttered photograph entitled "A peep into the home of Charles Sumner Greene."[12] This living room interior, like the Tomkins', is dominated by great swags of drapery, oriental rugs, furniture scattered here and there and books, paintings, and photographs everywhere. The great number and variety of objects in this room presumably reflected Charles' personal tastes. Throughout his life he surrounded himself with *objets d'art* which fascinated him. His own workspace expressed his many and varied interests and were a contrast to the strict restraint and order demanded in the buildings he and Henry designed for their clients.

A comparison of the interiors of the Tomkins house, Charles Greene's house and the interior of Frank Lloyd Wright's home at this time is particularly interesting in light of the thesis put forth by H. Allen Brooks and published in the *Journal of the Society of Architectural Historians*.

12. *Pasadena, California—The City Beautiful*, 1902.

As Mr. Brooks states:

> If you assumed [this was] illustrating a typical, cluttered Victorian interior, you were of course correct, because what this pre-1895 photograph indicates is Wright's taste in furniture and design before he came in contact with the Arts and Crafts Movement.[13]

If, as Mr. Brooks infers, the Arts and Crafts Movement caused various architectural contemporaries to "clean up" and bring more disciplined order to their work and to the arrangement of furnishings, then this might similarly have affected Charles Greene. That it only did so to a certain extent illustrates the searching duality of Charles' life and mind. Henry had a natural tendency for order in his life which easily fitted in with this trend.

The third and most prestigious of the three residences was "Torrington Place," the elaborate and costly Shingle Style mansion for James Swan.[14] A leader in church and civic affairs, Mr. Swan was a member of the wealthy eastern set who frequented the fashionable hotels. The Swan house on Colorado Street—Pasadena's main throughfare—soon became the showplace of the community. Because of Mr. Swan's desires the design was strongly traditional. However, the Greenes softened the traditional classicism of the entry portico and colonade with the bold unbroken line of the roof by continuing over the side porte cochere in much the same way as in the roof line of the Longley house and of the 1887 Low house by McKim, Mead and White.

The interiors of the Swan house exhibited an extensive use of oak paneling, sculptured plaster ceilings and ornate stained glass windows which showed the influence of Stanford White. The ceiling designs were flowing sinuous lines, the first known appearance of fluid Art Nouveau forms in the work of the Greenes.

13. H. Allen Brooks, "Chicago Architecture: Its Debt to the Arts and Crafts," *Journal of the Society of Architectural Historians*, Vol. XXX, No. 4, pp. 315-316.

14. In 1925, Mrs. Swan had Henry Greene do drawings for a major modification and it is possible that he was also involved in the moving of the house to its present site. In the process, the roof lines were dramatically changed to relate to the then popular style. The interiors were then changed by the owners.

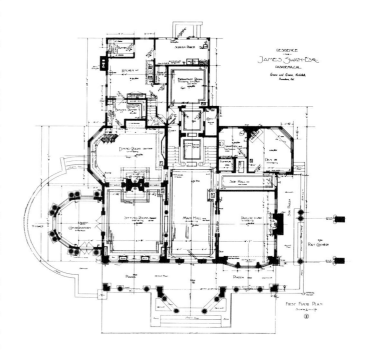

James Swan house, 515 E. Colorado Street, Pasadena, 1895. Courtesy of Avery Architectural Library.

The exterior design was influenced by the work of McKim, Mead and White. The house was moved to 2162 N. Holliston Avenue in 1925 and altered.

After the Fay, Tomkins and Swan residences of 1898, the Greenes designed the J. M. Smith house in 1899. The general outline of the house was in the Mission Style. The thin vertical "slit" windows which the Greenes used frequently added a play of light which helped break down the scale of their larger structures. Here too, in the Smith house, the strong flat dormer window was used, only in this case it took on a more forceful character because of the triangular gable which projected above the broad hipped roof. As in the Tomkins house, the Greenes were conscious of the transition between structure and site. Here for the first time they featured the large outdoor terrace created by incorporating the massive retaining wall into their design.

In the Charles W. Hollister house, also designed in 1899, the Greenes used the dormer as they did in the Smith house. But except for this feature the two houses were totally different and reflected the real struggles going on in the minds of the Greenes. This, the first of two houses for Hollister, while more Shingle Style, was simpler and cleaner than either the Longley or Swan houses. The plan was still tight even with the use of half-octagonal ends in the living and reception rooms. However, it was the straightforward quality of the exterior that was most noticeable in contrast to previous work. The single most notable feature was the chimney design. Although the drawings showed a quaint pattern of stone work along the edges, the chimney, as built, exhibited a much more direct and sculptural composition.

A similar chimney design expressing the stone boldly appeared in the design for the first house for Dr. William T. Bolton which, for the Greenes, was their singular venture with the Dutch Colonial style.

J. M. Smith house, 125 Terrace Drive, Pasadena, 1899 (Demolished).

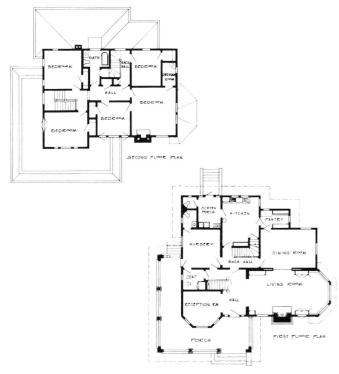

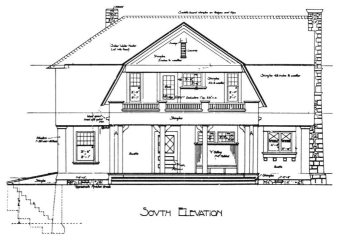

SOUTH ELEVATION

FIRST FLOOR PLAN

SECOND FLOOR PLAN

Charles W. Hollister house, 310 Bellefontaine Street, Pasadena, 1899. R. L. Makinson photograph.

This Shingle Style design is much cleaner than the previous designs for the Longley and Swan houses and illustrates a movement toward the Craftsman Style. Enclosure of porch roof terrace by others.

Dr. William T. Bolton house, address unknown, 1899. Courtesy of Avery Architectural Library.

In another change of direction, the design for the first of two houses for Dr. Bolton explores the Dutch Colonial Style with very slight hints of the oriental in the knee braces of the porch posts.

Wedding photograph of
Henry Mather Greene
and Emeline Augusta Dart,
1899.
Photograph courtesy of
Greene and Greene Library.

Just prior to the turn of the century Henry Greene was married to Miss Emeline Augusta Dart, a local girl formerly of Rock Island, Illinois where the wedding was held. By this time the Greenes' architectural practice was doing well. The firm had already completed some forty commissions, including some very large residences, in less than six years.

With the turn of the century came two non-residential designs—each of which avoided the restraints of traditionalism. The two clients, for whom they did numerous commissions, were to become long and lasting friends of the Greenes. The first commission for S. Hazard Halsted, was one of the first structures for the Pasadena Ice Company. The second was a two-story brick store building for the Bentz Antique Shop. Unlike the Kinney-Kendall building, just a few doors north, the Bentz building was nearly devoid of decoration and was basically a brick shell with large glass windows. More important than this store building, however, was the friendship which developed between Mr. and Mrs. Bentz and the Greenes. John C. Bentz was a prominent dealer in Oriental antiques. Throughout their most creative years the Greenes maintained a close association with the families of Mr. Bentz and his two brothers, who had shops in Pasadena, Santa Barbara and San Francisco. The Bentz association coincided with the major influences which most clearly affected the Greenes at the turn of the century: the Orient, the early publications expounding the Arts and Crafts philosophies, and their own manual training background. Through the Bentz families the Greenes had access to books, paintings and *objets d'art* from the Orient which stimulated their interests. In a letter to this writer Mrs. Bentz recalled:

> They were very fond of the stock of Japanese goods which my husband imported and often dropped in to chat and enjoy the various articles and reference books, nearly all of which concerned the temples. He [Charles] liked the heavy timber work in their construction.[15]

A careful study of the Greenes' later work suggests that they were also attracted to the Japanese Imperial Palace architecture where there can be found similarities of detail. Mrs. Bentz futher related:

> When I made my first trip to Japan in 1901 I brought back numerous little old books—mostly second hand and a number of prints, all of which he [Charles] loved, and I gave him many of them.

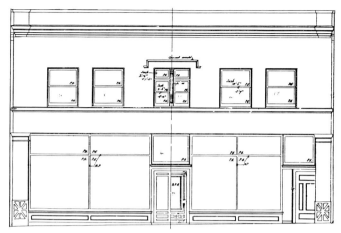

John C. Bentz building, 49-55 S. Raymond Avenue, Pasadena, 1900. (Demolished) Courtesy of Avery Architectural Library.

Much more modest than its neighbor, the Kinney-Kendall Building, the Bentz shop was nearly devoid of decoration and was basically a brick shell with extensive use of glass for show windows.

These were added to a collection of Oriental books, imported furniture and prints of historic Chinese and Japanese buildings which Charles and Henry, to a lesser extent, were to cherish all their lives. And while neither, much to their regret, ever had the opportunity to visit the Orient, Charles is known to have spent hours poring over the books, and is said to have gained inspiration for his own creations from these contemplations.[16] Charles Greene alluded to such inspirations in his unpublished novel, *Thais Thayer*:

> My eye fell upon the bronze urn. Presently I had a revelation...I laid out my scheme and began to build upon paper the essence of inspired thought....But strange as it may seem to the layman the spirit of that old bronze was the guiding motive of the design. I didn't draw a line or form a contour but my mentor stood before me, bathed in the still morning light where it always met my gaze...[17]

15. Letter to the author, November 30, 1958.

16. Interview with Alice and Charles Greene, 1955; Clay Lancaster, "My Interviews with Greene and Greene," *Journal of the American Institute of Architects*, XXVI, July, 1957, p. 204.

17. C. Sumner Greene, manuscript for the novel *Thais Thayer*; Documents Collection, Greene and Greene Library, The Gamble House.

About 1903 another and equally significant tie with the Orient emanated from the visit of an "itinerant bookseller." In an important interview with L. Morgan Yost in 1946, Charles related the incident. The bookseller

> had a set of books on travel. Idly Charles Greene leafed through the pages until his attention was arrested by pictures of Japanese homes and gardens. This is what he had been seeking. Here was the expression of post and beam and garden as one, an informal yet carefully conceived whole...No detail could be seen in the chalk and charcoal engravings of the time. But there was enough to start the flame of creation.[18]

To prove that this was not all his imagination, Charles turned and showed Yost the purported book. He "turned almost automatically to the page and remarked sadly that he had never gotten to Japan." This may, however, have been fortunate, for by assimilating all that they could from art objects and books, the Oriental influence for Greene and Greene filtered through the various cultures of California and consequently made their own work delightfully fresh.

The first of the many houses to be built on the Arroyo View knoll was designed for Katherine M. Duncan late in 1900.[19] The original single-story plan rambled about the small central courtyard. It was a simple house, its interior treatment of the study was an early hint of the Greenes' Craftsman Style and responded to the growing interest in the bungalow. It harkened back to the Manual Training School experience and the brothers' interest in wood as a flexible and naturally beautiful building material. The plan expressed a relaxation from the tight formality of previous plans but the Greenes were still searching...that character would not really appear again in their work until 1903 in the Arturo Bandini house.

18. L. Morgan Yost, "Greene and Greene of Pasadena," *Journal of the American Institute of Architects*, September, 1950, p. 123.

19. The Greenes did major alterations and additions on the structure in 1906 for Theodore M. Irwin and it was thereafter published widely under that name.

Katherine M. Duncan house, 240 N. Grand Avenue, Pasadena, 1900. Tournament of Roses Edition, *Pasadena Daily News*, 1905.

The design hints of the Greenes' leaning toward the Arts and Crafts Movement in its interior treatment. It was dramatically remodeled by the Greenes in 1906 for Theodore M. Irwin.

By 1901 Henry Greene and his wife were living in Los Angeles and, in the belief that a downtown office would broaden their practice, the Greenes opened a second office in the Potomac Block in Los Angeles. They maintained the original office in Pasadena for a while, however, and subsequent plans noted both the Kinney-Kendall and Potomac Block addresses.

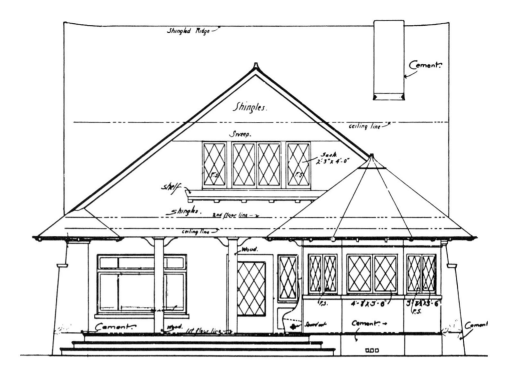

Metilde Phillips house, 151 S. Fair Oaks Avenue, Pasadena, 1901. (Demolished) Courtesy of Avery Architectural Library.

Here for the first time the Greenes injected the slightly oriental lift to the ridge line of the roof.

The brothers remained interested in octagonal geometry, but tended to interrelate it with square and rectilinear compositions. This was particularly evident in 1901 when nearly all of their work had the running theme of the half octagon form emerging from some portion of the design. In the house for Mrs. Metilde Phillips it became the dramatic feature of the front elevation and began to exhibit a unified control. The front elevations composed the bay windows of the first floor with a simple band of casement windows in the center of the second level organized under a strong, simple symmetrical gable. While the second level of the Phillips house began to take on a new sense of order in composition, the first floor still drew from Victorian historicism.

In 1901 Charles Greene was married to Alice White, who had emigrated from England several years before. As a present for his bride he designed and built a simple square table supported by a central square pedestal. The top of the table was inlaid in a geometric pattern of different woods. This was the first piece of furniture known to have been designed by the Greenes. That spring Charles and his bride honeymooned in England, which was then the center of the Arts and Crafts Movement. The timing was significant. The Greenes were receptive to a more "natural" expression which was beginning to emerge in their work. Charles' fascination with the English country house was clearly evident on his return to California.

Charles Greene's own house, "Oakholm," was designed in 1901 shortly before their early Craftsman ventures and related more to the Phillips house and the Lorenz P. Hansen house in terms of the Greenes' own development. The plan was tight, utilizing the half octagon to give space to the living and dining rooms. However, in the charming second-story studio Charles built for himself, the plan emerged upward with a fully expressed octagonal room. In later alterations the quality of this space was partially lost to rectilinear forms. As it developed, Charles' own house served somewhat as a center for experimentation. It was here that he would explore details that were later used, refined, and developed for other clients. As a result, a walk through this house is a moving and exciting experience as it becomes a walk back through the Greenes' development where at each turn of the way differing periods in their artistic development can be seen.[20]

20. It is encouraging that the current owners, Mr. and Mrs. James Richardson are carefully restoring the interiors with superb craftsmanship and authenticity.

Charles Sumner Greene, Alice Gordon White Greene and son Nathaniel about 1903.
Photograph courtesy of Greene and Greene Library.

Charles S. Greene house, 368 Arroyo View Drive, Pasadena, 1901. Photograph courtesy of Greene and Greene Library.

Charles Greene's own house, as originally built, relates more to the Phillips and Hansen houses and not until its additions and alterations later did it exhibit the quality of their Craftsman period.

Lorenz P. Hansen house, 968 or 1000 San Pasqual Street,
Pasadena, 1901 (Demolished).
Drawing by Donald Woodruff.

In 1901 two publications appeared which helped lead
the Greenes into the Arts and Crafts Movement and bring
forth distinct changes in their work. These were the Will
Bradley articles in the *Ladies Home Journal* and Gustav Stickley's magazine *The Craftsman*. Bradley's articles on the integration of interiors appeared with his furniture designs
periodically throughout 1901 and clippings from most of
these are found carefully placed in the Greenes' scrapbook
of the period.[21] While this indicates a genuine interest in

21. Scrapbook, Documents Collection, Greene and Greene Library,
    The Gamble House.

Greene and Greene scrapbook.
Courtesy of Greene and Greene Library.

Page from the scrapbook showing carefully entered clippings
from the Will Bradley articles published in the *Ladies Home
Journal* throughout 1901. Very little of the Art Nouveau character in Bradley's designs seems to have rubbed off on the
Greenes, however.

Bradley's work, very little of the Art Nouveau character in his designs seemed to rub off on the Greenes. What is far more important was the fact that Bradley was demonstrating the idea that architects could design and build furniture expressly related to their interior designs, a concept that was already being expounded in the *International Studio* magazine by the English Arts and Crafts architects. The initial issue of *The Craftsman* magazine in October of 1901 coincided with Charles' return from England and, coupled with Bradley's articles, gave real encouragement to the Greenes. This first issue dealt with the philosophy of William Morris which was now, through Gustav Stickley, actually being implemented in America. They must have been excited, to say the least, to find a man not only writing of the new Craftsman philosophy but also designing and producing items of the highest quality and workmanship. Stickley was indeed demonstrating what the Greenes had learned back in the Manual Training School. Having established his workshops as the "United Crafts of Eastwood, New York" Stickley wrote in the Foreword of the first issue of *The Craftsman*:

> The new association is a guild of cabinetworkers, metal and leather workers, which has been recently formed for the production of household furnishings....The United Crafts endeavor to promote and to extend the principles established by Morris, in both the artistic and socialistic sense.

There also appeared in that same issue an article entitled "An Argument for Simplicity in Household Furnishings" in which Stickley stated:

> Present tendencies are toward a simplicity unknown in the past. The form of any object is made to express the structural idea directly, frankly, often almost with baldness.[22]

22. "An Argument for Simplicity in Household Furnishings," *The Craftsman*, October, 1901, p. 47.

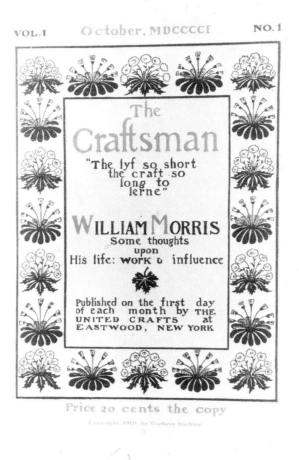

First issue of Gustav Stickley's magazine, *The Craftsman*.

Gustav Stickley was demonstrating what the Greenes had learned so well in the Manual Training School. *The Craftsman* provided real encouragement in the Greenes' orientation toward the Arts and Crafts Movement.

Entry and stairwell.

Interior.

The Greenes certainly saw and read these first publications of *The Craftsman* for within a few short months (early in 1902) they completely furnished the James Culbertson house in Stickley's furniture, even selecting the very pieces that had appeared in the October and November, 1901 issues.

However, in 1902 former New Jersey Senator George H. Barker called upon the Greenes to develop his vast estate, "Light Hall," in formal Colonial grandeur. This was a dramatic step back into historicism and was the one occasion where the brothers seriously worked in the Colonial Revival style; and, although it exhibits little of the individuality of their emerging directions, it demonstrates a kind of necessary versatility for an ongoing architectural practice. It is quite possible that this commission came into the office while Charles was in Europe, for in later years he would decline work rather than sacrifice his own artistic principles to the whim or demand of a client.

The grand design for the Barker house, while essentially Colonial, did suggest a Jeffersonian touch, again reflecting the work of McKim, Mead and White. Interiors were furnished with oriental rugs and included selections of neoclassical furniture. However, in a typical California manner, the classic design gave way in parts of the house to Craftsman ideas. The woodwork, the furniture and the lighting of a dining area and the peg detail over the fireplace in the study deferred to the Arts and Crafts as did the Art Nouveau forms in the leaded glass of the library.

George H. Barker house, 505 S. Grand Avenue, Pasadena, 1902. Photographs courtesy of Documents Collection, College of Environmental Design, UCB.

"Light Hall" was a dramatic step back into traditional styles
and was the one serious occasion when the Greenes worked
in the Colonial Style. However, the Colonial design is modified
in the Craftsman treatment of the den and its furnishings.

All Saints Episcopal Church rectory, 132 N. Euclid Avenue, Pasadena, 1902. (Demolished)
Photograph courtesy of Greene and Greene Library.

Their successful practice demanded further compromises which they were still prepared to make. In 1902 they designed a small rectory for the All Saints Episcopal Church in Pasadena, and also a rooming house for Rose J. Rasey. But also in 1902 Greene and Greene designed and built a house for James A. Culbertson. And here they brought together true Craftsman elements which were to become a distinctive part of their own unique vocabulary. Culbertson, a lumberman, had purchased a wheat field on a high bluff overlooking the Arroyo Seco from which cobblestones were taken for use in the foundation, garden walls and chimneys.

Mrs. Rose J. Rasey rooming house, 158 N. Euclid Avenue, Pasadena, 1902 (Demolished).
Pasadena, Illustrated Souvenir Book, 1903.

Known as Hotel El Morera, there is a pleasant symmetry and simplicity about this structure. This appears to be the only instance where the Greenes used white on door and window trim.

James A. Culbertson house, 235 N. Grand Avenue, Pasadena, 1902. Photograph courtesy of Documents Collection, College of Environmental Design, UCB.

Influenced by the half-timber country houses Charles had seen on his wedding trip to England, the Culbertson house also demonstrates the Greenes' interests in the use of clinker brick as a building material.

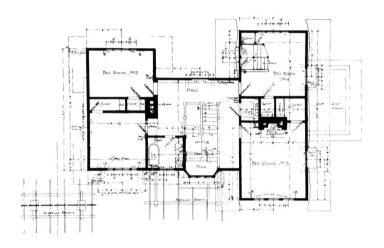

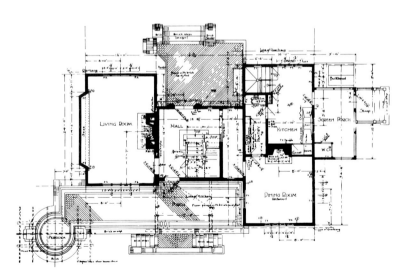

Plans, courtesy of Greene and Greene Library.

The Greenes, dissatisfied with the uniform gray of the cobblestones, added clinker brick, discards from local brick manufacturers. These were irregular in shape, having been too close to the fires of the drying furnaces, and they offered rich color tones of terra cotta, warm browns, purples and black. The blending of the clinker brick with the granite cobblestone, under the careful and sensitive guidance of Charles Greene, resulted in a combination of materials, scales, and forms which added a richness to the Greene and Greene style. Particularly interesting was the way in which they handled the transition of the masonry to the other materials and forms. As a means of terminating the irregularity to the clinker brick compositions they switched to a dashed stucco surface over a simple rectangular form in the chimney tops and foundation walls.

The Culbertsons had been annual visitors to Pasadena since 1898, spending the winters at the Hotel Green. With the construction of the new home, however, they began to spend a greater part of their time in Pasadena although maintaining their original home in Kenilworth, Illinois. But it was not only the climate and the beautiful site of the new home that lured them. It was the freedom and relaxed atmosphere of the life in California which was expressed in the design for the house.

The plan of the Culbertson house took full advantage of the corner site. The hallway and stairwell, with entries from adjacent terraces at each side, was the circulation core of the structure, with the living room on one side and the kitchen, dining and service area on the other. While the two-story plan was compact and rectangular in form, the Greenes' concern for outdoor living was expressed in the large porch overlooking the Arroyo. To one side a circular sitting alcove was sheltered by a simple wooden pergola atop cobblestone and clinker brick piers. Horizontal bands of casement windows in the living room were recessed into a shallow side area. This was the early form of the inglenook the Greenes were to exploit so deftly in later homes. In these windows the clear leaded glass composition was an abstract pattern of horizontal and vertical lines manifest as proportionately related square and rectangular forms.

James A. Culbertson house. Rear view.
Photograph courtesy of Documents Collection, College of
Environmental Design, UCB.

James A. Culbertson house.
Photograph courtesy of Mr. and Mrs. W. K. Dunn.

The Greenes combined here the orientalism of the ceiling trim with the linear abstraction in the clear leaded windows, the four-square directness of Stickley's oak furniture, carpets of American Indian design and accessories out of the Tiffany and Rookwood Studios. In spite of all these elements, it is simple, it is direct and it all seems to hang together.

These windows were in distinct contrast to the flowing Art Nouveau leaded window designs introduced to the house in a later addition. Although the exterior took the form of the English half-timber style, with the lower walls in a rough dashed stucco and the upper clad in shingle, the interiors were more imaginative and expressed the Greenes' growing confidence as they began to embrace the Arts and Crafts Movement. The ceiling and wall patterns of the trim of the living room showed, for the first time, the strong influence which Japanese timber construction had upon their designs. Even the colors took on Oriental overtones. The walls of the living room were of rough plaster stained a "Japanese" gray contrasting with the patina of the natural wood trim and furniture.

Although the Greenes had not yet reached the architectural expression they are now known for, they were already leaning toward a "total" architecture where the architect was involved with all aspects of the design. Through *The Craftsman* magazine they were lured by the simplicity of Stickley's oak furniture. Here were furniture forms that seemed to come directly from the worker's craft, to be designed according to the same priniciples the Greenes had absorbed in the Manual Training School. A major article about the Culbertson house appeared in *Good Housekeeping* magazine in 1906, and described the charms of an inexpensive house reflecting the spirit of life in California:

Here is a house...which cost about $6000 to build, yet it serves admirably as a model for more expensive mansions, while its simplicity and the abundance of its pleasing ideas hold out many possibilities to the builder of the veriest cottage.[23]

This was indeed a distinction between the Greenes and many of their contemporaries. Although the Culbertson house was a design of English extraction, it clearly had its roots in the nature of its California site and in the easy pace of California life. The weaving of the personalities of the clients and the characteristics of the regional environment, regardless of style or form, was inherent in later Greene and Greene designs. They were able to accomplish this with such ease that the resulting house blended into the landscape with a natural grace. The author of the *Good Housekeeping* article, Una Nixson Hopkins, recognized these same qualities when she wrote of California as: "a region in which native domestic architecture is flowering with a beauty and sincerity hitherto unknown on this continent." She described the conditions for building on the "Coast" as "peculiarly favorable to the free development of good domestic architecture—the climate, the seasons, the supply of building materials, (and) a generation of talented and enthusiastic young architects."[24] Although the Hopkins article was written four years later, it portrays the spirit of the Greenes in 1902. For the better part of a decade they had explored the traditional styles, and had experimented with some of their ideas in search of architectural expressions which, to them, made sense in a young and growing land. The Culbertson house more than any other provided a hint of what was to come.

23. Una Nixson Hopkins, "A Study for Homebuilders," *Good Housekeeping*, March, 1906, p. 259.

24. *Ibid.*

Terrace pergola overlooking the vast Arroyo Seco valley. Photograph courtesy of Greene and Greene Library.

Mr. Culbertson is seated beside the timbered pergola used here for the first time by the Greenes. This is an early example of their handling of heavy timbers with the cobblestone and clinker brick piers, although here they had not yet begun to soften the timbers by gently rounding the ends.

III

A Style Emerging 1903–1907

Nearly a decade passed after the Greenes' arrival in California before the blossoming of their creative imagination. Then, with surprising speed and vigor, they developed and refined the style which was to have such an impact on California domestic architecture. Within a year a new spirit was expressed in the plan forms of the Bandini house of mid-1903 and in the detail of the Reeve house of early 1904.

The second decade of their work opened with a major change in operations which was officially announced in January, 1903.

> Messrs Greene and Greene, Architects, announce that on and after February 1, 1903, their office will be in the Grant building, N. W. corner Fourth and Broadway, Los Angeles, rooms 722 and 723. The Pasadena office will be discontinued. Mr. Charles Sumner Greene will be found at his studio, Arroyo View Drive, Pasadena, Monday, Wednesday and Friday afternoons.[1]

While the larger office in Los Angeles suggested a desire for a more extended and diverse practice, immediate events were to ultimately draw all office activity back to Pasadena. Charles maintained his artist-patron relationship with clients by keeping his studio in his home in Pasadena. It was there that Arturo Bandini presented the firm with a simple commission which invited unlimited opportunities of open patio planning—a concept which freed the Greenes from the tight formality of traditional plan forms. Arturo Bandini was the son of Juan Bandini, one of the old Spanish dons whose family roots lay in the life, government and environment of early California. He and his wife had a natural feeling for the early Spanish way of life and for the structures found scattered about the southland. They asked the Greenes to build them a simple bungalow which would express the charm of those early adobe structures, take its form from their central courtyard plans, and be constructed from economical materials. A plan expressive of a gracious unhurried life was the important consideration. The material of construction was secondary; wood was chosen. The natural feeling of a way of life was to be evoked, not a sterile image of a conception of that life. As Charles described the concept in a letter to another client,

> We are just beginning a house on the old mission plan that is to have a court about 60 feet square. It is all of wood and very simple—not in the so called Mission style at all.[2]

The Arturo Bandini house, named "El Hogar," the hearth, was a series of spaces one room deep arranged around three sides of a spacious central court.[3] The two side wings contained the separate chambers and were connected at the rear by the living, dining and kitchen areas. Each of the rooms opened onto the covered veranda which defined the central court. This court, screened from the front of the property by a free standing flower covered pergola, was given added charm by trees, flower beds, paths and a central fountain.

1. Newspaper clipping; undated, found in the Greenes' scrapbook.
2. Undated letter by Charles Greene to Mrs. James A. Garfield. Documents Collection, Greene and Greene Library, The Gamble House.
3. Two of the three wings of the Bandini house were destroyed by fire in 1923. The rebuilding by other architects followed the general form of the original structure but not the architectural character. The third wing remained in original condition until its demolition in 1961.

Arturo Bandini house, 1149 San Pasqual Street, Pasadena, 1903.
(Demolished) Drawing by Donald Woodruff.

The central courtyard plan allowed for comfortable outdoor
living in the arid Southern California rolling countryside and
opened the door to other casual plan forms which Greene
and Greene developed with considerable variation in their
designs for both large and small houses.

Detail of interior patio.
Photograph courtesy of Mrs. Elliott Bandini.

The adobe and tile-roofed structures of early California
were here interpreted modestly in redwood and cobblestone.
Landscaping was kept informal.

The Greenes chose redwood as the basic construction material because of its lasting qualities, ease of working, and response to subtle earth-toned stains. They developed a basic structural system fabricated entirely on the ground and then hoisted into place as a finished wall inside and out. The redwood boards, rough on the exterior and smooth on the interior, were covered at the joints with three inch battens. The exterior was left in a rough stain while the inside was given a thin light oil finish to prevent spotting of the wood and yet retain as nearly as possible its natural color.[4] Wood roof trusses, fully expressed in the interior design, were built right on the site and hoisted into position as soon as the walls were raised. The ceiling was sheathed with the same batten detail as the walls. The two massive fireplaces were built of cobblestones and had heavy wooden mantels. Large projecting boulders formed seats on each side of the firebox. Two large flat handmade bricks from the old San Fernando Mission were carefully placed in the hearth of the living room.[5]

The most important element was the "U" shaped plan organization which allowed for a free association of indoor and outdoor spaces complementary to one another, and brought the garden into the total living pattern. The interiors had an intimate, sheltered and cave-like atmosphere; they were cool and comfortable during the day and provided an escape from the hot burning rays of the sun and the dry air. The doors and windows were opened in the late afternoons to take advantage of the cool breezes of the evening. Seating space under the veranda served as a transition between the garden and the interiors and gave protection from the elements. The structural columns supporting the veranda rested upon granite boulders from the arroyo.

4. Seymore E. Locke, "Bungalows; What They Really Are," *House and Garden*, August, 1907.

5. M. Laura Jodon, "El Hogar—A Quaint and Interesting Home in Pasadena," *Los Angeles Times Illustrated Weekly Magazine*, September, 1904.

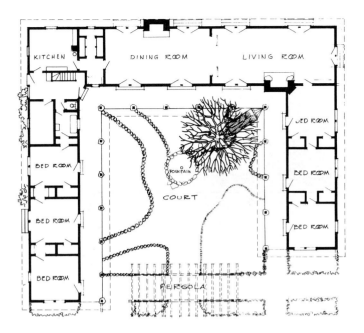

Arturo Bandini house.

Living room and dining room.
Photograph courtesy of Mrs. Elliott Bandini.

The interiors were developed in the same materials as the
exterior and the natural character of the foothills and arroyos
became an integral part of the design. The bench to the
left in the opening to the dining room represents one of the
earliest Greene and Greene furniture designs.

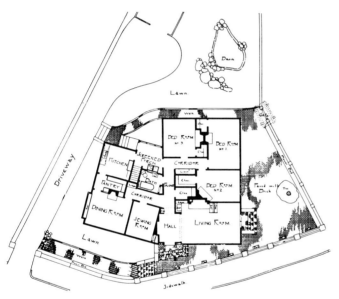

Martha, Violet and Jane White house, 370 Arroyo View Drive, Pasadena, 1903. *The Western Architect*, July, 1908.

An early attempt to break from traditional linear forms, the design for Charles' sisters-in-law evolved from the irregular configuration of the site. For the first time structural elements of the roof overhangs, porch and cantilever details were expressed as a contributing part of the articulated design.

Although the Greenes looked upon the Bandini house as a turning point in their work, its actual significance was related more to its planning relationships and utilization of outdoor spaces. The open plan concept which defined and utilized outside space provided the Greenes with that seemingly missing element which would introduce less formal plan concepts to their future designs.

At this same time Charles' three sisters-in-law purchased the property directly east of his own home on Arroyo View Drive where the angled configuration of the front property line and the pie-shaped lot necessitated a break from the tight Victorian plan. Although not as open and free as some of their later designs, the scheme for the house for Martha, Violet and Jane White was inspired by the angle of the street and bent on the central axis. The bent plan related well to the irregular and sloping site and accented the low horizontal lines by cantilevering the shingle-clad main floor beyond the rock and clinker brick foundation wall which enclosed the small quarters below. This structure suggests that the timing of the design may have been related to the appearance of the "itinerant bookseller" with his publications on Japanese timber structures. Here for the first time the Greenes put special emphasis on the projecting beams and timber structure of the entry roof. Although the ends were not rolled or shaped, as they often were in later designs, the cut detail and the imprint of the post and beam was now a dominant element of the Greenes' architectural palette.

During the construction of the White sisters' house, plans were proceeding on a small two-story rental house for Josephine van Rossem next door to the east.[6] The Arroyo View knoll was becoming a Greene and Greene village. This rental house originally possessed little of the expressed timber nature of the White sisters' house next door, but its low budget plan had a simplicity and order which were both efficient and appealing. Its unique quality appeared on the interior where the low ceilings—which also formed the flooring above—were built of rough sawn timbers which were left exposed and stained to a soft brown. The smooth redwood board and batt walls were wainscotted to a height of six feet and stained a darker brown. Consequently, the whole interior took on the warmth of the natural materials. Above the redwood paneling, burlap enhanced the frieze and carried out the natural quality of the interior. Upstairs, space was conserved by single width board and batt walls built on the flat and lifted into place. And here for the first time, the brothers designed lighting fixtures for the interior of the bedrooms. Although crude in comparison to later designs, these simple wall brackets were carefully integrated into the board and batt design.

6. Following major additions and alterations in 1906 the house was thereafter identified as the James W. Neill house.

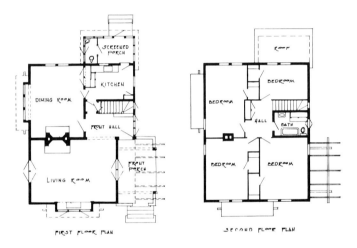

FIRST FLOOR PLAN   SECOND FLOOR PLAN

Josephine van Rossem house, 400 Arroyo View Drive, Pasadena, 1903. Photograph courtesy of W. J. van Rossem.

The first of three houses for Mrs. van Rossem, all built around the Arroyo View reservoir, this design remained for only three years, at which time the Greenes made substantial additions and alterations for Mr. and Mrs. James W. Neill. The plan, compact and straightforward, offered sizeable spaces, and good lighting and air circulation for a small house design.

Outside of the Pasadena newspapers and local souvenir books the first major publication of the Greenes' work featured Charles Greene's renderings for the Mary R. Darling house at Claremont, California published in London's *Academy Architecture*, 1903. Quite compact and totally unlike the rambling Bandini plan, the Darling house had a rustic Craftsman quality throughout. This quality is best expressed in the memoirs of Kenneth Glendower Darling entitled "Our New Home":

> The broad front was allotted to the living room, the so-called study (eventually my own private sanctum for pursuits scholastic), and an entrance hall. When the sliding doors were thrown aside, the entire length of the house could be converted virtually into a single room — an arrangement admirably suited to the requirements of entertaining on a large scale. These rooms were lighted by casement windows built out from the line of the walls and resting on huge native boulders—a device permitting the installation of snug upholstered window seats. Among other individual touches were the redwood beams of the ceilings, left essentially in the rough (with the original adze marks still in evidence) and the dado and raised dais of the 'study'.[7]

7. Kenneth Glendower Darling, *My Early Life in California and My First American and European Tours (1890-1908)*, Honnold Library, Claremont Colleges, pp. 15-16.

ALCOVE IN STUDY.

Mary R. Darling house, 807 N. College Avenue, Claremont, 1903. *Academy Architecture*, 1903.

The watercolor sketch of the exterior by Charles Greene for the English publication *Academy Architecture* represented the first foreign publication of the work of the firm. Charles' sketch of the study alcove indicates the Greenes' avid interest in the early issues of Gustav Stickley's magazine *The Craftsman*. The interior fittings closely emulate Stickley's own mission oak furniture as well as the fine hammered copper lamp designs of Dirk van Erp. Although published as the work of Charles, the plan expresses a sense of order and symmetry which is more often identified with the designs of Henry.

The Greenes' interest in *The Craftsman* is clearly evident in Charles' sketches of the interior picturing furniture, lamps, rugs, etc. which very closely resemble Gustav Stickley's furniture designs and accessories advertised in his magazine. But most significant is the concern for the total design. The exterior watercolor sketch deals with the landscaping and the interior drawings show the relationship of interior furnishings. This is particularly interesting inasmuch as the work of Harvey Ellis first appeared in the July and August, 1903 issues of *The Craftsman*.[8] The Ellis illustrations exhibited a feeling for the work of Charles Rennie Mackintosh, C. F. A. Voysey, and Joseph Hoffman and contained the two-dimensional graphic design quality sometimes felt

in their work. But there was also an overriding strength in the unity of the overall design and furnishings which had a significant effect upon the Greenes' work. Although the Greenes had been following the *International Studio* magazine since 1897, it seems to have strongly influenced their own work only after the Ellis articles. In any case, the Greenes' first-hand knowledge of manual training, materials, construction and woodworking techniques gave their handling of detail a powerful three-dimensional realism with the same degree of integrity found in Japanese joinery.

8. Harvey Ellis, "A Craftsman House Design," *The Craftsman*, July 1903, Vol IV, No. IV, pp. 269-277; Harvey Ellis, "An Urban House," *The Craftsman*, August 1903, Vol. IV, No. V, pp, 312-327.

Harvey Ellis, sketch for an article entitled "An Urban House." *The Craftsman*, August 1903.

The Greenes' later three-dimensional use of the square peg as a functional and aesthetic detail may have been inspired by Ellis' decorative use of the square pattern in the wall behind the piano.

F. J. Martin studio apartments, 225 N. Madison Avenue, Pasadena, 1903. (Demolished) Courtesy of Avery Architectural Library.

The clean direct composition of the plans is disguised by the facade designed just prior to the Greenes' major break from the popular adaptations of the Mission Style.

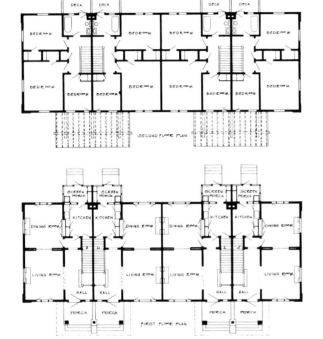

Emma M. Black house, 210 S. Madison Avenue, Pasadena, 1903. R. L. Makinson photograph.

The use of clapboard siding and the square bay window relate this small bungalow design to the first van Rossem house.

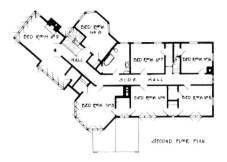

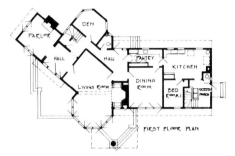

Other work emerging from the office in 1903 reflected previous practices and influences as well as variations on the newer concepts. These structures included the Frank J. Martin apartments, houses for Emma M. Black, Philip L. Auten, Samuel P. Sanborn, Dr. Edith J. Claypole, and the Dr. Francis F. Rowland house and office.

Samuel P. Sanborn house, 65 N. Catalina Avenue, Pasadena, 1903. Marvin Rand photograph.

The varied geometric forms of the plan were carefully composed and contribute to the free and playful three-dimensional character of the overall structure. Originally built at 999 E. Colorado Street, the house was moved to 65 N. Catalina Avenue as the boulevard developed commercially.

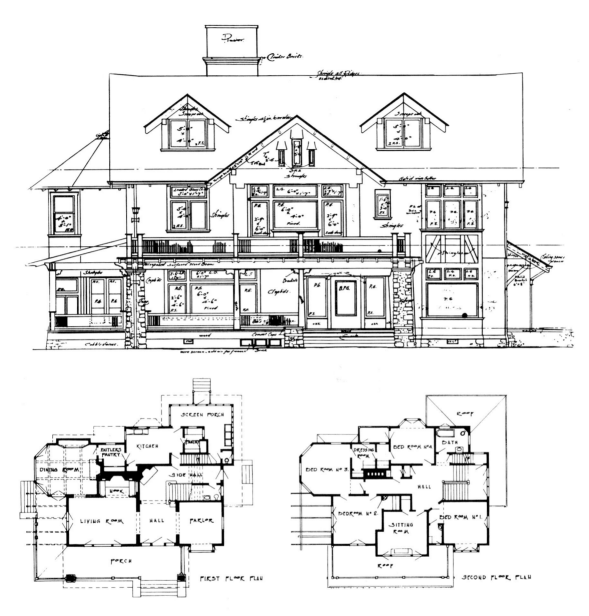

Philip L. Auten house, 119 N. Madison Avenue, Pasadena, 1903. (Demolished) Courtesy of Avery Architectural Library.

This "transition" house reveals elements of both the "old" and the "new." These include the octagonal bays, the clustered traditional plan, clapboard siding and cobblestone masonry composed with the emerging wooden structural vocabulary of projecting timbers, balcony railing detail, bold gabled roof forms and slit windows.

Dr. Edith J. Claypole house, 50 S. Grand Avenue, Pasadena, 1903. (Demolished) Photograph courtesy of Documents Collection, College of Environmental Design, UCB.

The plan of the Claypole house came as close to a stock design as ever utilized by Greene and Greene and was repeated in variation on several occasions.

Dr. Frances F. Rowland house and office, 225 State Street, Pasadena, 1903. Photograph courtesy of Documents Collection, College of Environmental Design, UCB.

The first of only two designs in which the Greenes struck the ridge across the narrow dimension of the plan to allow the roof of the two-story structure to sweep low over the entry thus giving a more modest frontal appearance. Roof openings allowed light and ventilation into the second floor spaces. The front pergola was added when the house was moved from 55 S. Marengo Avenue.

Jennie A. Reeve house, originally at 306 Cedar Avenue, Long Beach, 1904.

In contrast to the open sprawling patio designs for the climate of the San Gabriel Valley, the restricted corner lot of the Reeve house, three blocks from the Pacific surf, called for a compact plan which the Greenes developed with a strong central core, broad banks of bay windows to borrow the welcome sunshine, and fireside inglenooks when the fog and the chill of the ocean breezes came in.

Photograph courtesy of Greene and Greene Library.

In this design, Greene and Greene brought together most of the architectural elements that would become readily identified with their own unique vocabulary. It is the pivotal structure in their embrace of the Arts and Crafts Movement. The two-story, shingle-clad bungalow contained the Greene's characteristic articulated timber structure, multiple-gabled, deeply overhanging roofs (with the projecting support beams now shaped on the ends), open sleeping porches, vertical slit windows for closet ventilation, horizontal bands of casement windows, a sensitive combination of boulder and cobblestone with clinker brick masonry, Tiffany glass designs in doors, windows and lighting fixtures, and the coordination of landscape, walks, fencing and garden gates.

In 1902 and 1903 the various elements contributing to the Greenes' evolution as Craftsman architects appeared only as parts of one structure or another. But in January of 1904 the design for the Jennie A. Reeve house in Long Beach, California brought the full range of their new architectural vocabulary together for the first time. Here in this simple two-story, shingle-clad bungalow was the articulated timber structure, multiple-gabled overhanging roofs with projecting support beams now shaped on the ends, open sleeping porches, vertical slit windows, horizontal bands of casement windows, the sensitive combination of cobblestone with brick masonry; special door, leaded glass and lantern designs; the coordination of landscape, walks, fencing and garden gates and a full development of interior furniture and accessories. Although the patio plan ideas were fresh in their minds, the Greenes responded to the corner ocean front site and the chilly, sometimes foggy, environment with a carefully composed and compact plan which paid special attention to the seaside climate. Three massive fireplaces formed the axial core of the plan, and the living room and a flexible bedroom on the ground floor (often used as a related family room) were oriented to the ocean view and featured great bands of glass window walls and window seats to catch the rays of sunshine and brighten the detail of the interior wood paneling. In contrast, the corner inglenook of the living room provided a cave-like quality and was an invitation into a smaller protected space with corner seating built into a hearth of the grand firebox. Imaginative attention was paid to every aspect of the house. On the beautifully crafted interior, the Greenes' imprint was easily recognized in the carefully detailed panelling and built-in cabinetwork where the expressed pegs were softly rounded and the finish of the wood had a waxed patina. Leaded glass designs coordinated the panes of doors and windows with the china cabinets and interior storage units. Here was craftsmanship and design quality anticipating the masterpieces of 1907-09.

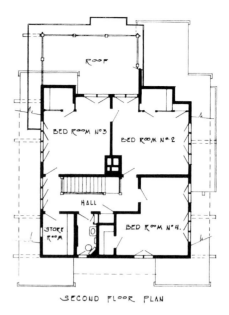

SECOND FLOOR PLAN

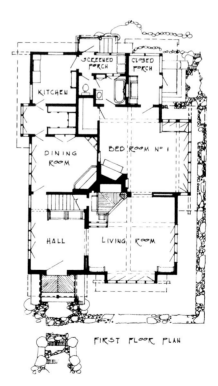

FIRST FLOOR PLAN

Living room inglenook and dining room interior.
Photographs courtesy of Documents Collection, College of
Environmental Design, UCB.

No part of the Reeve house escaped the imaginative attention
of the Greenes who coordinated every aspect of the beautifully crafted interior. Their unmistakeable imprint is easily
recognized in the careful handling of finish and detail where
the craftsmanship and design integration, here in 1904,
is a preview of their larger masterpieces of 1907-09. The
Greenes' furniture designs continue to show the influence of
Gustav Stickley, although with a bit more tenderness. The
pegs in the ash and cedar woods were left to protrude and the
edges and corners eased to soften the straight lines. Faint stains
were used and the finish was rubbed to a glass-like sheen.

Special attention was given to the new electric lighting. For the first time the Greenes designed hanging and bracketed lanterns of "Tiffany" glass with vine-patterned leaded overlay capped by broad canopys, not unlike the oriental lantern. Some were suspended from ceilings by chains and others were fastened to wall brackets where they were complemented by gas light jets in case the newly developed power plants broke down. The furniture, too, was designed for the house and styled very much after Gustav Stickley pieces. The archive photographs of the liv-

ing room inglenook and the dining room reveal a creative vigor. Such totality of design and craftsmanship establishes the Reeve house as one of the most significant of the Greenes' works. Were it in its original condition today it would certainly stand as one of this nation's monuments of American domestic architecture.[9] Mrs. Reeve was obviously pleased. In addition to her own house, the Greenes did two very small speculative houses for her, another in 1904 in Long Beach and one in 1906 in Sierra Madre.

9. The Reeve house has been moved twice in its long history of changing ownership. In 1917 Dr. V. Ray Townsend found the house on blocks ready to be carted away from its original site. He bought it and moved it several blocks inland to its second site in Long Beach. Shortly thereafter he moved to the Claremont area but, unwilling to give it up, rented it out for the next ten years. Meanwhile, in Claremont, the Townsends located the Darling house (1903) in which they resided until 1927 when Henry Greene was engaged to move the Reeve house a second time and to handle its additions, alterations and landscaping in readiness for the Townsends' return to Long Beach. Such devotion to architecture is unusual. The Greenes' buildings conveyed a spirit that is still communicated to their inhabitants.

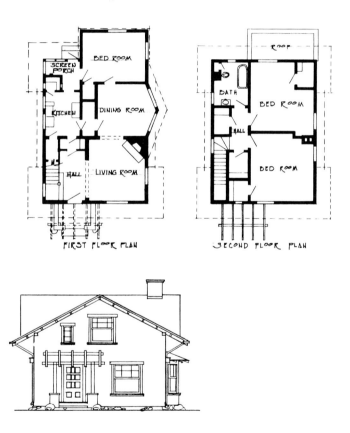

Jennie A. Reeve house No. 2, address unknown, Long Beach, 1904. Courtesy of Avery Architectural Library.

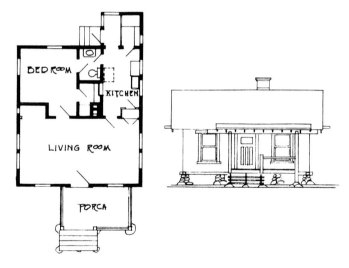

Jennie A. Reeve house No. 3, address unknown, Sierra Madre, 1906.

The second of two small speculative houses designed for Mrs. Reeve.

Although the firm retained the office in Los Angeles, the lure of the rolling countryside drew Henry Greene back to Pasadena in 1904 where he designed and built his own family home. Recognizing the strong bond between his wife Emeline and her mother, Charlotte A. Whitridge, Henry developed a special plan which provided an apartment enabling his mother-in-law to live in the same house with her daughter. A central hall bisected the two portions of the design which had dual facilities throughout with the exception of the large dining room at the end of the central hall. The rear line of the house was stepped to capture afternoon sunshine and the view of the valley to the south.

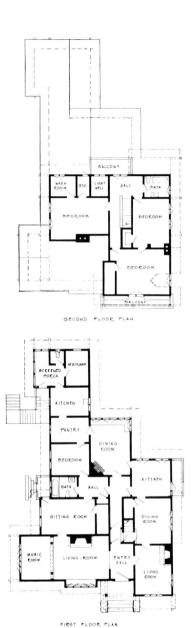

SECOND FLOOR PLAN

FIRST FLOOR PLAN

The unusual arrangement of this plan was prompted by the provision for Henry Greene's mother-in-law's apartment within the house. The house was stepped to capture the panorama of the San Gabriel Valley.

Henry Greene's disciplined touch was felt in the straight-forward lines of the exterior elevation. There was no hint of frivolity found in the entire composition. The chimneys were pure vertical stacks and the horizontal siding accentuated the crisp character of the design. The volumetric composition of the elements, particularly as viewed from the northeast, revealed that the architect was in full control. The exterior lines of the elevations moved in and out with purpose and integrity and there was a distinct unity about the overall composition. The roof planes were a quiet expression of overlapping and interrelating low gables woven together with a quiet grace, reminiscent of the nearby hills. As early as the mid-1890s, the Greenes had demonstrated a great concern for roof forms. This concern, crystallized in the construction of Henry's own home, became one of the most effective elements of their design vocabulary.

Henry M. Greene house, 146 Bellefontaine Street, Pasadena, 1904. (Demolished)
Photograph courtesy of Greene and Greene Library.

Strong overlapping roof lines and a sensitive composition of simple mass forms are accentuated by the horizontal clapboard siding.

Charles W. Hollister house, west side of Cahuenga Boulevard north of Hollywood Boulevard, Hollywood, 1904. (Demolished) Drawing by Donald Woodruff.

Henry Greene's crisp lines of the Hollister elevations were a dramatic contrast to the eclectic popular tastes of 1904.

The varied and rapidly evolving designs of 1904 continued with the second house for Charles W. Hollister, located in Hollywood. The quality of Henry Greene's taste obviously influenced its extraordinarily clean, contemporary quality. In both the front elevation and the plan there was a restraint and a simplicity which gave a new dignity to small house design. Here the first use of the courtyard principle since the Bandini house was more refined. The plan was reversed and the base of the "U" form placed to the front of the property and defined with a central entry hall. The living room and an optional bedroom-study constituted the front section. Dining, pantry, kitchen, porch and servants' quarters constituted the left wing, and bedrooms the right. Unlike the Bandini house, however, this plan included an interior passage connecting the separated spaces of the bedroom wing so that there was no need to go through the private rooms or enter from the exterior as in the Bandini house. This plan was much more workable and the concept was later refined in numerous designs, most of which reveal Henry's imprint and his fascination with the "U" plan. In the Hollister scheme, the interior spaces, the inglenook development, the fireside seating and the concern for furnishing all demonstrate the blending of Charles Greene's artistic touch. This mutual effort with the talent of one brother complementing that of the other was distinctive of the Greenes' work.

Inglenook detail of living room, watercolor sketch by Charles Greene. Courtesy of Documents Collection, College of Environmental Design, UCB.

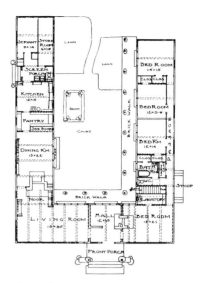

Floor plan, *Country Life in America,* October, 1905.

View of interior patio. Courtesy of Documents Collection, College of Environmental Design, UCB.

For the Hollister house the "U" plan form of the Bandini house was reversed; the entry was at the base of the "U" and the plan incorporated an interior passageway. While smaller in scale than the Bandini courtyard, the design for the Hollister house is made more formal by the rectangular pond and the use of green lawn areas.

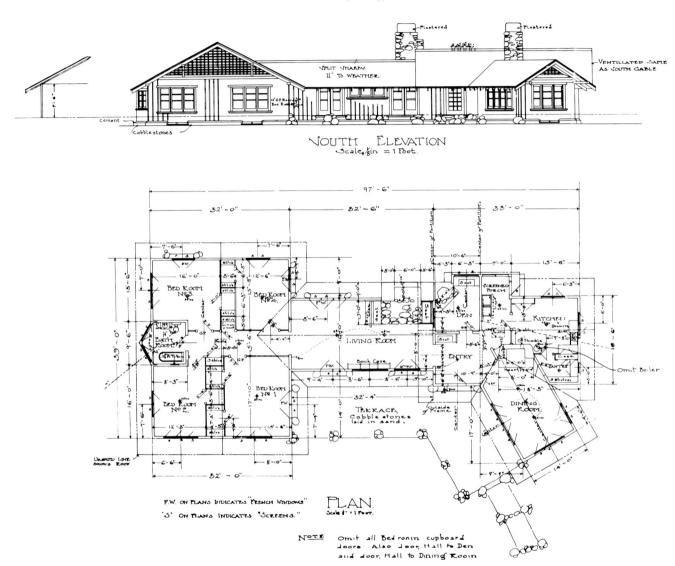

BUNGALOW FOR EDGAR W. CAMP ESQ. AT SIERRA MADRE CAL.
GREENE & GREENE ARCHITECTS, GRANT BLDG., LOS ANGELES CALIFORNIA.
No 1.

SOUTH ELEVATION
Scale ⅛in = 1 Foot.

PLAN.
Scale ⅛ = 1 Foot.

F.W. ON PLANS INDICATES "FRENCH WINDOWS."
"S" ON PLANS INDICATES "SCREENS."

NOTE: Omit all Bed room cupboard doors. Also door, Hall to Den and door, Hall to Dining Room.

Edgar W. Camp house, 327 Sierra Woods Drive (originally addressed as 497 W. Grandview Avenue), Sierra Madre, 1904. Courtesy of Avery Architectural Library.

The Camp bungalow, built on the rocky foothills of Sierra Madre, further elaborated on the Bandini plan. Its board and batten construction methods created a handsome and natural dwelling from the most basic materials native to the area.

The Craftsman, December, 1909.
Courtesy of Documents Collection, College of Environmental Design, UCB.

Living room fireplace. Courtesy of Documents Collection, College of Environmental Design, UCB.

Natural boulders from the nearby terrain were boldly expressed on the interior in the fireplace, seat and hearth design; and furnishings were expanded to include bookshelves and picture frames as well as seating and tables.

The influence of the Bandini house was again felt in the rambling design of 1904 for Edgar W. Camp in Sierra Madre. Built on a large rolling piece of land at the foot of the San Gabriel mountains, the plan modified the "U" principle and, by slightly angling the east wing, created a terrace for outdoor living with a view over the valley below. Again, board and batt were used and expressed on the interior and the furniture design continued to reveal the strength of Stickley's influence. The major feature which distinguished the Camp house was the massive fireplace and hearth. No longer just cobblestones, this great rock sculpture brought the bold raw character of the Sierra Madre foothills right into the hearth where giant boulders projected to form seats. As in the Bandini house, a great timber mantel brought horizontality to the composition and helped to relate the masonry to the wood truss character of the living room. On the exterior, the chimney, which was extremely wide at the base, rose from the ground as though it were a part of nature's magnificent rockpile.

As the Greenes gained confidence in their new art they developed a reputation for being extremely demanding of their workmen. They maintained absolute control over construction. Eventually contractors found it necessary to insert an additional amount in their bids to compensate for work the young architects would order "ripped out" and re-done. At the same time, the Greenes recognized the stimulation of a client's personal challenges and attempted to integrate their own principles with the client's desires. The correspondence leading to the house designs for Mrs. James A. Garfield reflect a cordial and willing rapport between architect and client. The letters, which begin in early 1903, provide a clear perspective of these delicate architect-client relations.[10] They show that the Greenes refused to compromise their artistic convictions, but worked instead to fuse their client's point of view with that of their own. The widow of the former President was pleased with the original, but too costly, design, and she, with the aid of her architect son, became intimately involved with the entire operation. She questioned the roof forms, made suggestions for window alignments, for various adjustments and for changes of materials which would help to bring costs into line. Several exchanges in the letters point out the strong will of the brothers. In an exchange in early June Mrs. Garfield wrote:

What do you think of omitting the skylight? Cannot ventilation be arranged without the light and still look well?

Charles' terse answer was:

Retain skylight – reason will follow!

In the final construction the skylight remained. One exchange seems particularly significant for it answers the often asked question about the Greenes' dramatic use of great projecting timbers. Mrs. Garfield asked:

Will it interfere with the effect you are striving for to let the girders in the gables of the roof extend only to the edge, instead of reaching beyond? I prefer that treatment.

Charles Greene's calm reply ended the discussion:

The reason why the beams project from the gables is because they cast such beautiful shadows on the sides of the house in this bright atmosphere.

This statement spoke for the whole of the Greenes architectural expression. In each timber and at every turn of the building they were responding to the site, the breezes, and the sun; and they were accepting these natural elements as giving firm direction to their individual designs.

The Garfield house, unlike the low, rambling character of the preceeding houses, was a two-story rectangular gabled structure which represented yet another expression used by the Greenes when the site or the client's needs dictated such compact form. It was the various use of this form which prompted writers to liken the Greenes' work to the Swiss Chalet.

10. The series of letters between Mrs. James A. Garfield and Charles Greene are a part of the Documents Collection, Greene and Greene Library, The Gamble House.

Mrs. James A. Garfield house, 1001 Buena Vista Street, South Pasadena, 1904.
Entry and canopy detail, Marvin Rand photograph.

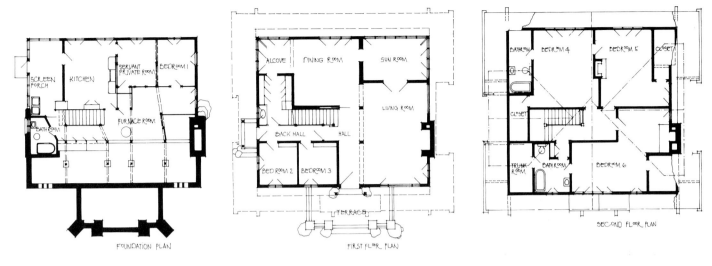

FOUNDATION PLAN

FIRST FLOOR PLAN

SECOND FLOOR PLAN

Plans, drawings by Peter Wohlfahrtstaetter.
Photograph courtesy of Greene and Greene Library.

Following several more elaborate designs in which Mrs. Garfield took an active part, the final scheme made use of the large understructure space by placing the kitchen in the basement. The photograph reveals the 1897 Longley house to the left.

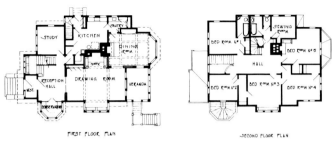

FIRST FLOOR PLAN

SECOND FLOOR PLAN

R. Henry C. Green house, 1919 Robson Street, Vancouver, British Columbia, 1904. (Demolished)
Courtesy of Avery Architectural Library.

While lacking the relaxed character of plan forms which the Greenes had been developing in Southern California, this plan explored the cruciform of the living room as a multi-purpose space providing the contrasts of the solarium and the fireside inglenook—a concept refined in the Gamble house of 1908 and experimented with by English architect M. H. Baillie Scott as early as 1906.

In Vancouver, British Columbia, the English half-timbered stucco house for R. Henry C. Green stands in dramatic contrast to the Greenes' work in Southern California. Roger Henry Carleton Green, a barrister from Ireland, had come to Vancouver in 1904. He had become acquainted with the Greenes' work and engaged them to design his home in the West End. The first impression of this Vancouver house suggests the less distinctive work by the Greenes at the turn of the century. But on closer inspection it becomes obvious that the demands of the locale, the weather and the client greatly affected the ultimate decision. The cruciform configuration of the living room (predating its use in the Gamble House by four years) provided a flexibility in mood and use of space; the cavernous inglenook contrasts with the windowseat in the morning sunlight. The axial geometry of the living room design was distinc-

tive. The less imaginative planning of the balance of the house, however, was singularly out of character with the Greenes' changing new directions during 1903 and 1904.

Back in California, more and more individual tones became a working part of the Greene and Greene architectural palette. As the expressed timber structural system became more pronounced, their plans exhibited a modular order within which they found great opportunities for flexibility. A new sense of geometry combined with the open planning concepts freed them from the inhibitions imposed by the stilted, tight Victorian style.

Continuing the direction and excitement expressed in the earlier work of 1904, the Adelaide Tichenor house wove together the "U" plan, the inglenook-solarium geometry of the Vancouver house, the total interior concepts of the Reeve house, the expressed timber structural system and, for the first time, provided an opportunity to design nearly all of the household furniture. Mrs. Tichenor was an intelligent and determined woman who did not hesitate to voice her opinions. She played an active role in the design and development of the house and the challenge she presented was a constant stimulus to the architects. However, Charles was beginning to exhibit a creative stubbornness which on occasion prompted his client to dramatic outbursts in their correspondence.[11] Despite their disagreements, however, and the delays in construction which were increasingly typical of the Greenes' work, the end product in 1905 was a house of superb design. The association with Mrs. Tichenor also opened the doors to a wealthy clientele who were to indulge the Greenes with large budgets and, consequently, to a degree, permitted a disregard of financial restraint.[12]

11. Correspondence between Mrs. Tichenor and Greene and Greene is part of the collections of Documents Collection, College of Environmental Design Library, University of California, Berkeley.

12. Interview with Henry Greene's daughter, Mrs. Alan R. McElwain.

Adelaide M. Tichenor house, 852 E. Ocean Blvd., Long Beach, 1904.

The Tichenor variation on the court plan concept further narrowed the interior space to that of a protected terrace, and a visual garden developed in accord with the interests in the Orient of both client and architects.

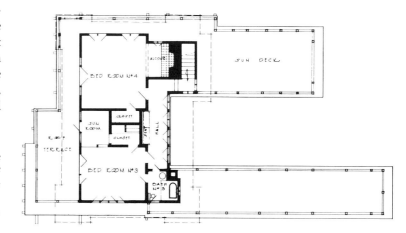

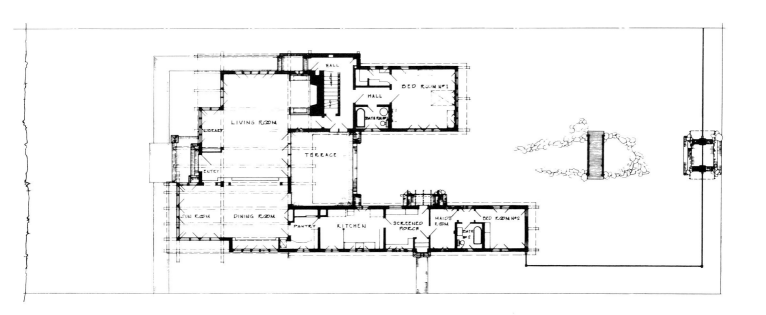

The "U" shaped plan was developed with a second story across the base, and the legs were brought closer together to form a more intimate terrace. Because of the chilly winds on the ocean front, the space beyond the terrace was essentially treated as a visual garden and the eaves were clipped back closer to the house. The mutual interest in the Orient of both client and architects led to the selection of green tiles for the roof, an arched bridge over the pond in the garden, and a ceremonial roofed gateway from the main street into the rear garden.

In spite of the delicacy of the other portions of the design, the ground floor was carried out in a bold half-timber fashion with rugged clinker brick filling in the exterior walls. Roofs of the one-story portions were kept at a very low pitch and low railings were provided to allow their use as sun decks. The flatness of these roofs and the extremely brief overhangs of the two rear wings make these portions of the structure resemble two giant railroad pullmans backed up to the two-story frontal portion of the house.

Adelaide M. Tichenor house.
Photographs courtesy of Documents Collection, College of Environmental Design, UCB.

The early photograph of the rear of the house under construction reveals the "Japanese" bridge and the Oriental character of the structure. That character was not hidden with time and plant growth, but was rather enhanced as shown in the later photograph of the torii gate.

Watercolor drawing by Charles Greene.
Courtesy of Greene and Greene Library.

Although perspective sketches were seldom developed for
the Greenes' clients, this watercolor masterfully characterizes
the rich detail of the Tichenor house.

On the interior, the plan was by far the most sophisticated of the new Greene and Greene style. The refined "U" plan was far removed from the inexpensive ranch house. By virtue of the flexible modular structural system the living room, inglenook, solarium, sun room, entry and dining room each had a separate identity and yet were all part of the vast open sunlit interior. By use of slight changes of level and configuration the Greenes gave variety and definition to the spaces without altering the interpenetration of open space. The fireside inglenook and the contrasting windowed solarium achieved a more relaxed and informal living pattern than was found in the axial balance of the R. Henry C. Green living room in Vancouver.

The interior, almost exclusively carried out in wood, was a fortunate blending of client-architect interests. Mrs. Tichenor, who was attending the Louisiana Purchase Exposition in St. Louis, wrote to Charles:

> We arrived here only yesterday, but the more I see of it, the more I feel that I do not want to go on with my home until you see this…I think you will never regret it if you arrange your affairs to come at once…you will be able to get so many ideas of *woods* and other things for finishing what you now have on. Please consider this; as I said before, I am anxious to have you use the knowledge you may gain here on my own house. It will be impossible for me to describe to you the effect of the *woods*. There are things I would like to buy too, but I dare not until I know what you are going to do.[13]

Subsequent correspondence reveals that Charles did make the trip to the Exposition. Records show that terra cotta work and Grueby pottery were ordered for the Tichenor house, a significant tie with the eastern Arts and Crafts Movement. The Greenes' furniture and lighting fixture designs were now going beyond the influence of Gustav Stickley. Their softened lines began to show not only a maturity but also a relaxation which occasionally led to a little frivolity as, for instance, in the "owl" motif in the special door handle escutcheons for Mrs. Tichenor.

13. Correspondence of June 10, 1904. Courtesy Robert Judson Clark and the Documents Collection, College of Environmental Design, UCB.

Adelaide M. Tichenor house, first floor bedroom.
Courtesy of Greene and Greene Library.

Interior detail of living room and raised dining room.
Architectural Record, October, 1906.

Facing Page:
Living room opening to central court with inglenook to left.
Courtesy of Documents Collection, College of Environmental Design, UCB.

Seagulls at sunset were cut from sheet lead and fastened to the stained leaded glass windows in sunset colors of blue and orange Tiffany glass. Greene and Greene had here the opportunity to fully explore their abilities with furniture, stained glass lighting fixtures and windows, hardware design and the selection of many art objects and pottery for the interiors. Charles Greene designed an owl pattern at Mrs. Tichenor's request for the door handle escutcheons and certain metalwork in the bedroom furniture.

As the Greenes' practice grew their insistence upon paying personal attention to each detail created delays at both design and construction stages. As a result, waiting clients often expressed anxieties. This was particularly true with the Tichenor house. The work was still unfinished in September of 1905 which prompted another revealing letter from Mrs. Tichenor:

I must insist that every design be given to the proper party for art glass lighting fixtures, etc. before Friday. Whether you have time or not I want you to take it. I am not willing to wait until your brother returns. He may not come Monday, and if he does it will take time for him to adjust himself, etc. again. That is only another excuse for postponing …Can you leave your Pasadena customers long enough so that I may hope to have my house during my life time? Do you wish me to make a will telling who is to have the house if it is finished? From August 1st to December 7th is a long time—and the glass not in, hardware not in doors, etc.…I have told you often enough, it seems to me, for you to know by this time that the sun room is to be a reception room and as such must be shut off. I have told you that all sorts of persons who are strangers to me, come and ask for me by name. The maid must not allow them to enter my living rooms. I have told you I had had things stolen in that way. I told you that was one reason I wanted a partly enclosed porch but you enclosed it, contrary to my wish and I was obliged to put a porch on the second floor. Now the only way seems to be to have a screen large enough to be a screen, not a mere ornament. I have explained this to you so many times; showed you how I must have the step made an entrance door etc.…P.S. These little book shelves you have made will hold about 1/5 of my books. Do you wish me to put the others in the fire? I suppose I am to burn all of my pictures too? I see no place to hang any except in the bedroom and I do not believe that bedrooms should have them.[14]

Her last comment regarding the lack of space or opportunity for hanging paintings was most appropriate. The total extent to which Greene and Greene designed their interiors often left little opportunity for the owner to insert his or her own personality or belongings. However, in the Tichenor design, there were adjustments made by both parties and the end result possessed a rare unity and spirit. It was as though here the Greenes put together in one package the entire ideals of the Arts and Crafts Movement.

14. *Ibid.* Correspondence of September 27, 1905.

Josephine van Rossem house No. 2, 210 N. Grand Avenue, Pasadena, 1904. Courtesy of Pasadena Historical Society.

Mrs. van Rossem engaged in real estate and built this house for specific clients in the East.

FIRST FLOOR PLAN   SECOND FLOOR PLAN

While the Tichenor house dominated the later months of 1904 as well as 1905 there were other clients to be considered. Design and construction included another speculative house for Josephine van Rossem, a tidy bungalow for Mrs. Kate A. White, and a curious design for the home of the Reverend Alexander Merwin.

Below:
Kate A. White house, 1036 Brent Avenue, South Pasadena, 1904. Drawing by Donald Woodruff.
Plan drawing by Philip Enquist.

Illustrated prior to major alterations, the White house demonstrated the charm and livability which the Greenes' talents could bring to modest designs.

Rev. Alexander M. Merwin house, 267 State Street, Pasadena, 1904. Courtesy of Documents Collection, College of Environmental Design, UCB. Drawings by Peter Wohlfahrtstaetter.

The classic affectations applied to this clean bungalow were extraordinary for the Greenes who here made special concessions to the desires of Rev. Merwin. The strong central hall bisecting the ground floor accommodated the major rear entry which provided access to the circular drive where Rev. Merwin kept his electric automobile.

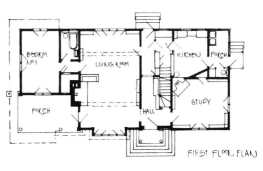

An artist's philosophy is revealed both by his creation and by what he has to say about his own art. The ideas of the Greenes were presented with great sincerity and conviction in the article by Charles Sumner Greene, "California Home Making," which appeared on January 1, 1905 in the Tournament of Roses Supplement of the local Pasadena paper. The article contained numerous illustrations and drawings by Charles; the essay was somewhat folksy and conveyed in a rambling way his feelings about the different kind of life in California and the ways in which this life style should affect architecture. His descriptions revealed his interest in the small bungalow and suggest that it was written with the Bandini bungalow rather than the more sophisticated Tichenor house in mind. The following excerpt from the article relates to the changing direction of their work:

> For the better side of California building we must look to the medium cost houses. Here there is great range and adaptiveness. Wood is the principle building material of the country as yet, and certainly a wooden house may be made exceedingly habitable and attractive. Small houses with all or nearly all rooms on one floor, seem to fill the needs of very many people. To leave out the stairs not only saves expense but adds to convenience as well. To arrange a large living room with entrance direct from the street is not so popular as it once was. Neither is a dining room and living room combined considered a complete success. There is a slight tendency to design for the privacy of the family, though the English idea of the house is not in vogue. It is probable that the American distaste of anything secluded or shut off will prevail in this type of building. The attractiveness of this kind of house depends upon simplicity and adaptiveness to surroundings for the outside and deftness of arrangement inside. When one approaches such a house it must not obtrude itself upon one's sight, but rather fit into the things about it. Good things are not always seen at once, but they do not need advertising when they are found. Pasadena is fortunate in having so many beautiful bungalows. This term is stretched to include anything of a house with a long simple roof line. Only the people who have visited India may appreciate the dictionary meaning of the word bungalow, i.e., a Bengalese house. One may often see pictures in the current magazines of California bungalows and much might be said in their praise. It is not so much what one does as how one does it.[15]

In answer to a questionnaire from Charles F. Lummis of the Los Angeles Public Library Department of Western History, Charles stated:

> Our attempts mostly in [the] line of domestic architecture, may be arranged in three grand divisions. 1st to understand as many phases of human life as possible; 2nd to provide for its individual requirement in the most practical and useful way; 3rd to make these necessary and useful things pleasurable. As it may be conjectured, our ambition overreaches our powers...[16]

Much of the philosophy of the New Year's Day article was transmitted to the Greenes' small bungalows that were built in the Pasadena area through 1905. In Altadena, the William A. Bowen house demonstrated the interests in symmetry in the plan form.

15. Charles Sumner Greene, "California Home Making," Tournament of Roses Edition, *Pasadena Daily News*, January 1, 1905, p. 26.

16. Circa 1906. Janann Strand located this document in the archives of the Los Angeles Public Library.

William A. Bowen house, 443 E. Calaveras Street, Altadena, 1905. Drawing by Donald Woodruff.

This plan organization is closely related to the Bandini plan in the handling of the circulation of the bedroom wing. The details of the construction, however, are far more sophisticated and the bilateral symmetry of the library, entry hall, dining room and corner window seats is direct and refreshing.

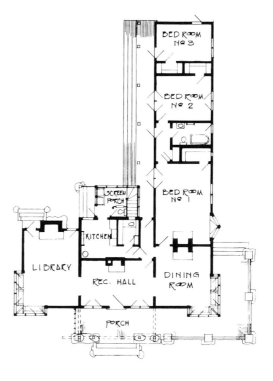

S. Hazard Halsted house, 90 N. Grand Avenue, Pasadena, 1905.
Photograph courtesy of Greene and Greene Library.

For a previous client, S. Hazard Halsted, the final design was modest but featured a large living room with very handsomely designed hanging lanterns very different from the Greenes' earlier lighting techniques.

The following year the Greenes continued their work for Mr. Halsted by designing two modest office bungalows for his Pasadena and Pomona Valley Ice Companies.

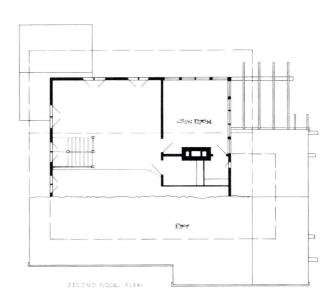

Living room detail.
Photograph courtesy of Greene and Greene Library.

The final design of the Halsted bungalow retained the spacious living room of earlier larger schemes. The ability to adjust the height of the cleanly designed overhead lighting fixtures was one of the subtle but important elements of the Greenes' detail concerns.

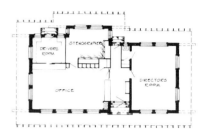

Pasadena Ice Company office, photograph and plan, east side of South Broadway, Pasadena, 1906. (Demolished)

Pomona Valley Ice Company office, 1163 East 2nd Street, Pomona, 1906. (Demolished)
Photographs courtesy of Greene and Greene Library.

For his expanding ice company, S. Hazard Halsted called upon the Greenes in 1906 to design small offices for both his Pasadena and Pomona ice plant operations.

Charles J. Willett house, 424 Arroyo View Drive, Pasadena, 1905. Photograph, *The Western Architect*, July, 1908.

The modest but tasteful grace of this scale of the Greenes' work set patterns for bungalow home designs which were ultimately reflected by builders and architects throughout the country. The brothers also had earlier designed a unique "T" plan house for Judge Willett which, unfortunately, was never constructed.

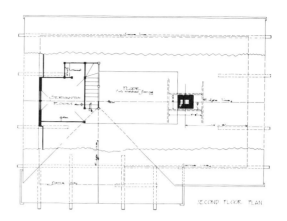

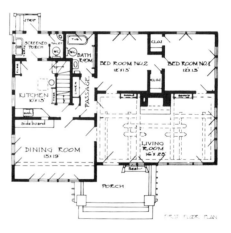

Below: Charles J. Willett project, Pasadena, 1904.

One of the most beautifully detailed little bungalows was built for Judge Charles J. Willett.[17] Here the Greenes demonstrated that their approach to design could bring real dignity to even the smallest of speculative bungalows.

17. Earlier a unique "T" plan had been developed for Judge Willett, but, unfortunately was never built. This is the only known use of such a plan by the brothers and they handled it remarkably well. The more modest Willett bungalow built was so totally remodeled in 1928 that the present structure cannot be regarded as the work of Greene and Greene.

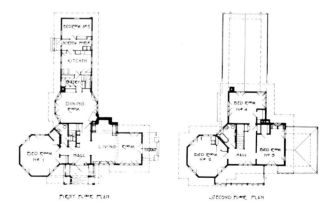

Just two doors from the Willett bungalow, around the corner, Josephine van Rossem called upon the Greenes for a third time. In this instance the design was for Mrs. van Rossem's own home and the Greenes gave it considerable attention, especially with regard to the interiors and the natural wood finishes. One of the brothers scoured the Redwood Highway of Northern California for the clear unblemished 20" redwood boards for the living room ceiling. These were then rubbed down with a chemical, leaving a green streak which was then rubbed out with oil and brought back to natural color and grain with absolute protection against infestation. This space was always a source of great pride for the brothers. Great cobblestone walls were designed along the Orange Grove Avenue side of the house and the irregular site adjacent to the reservoir, which brought about an angled "V" shaped plan that resulted in a pleasant configuration of the gabled roof design.

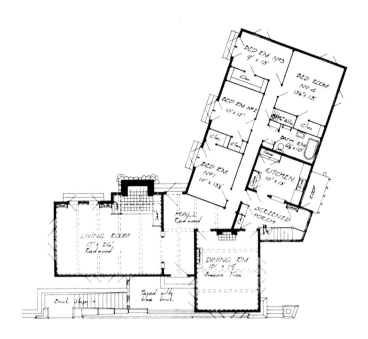

Josephine van Rossem house No. 3, 223 Orange Grove Avenue Pasadena, 1905. (Demolished)
Plan, *The Western Architect*, July, 1908.
Photographs courtesy of W. J. van Rossem.

Largest of the three houses built for Mrs. van Rossem, this was the only one designed for her own occupancy and contributed to the series of Greene and Greene structures popularly know as "Little Switzerland" built around the reservoir. The Greenes traveled to the timber areas of Northern California to personally select the planking used for the naturally finished ceiling.

Living room detail.

Dining room detail.

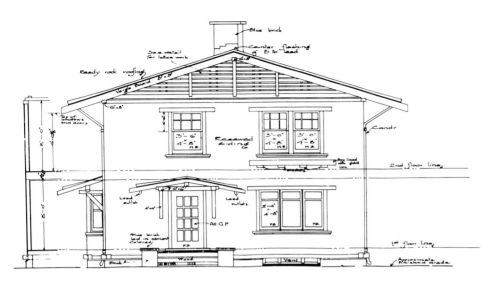

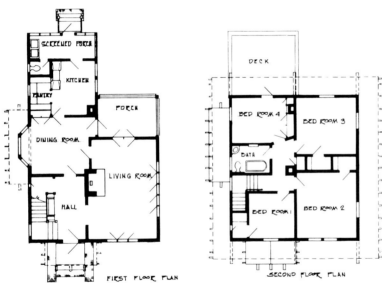

Lucy E. Wheeler house, 2175 Cambridge Street, Los Angeles, 1905.
Courtesy of Avery Architectural Library.

This modest two-story residence was one of the few Greene designs built in the city of Los Angeles.

By the end of 1905 Greene and Greene had produced sufficient work to attract prospective clients and impress builders; as a result, copies of their details and designs began appearing in the work of others. Other new work in 1905 included the Lucy E. Wheeler house, the Iwan Serrurier house, the A. C. Brandt house, the L. G. and Marion Porter house, and numerous projects.

As significant as the small bungalows, however, were the larger and more varied commissions coming into the office. The first of these actually had its beginning the previous year. This was the design for the entrance portals and the bridge for the South Pasadena "Oaklawn" tract development. Charles' drawing for the portals appeared in the New Year's Day article of 1905.

PLAN

Left:

A. C. Brandt (Iwan Serrurier) house, originally located at N.E. corner Maiden Lane and Mariposa Streets, Altadena, 1905. Marvin Rand photograph.

An unusual plan for either of the Greenes, the house was developed for builder A. C. Brandt and was first occupied by Iwan Serrurier and his family. This design immediately followed the design for Mr. Serrurier's speculative house.

Below:

Iwan Serrurier house, 805 W. California Street, Pasadena, 1905. (Demolished) Photograph courtesy of Greene and Greene Library.

Built as a speculative venture for Mr. Serrurier, the design is simple, makes use of zoned areas for interior functions and is a rare instance where the Greenes made use of the long central hallway to organize the plan.

FLOOR PLAN

111

EAST ELEVATION

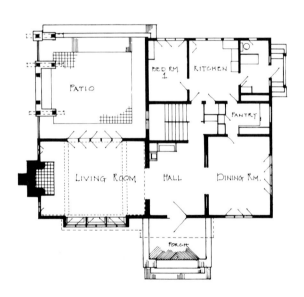

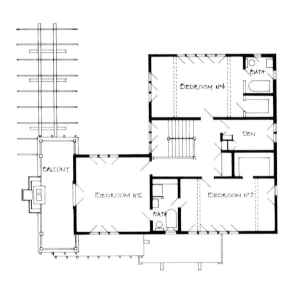

L. G. and Marion Porter house, 1957 Hobart Boulevard, Los Angeles, 1905. (Demolished) Courtesy of Avery Architectural Library. Plans, drawings by Philip Enquist.

The compact "L" form plan offered a handsome outdoor living patio on a tight city lot through the utilization of the pergola.

The bridge, which spanned the railway, cycleway and private road to connect the Oaklawn tract with the main thoroughfare, took considerable time to design, and numerous schemes were developed. The Greenes' final design consisted of five long simple flat arches, a total of 340 feet in length. Electric lanterns were placed at each end of the bridge, and along the Fair Oaks entrance a handsome timber and tiled roof waiting station was built of great cobblestones. Henry was particularly interested in the bridge design and in the new reinforced concrete construction methods. Because of this structural system, the Greenes engaged a consulting engineer, Michael de Palo, who had just completed the design and construction of the long arch-bridge across the waters at Playa del Rey, California.

The *Los Angeles Times* printed an extensive story on the "Oaklawn" bridge on February 8, 1906, just a few days before the construction by Carl Leonhardt was begun. But when the contractor removed the shoring from under the arches, the Greenes' dreams for the long, graceful, arched bridge were shattered. Cracks appeared near the supports of the arches. Because of the widespread attention given to the bridge, the reputations of all involved suffered. Ultimately, the consulting engineer and contractor were held responsible. When extensive tests were made by subjecting the arches to eighteen tons of extra load a deflection of only 3/16 inch appeared. There did not seem to be any danger, and the 1/4 inch cracks closed as evening came on. Nevertheless, the railroads would not accept the bridge construction over their tracks until an extra pier was placed in the center of the longest span. This destroyed the grace of the original design. The brothers were deeply disappointed. Members of the family recall Henry saying on numerous occasions, "we really went through hell over that bridge."

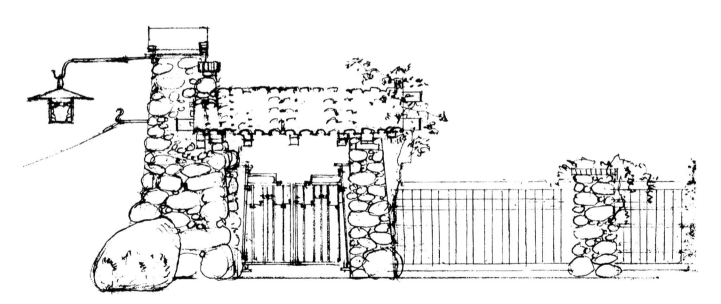

South Pasadena Realty and Improvement Company entrance portals and fence for Oaklawn Park tract development, Oaklawn Avenue and Columbia Street, South Pasadena, 1905. Sketch by Charles Greene, Courtesy of Greene and Greene Library.

Oaklawn Park.
The abstract detail of the gate design bears the unmistakable
imprint of the Greenes.
Marvin Rand photograph.

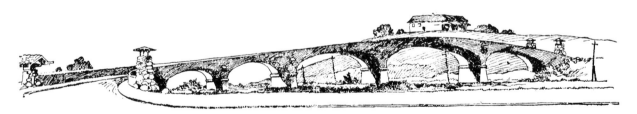

Bridge for Oaklawn Park tract development.
Los Angeles Times, February 8, 1906.

The graceful design composed of five simple arches was
developed by the Greenes in association with Michael de Palo,
an Italian expert in reinforced concrete.

Detail of waiting station at Fair Oaks Avenue.
Marvin Rand photograph.

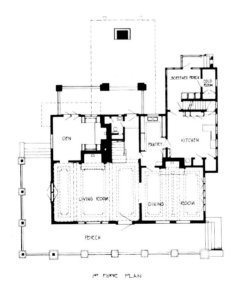

1ST FLOOR PLAN

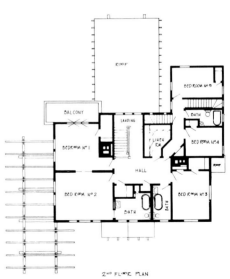

2ND FLOOR PLAN

About the same time that Greene and Greene were beginning their work on the ill-fated bridge they were selected as architects for the Arthur A. Libby house on fashionable South Orange Grove Avenue in Pasadena. The most distinguishing feature of the design was the great elongated porte cochere which the Greenes used here for the first time and for the very practical purpose of sheltering the circular drive and secondary entrance at the rear of the house. Thus the most dramatic feature of the entire house was out of sight at the rear. Nonetheless, the great porte cochere was later to become one of the major features of some of their most distinguished houses.

The Libby house was dramatized by the severity of the landscaping. In transition between house and site, the long frontal terrace was lined with potted plants. *Ficus repens* crept up the low brick retaining wall and vines ascended the side pergola. The Libby house, surrounded by its wide, flat lawns, stood out in quiet dignity amid the Victoriana of South Orange Grove Avenue.

Attic gable and shutter details.

Facing page:
Dr. Arthur A. Libby house, 665 S. Orange Grove Avenue, Pasadena, 1905. (Demolished) Courtesy of Documents Collection, College of Environmental Design, UCB.

Until its unwarranted demolition in 1968, the strong simple form of the structure and the extraordinary restraint of the landscaping of the Libby house represented a significant and tasteful departure from both the fussiness of early fashionable South Orange Grove Avenue as well as its later high density apartment neighbors. The Greene and Greene porte cochere was first developed here to shelter the rear entry and bridged across the handsomely designed circular brick drive and motor court, a refinement of the concept developed for the earlier Merwin house.

Exterior railing details.
Marvin Rand photographs.

During this same year the Greenes met Peter Hall, who was to become virtually their personal contractor and their most significant associate. It was becoming increasingly difficult for the Greenes to find builders or craftsmen willing to meet their exacting standards. But Peter Hall and his brother, John, responded to their artistic demands and there quickly developed between the Greenes and the Halls a close relationship in which both architects and contractors worked together harmoniously.

Peter Hall was born in Stockholm, Sweden in 1867 and was brought to the United States at the age of four. He was a self-taught craftsman who gained a reputation as the best stair builder on the Pacific Coast. He went into the contracting and building business for himself and was joined by his brother who ran the mill and also worked closely with the Greenes on furniture in later years. Some have claimed that the Greenes set Peter Hall up in business and trained his craftsmen because they could not find a mill suited to their demands. Records show, however, that he was working with other architects in 1905 before his first association with the Greenes. The brothers were largely responsible for the expansion of Peter Hall's business, reputation and shop facilities, however. Leonard W. Collins, a draftsman for the Greenes, recalled that Charles would spend several hours each morning at the Peter Hall shops working alongside and directing the craftsmen. With his long flowing hair and his work smock he was a colorful and arresting figure.[18]

Greene and Greene first employed Hall as a contractor on the alterations for the Tod Ford house on South Grand Avenue. Small as the job was, it led not only to the long association between the Greenes and the Halls, but also to an acquaintance with various members of the Ford family, among whom were the Henry M. Robinsons and the Freeman A. Fords, later important clients.

18. Interviews with Dr. Leonard W. Collins.

Henry M Robinson house, 195 S. Grand Avenue, Pasadena, 1905. Photograph and plans courtesy of Greene and Greene Library.

Equal in all respects to the widely recognized masterworks of 1907-1909, the 1905 design of the Robinson house is fully representative of the Greenes' talents. The plan is casual, free and airy, the exterior materials natural to the Southern California environment, and the siting and landscaping take full advantage of the beautiful location atop the bluffs of the Arroyo Seco.

The Henry M. Robinson house (1905) was another major achievement for the firm of Greene and Greene. Although basically related to the bungalow and Arts and Crafts ideas, its scale and exterior materials projected an entirely different quality. The plan resembled the modest Camp bungalow, but there all similarity ends. The two-story structure was brick on the ground floor and frame on the second level with a blown stucco finish over the entire exterior; the roof and the expressed timber structure of the porches and pergola tied the design to the Greenes' personal architectural vernacular. The use of more massive and substantial materials gave the Robinson house a new spirit and added greatly to the stature of the Greenes' work.

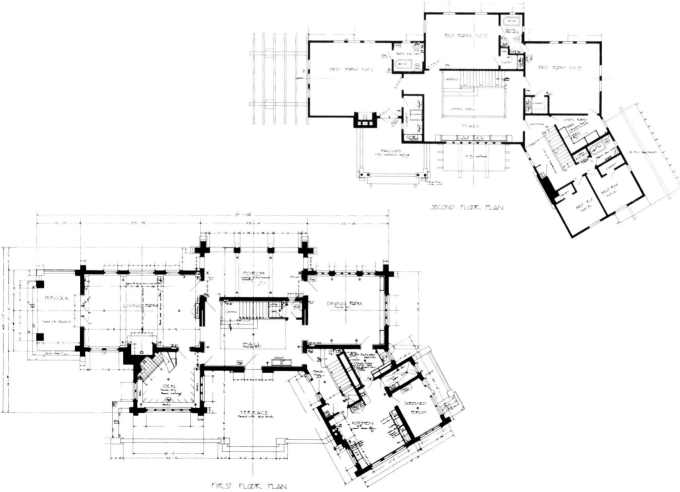

SECOND FLOOR PLAN

FIRST FLOOR PLAN

119

EAST ELEVATION

Henry M. Robinson house, elevation drawing.
Courtesy of Greene and Greene Library.

The handling of the foundation, the use of corner supporting
buttresses and the positioning of the open covered porch
were bold responses to the challenging site. The unusual
ribbed detail of the roof evolved from the Greenes' analysis of
the available size rolls of "Malthoid" asbestos roofing material.

Detail of two-story entry space
and stairway.

Dining room detail of table, chairs and adjustable chandelier
of Tiffany glass with leather straps and weight design.
Photographs courtesy of Documents Collection, College of
Environmental Design, UCB.

Detail of sculptural brickwork of the fireplace. Photograph courtesy of Documents Collection, College of Environmental Design, UCB.

The distinctive quality of the Robinson house began with the selection of the large site on South Grand Avenue which backed up to the steep bluffs of the vast Arroyo Seco, the beautiful natural valley which was one of Pasadena's most treasured assets. The house was situated far back on the site, at the brow of the bluffs so that the major interior spaces overlooked the Arroyo.

On the interior, the Greenes continued their long love affair with wood, and their work of the previous two years was here further developed and refined. Again, they were given a free hand with the design of elaborate lighting and much of the furniture. However now, in early 1906, their tastes were changing. This was most clearly expressed in some of the furniture designs in the living and dining rooms which broke further away from the Stickley influence. In some pieces the Greenes' interest in Chinese household furniture was clearly expressed. Although this style was not retained in their later work, it helped lead them away from the harshness of early Craftsman designs. Lighting also took on a new refinement. Great chandeliers were designed of wood and "Tiffany" glass, and in the dining room there was an elaborate system of weights and leather straps which enabled the fixture to be raised and lowered to suit the occasion.

James A. Culbertson house, view of first garage added to the
property in 1906.
Photograph courtesy of Greene and Greene Library.

During this same period a series of major modifications
to the James A. Culbertson house was begun. These continued over a number of years. Charles' lifelong interest in
wood carving is illustrated in the elaborate carvings for the
frieze in the entry hall. The designs were strongly Oriental
in character and repeat patterns of plant forms. In the bay
of the new stair landing there were added special windows
of clear glass with a leaded design of sinuous lines which
had seldom entered the Greenes' designs. These windows
were a dramatic contrast to the linear design of the living
room windows which were probably designed in 1902 by
Henry Greene. The first garage addition of 1906 was

handled with such skill by the Greenes that its addition
enhanced the entrance garden as well as the house itself.

In 1915 a great two-story leaded bay window was added
to the front elevation of the living room and another of one
story to the end of the new dining room. On the exterior
all of the alterations emphasized the refinements in the
Greenes' use of heavy timbers, bold joinery and softly
shaped beam ends. This gave the Culbertson house the
hint of the Orient; yet the various remodelings were so
sensitively handled that they did not destroy the rich
English half-timbered character of the original design.

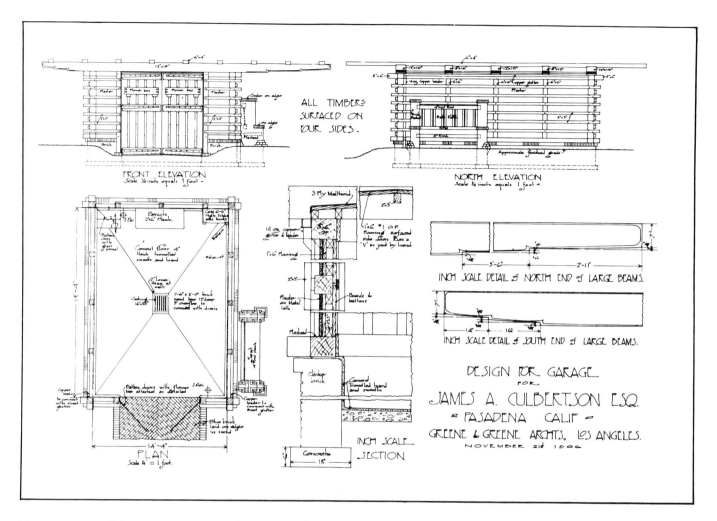

The appearance of the garage was extremely important because of its location in the front yard, directly opposite the entry terrace. It serves as an example of the Greenes' ability to create extraordinary beauty from a potentially disasterous situation. The creative imaginations of the brothers combined the utilitarian function with a light and airy garden pergola. Courtesy of Greene and Greene Library.

James A. Culbertson house, view showing bay window additions in 1915. Lloyd Yost photograph.

Facing page, upper left:
James A. Culbertson house, interior of entry hall as remodeled by the Greenes in 1906. (Demolished)
Photograph courtesy of Greene and Greene Library.

The refinements of the lighting fixtures and the Greenes' interest in the Art Nouveau movement were carefully blended with the carvings, panel detail and furniture of the original 1902 design.

Facing page, upper right:
Detail of remodeled stairwell and upper hallway.
Julius Shulman photograph.

Nowhere was the Greenes' rare use of the sinuous line of the Art Nouveau movement so beautifully or effectively used as in these clear leaded glass windows of the stair landing.

Facing page, lower left:
Detail of dining room fireplace.
Julius Shulman photograph.

Facing page, lower right:
Living room fireplace with carved lettering.
Photograph courtesy of Mr. and Mrs. William Dunn.

Pergola and gate to second garage.
Lloyd Yost photograph.

Caroline S. DeForest house, 530 W. California Street, Pasadena, 1906. Marvin Rand photograph.

The DeForest design presented a modest front elevation by turning the gable the short direction of the plan and allowing for second floor light and ventilation through special openings in the roof. The house today is the Greene and Greene structure most nearly in its original condition.

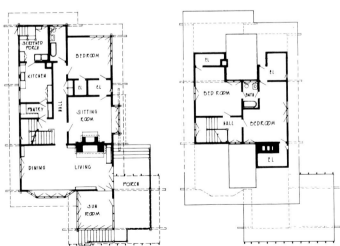

One of the most delightful smaller houses of this period was designed in 1906 for Caroline De Forest. The Greenes turned the entire plan around, placing the living room at the rear of the narrow site which sloped away from the street. The entrance was located at the side near the rear where the porch had a comanding view over the San Gabriel Valley. Thus, noise and activity from the street was minimized and a high degree of privacy provided. For the second time, the Greenes used the long single gable across the short axis of the house which gave a low front elevation profile. The use of openings in the roof allowed light to enter into the second story areas. Today the De Forest house is the Greene and Greene structure most nearly un-altered since its construction. Even the original wooden drainboards and cabinetwork are found in the kitchen.

Detail of original kitchen design.
Marvin Rand photograph.

Detail showing special treatment of underfloor openings and ventilation grills.
Marvin Rand photograph.

FIRST FLOOR PLAN

SECOND FLOOR PLAN

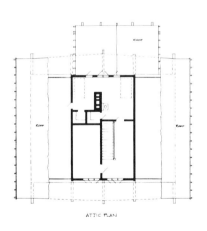

ATTIC PLAN

Apart from the open sprawling floor plan concepts, there were still situations calling for designs developed with the basic box or rectangular plan. In the designs for the houses for John B. Phillips, the second for Dr. William T. Bolton and for Robert Pitcairn Jr. differing interpretations evolved from varying client and site concerns. In the Phillips scheme abundant space was achieved by the centralization of the circulation and stair patterns and utilization of the vast attic space created by the long broad single gable roof. For the Bolton house the gable was run the width of the house, resulting in a totally different quality but requiring greater space devoted to hallways for interior movement.

Facing page and above:
John B. Phillips house, 459 Bellefontaine Street, Pasadena, 1906. Marvin Rand photographs.

The Phillips house demonstrated the charm and flexibility which the Greenes could bring to a basic rectangular plan under a broad simple single gable allowing for maximum use of all available space.

Dr. William T. Bolton house, 370 Del Mar (formerly Elevado Drive), Pasadena, 1906. Photograph courtesy of Documents Collection, College of Environmental Design, UCB.

The flexibility of the Greenes' structural concepts was explored exceptionally well in the 1906 house design for Robert Pitcairn Jr. They began with a basic two-story rectangle and, by the superb use of the cantilever and carefully placed projections and recesses, produced a design with the individual character of more costly houses. They completely divorced the service wing from the basic living plan and, by adjoining it to the corner of the rectangular plan, provided maximum use of outdoor terraces to the main portion of the house. Brick terraces and second-level cantilevered sleeping porches added interest to the basic box form while also providing valuable outdoor living spaces. The terraces in particular added a handsome transition to the site. The bungalow was no longer merely overgrown as in the Libby house, but took on a new and exciting quality which indicated that the principles of the bungalow could be equally effective for larger structures.

Below:
Robert Pitcairn, Jr. house, 289 N. State Street, Pasadena, 1906. Drawings by Philip Enquist.

Here Greene and Greene dramatically and effectively demonstrated that their architectural vocabulary was adaptable and appropriate for the large as well as the small bungalow.

By careful juxtaposition of spaces this plan achieved an excitement and scale which gave inspiration to the large masterworks of later years.

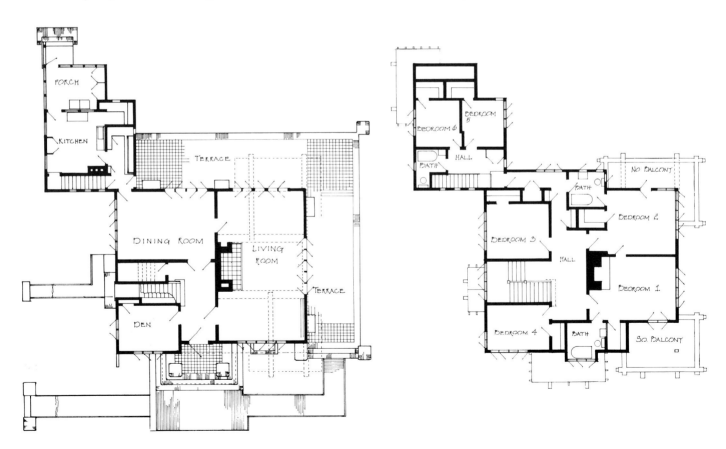

Robert Pitcairn, Jr. house.
Marvin Rand photograph.

At the same time there was a project for F. W. Hawks on the boards which was a still more sophisticated version of the "U" plan. A study of the drawings suggest that the house might well have been one of the Greenes' great masterpieces. The living room had a two-story ceiling with stairs and balconies projecting from the great space housing the sleeping loft at one end. Equally exciting was the subtle composition of interrelating roof planes which extended the two rear wings. But the excitement of the narrow low entry exploding into the great central timbered living room space with its two-story fireplace was like no other design by the Greenes. If they had one great failing it was the non-utilization of vertical interior space. In the Hawks project it was beautifully developed but for unknown reasons was never carried out.

Project: F. W. Hawks house, Pasadena, 1906.
Courtesy of Avery Architectural Library.

The excitement developed in the design of the two-story high living room with the expressed roof trusses and balcony projections distinguishes this project. It was a great loss that it was never built.

Robert Pitcairn, Jr. house, balcony structure and drainage detail. Marvin Rand photograph.

Greene and Greene had an uncanny way of making the smallest necessity an important design element in their work.

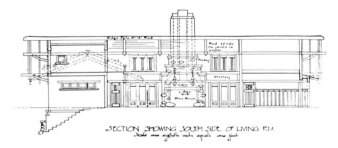

SECTION SHOWING SOUTH SIDE OF LIVING RM.
Scale one eighth inch equals one foot

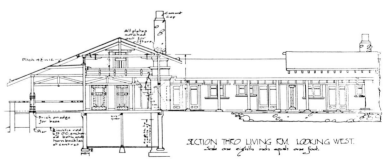

SECTION THRO LIVING RM. LOOKING WEST.
Scale one eighth inch equals one foot

Theodore M. Irwin house, 240 N. Grand Avenue, Pasadena, 1906. Photograph courtesy of Documents Collection, College of Environmental Design, UCB.

The Greenes juxtaposed the Irwin features to the Duncan design so well that it is only in the interior detail of the original rooms that the variations are evident. The time difference does express the brothers' changing attitude about the use of cobblestone in earlier designs and their later incorporation of clinker brick to add color and warmth.

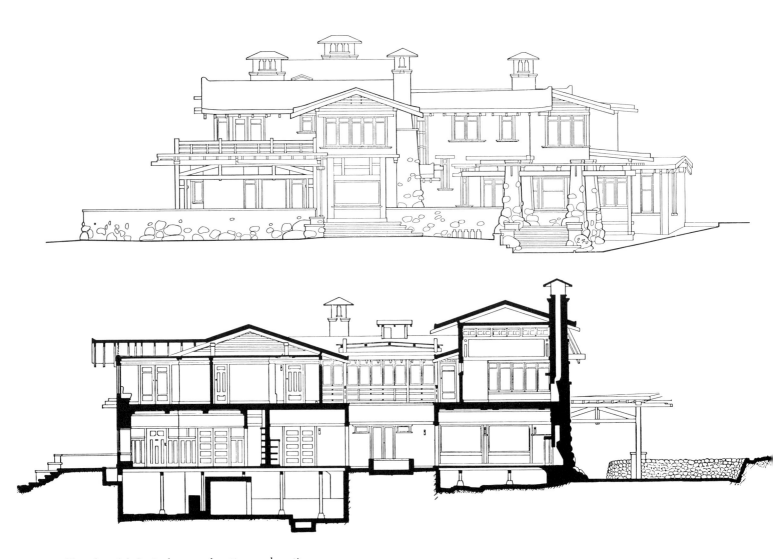

Theodore M. Irwin house, elevation and section.
Courtesy of Historical American Building Survey.

The earlier Duncan house was totally enveloped by the
second-story and major additions and alterations for the
Irwins. The original central court provided a challenge to the
architects who capitalized on the narrow space, broadened
it at the second level by providing terrace setbacks off the
upstairs bedrooms and then contained the space overhead with
a light wooden pergola. The Greenes were stimulated by
the potentially awkward situation and transformed it into
some of the most exciting parts of the design.

By this time Greene and Greene were noted for their creative designs for wooden bungalows, and various earlier clients and new owners of their earlier houses were calling upon them for alterations and additions which would reflect the Greenes' new style and accommodate growing families. In late 1906 they undertook the remodeling of the Duncan house for Theodore M. Irwin, the second of the van Rossem houses for James W. Neill, and Charles Greene's own home—all of which were in the same block. Each involved major alterations and dramatically changed and updated the character of each to such an extent that they virtually became different houses.

The addition of a complete second floor and related alterations to the original ground floor of the Duncan house for Theodore M. Irwin demonstrated the skill of the Greenes in the handling of the many interrelated forms and spaces.[19] In the original one-story plan there was a central courtyard; the major dramatic feature of the new design was the two-story court in the center of the house. The Greenes capitalized on the unique space, defined it with a pergola structure over the second-level roof and opened bedrooms and decks out onto the intimate outdoor space which supplied both light and ventilation.

19. Following the major additions and alterations of 1905 the Duncan house is hereafter identified as the Theodore M. Irwin house.

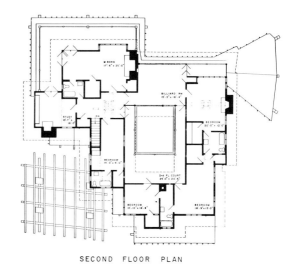

SECOND FLOOR PLAN

FIRST FLOOR PLAN

Plans, courtesy of Historical American Building Survey.

135

Charles S. Greene house, 368 Arroyo View Drive, Pasadena, 1906. Marvin Rand photograph.

In 1906 Charles expanded his own house to accommodate his growing family and developed the full second floor and his own private studio and reading room above that. In so doing the octagonal configuration of the original studio was radically altered.

Just across the reservoir from the Irwin house, Charles Greene added three rooms to his own home. This developed a full second floor. The structure thus became more related to the Arts and Crafts period.

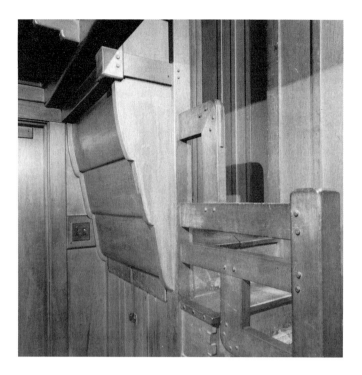

Right:
Detail of second floor
hall stairway to studio and
tree-top reading room.

Below:
Detail of master bedroom fireplace.
Marvin Rand photographs.

Charles carefully selected the soft tan granular bricks and precisely composed them to contrast with the delicate inlay of the bronze and steel firebox header.

Charles S. Greene house, detail of master bedroom added in 1906. Marvin Rand photograph.

The combination of brick and stucco cubistic forms with the playful detail of the door and the rich natural patina of the wood paneling, flooring and ceiling resulted in one of the Greenes' most pleasing spaces.

View of second floor hallway and third level narrow stairway.
Marvin Rand photograph.

The extraordinary composition of form, line, light, material,
patina and space which dramatically distinguished the Greenes'
personal genius can be felt in this beautifully sculptured
upper hallway.

James W. Neill house, 400 Arroyo View Drive, Pasadena, 1906.
Marvin Rand photograph.
Plans, *The Western Architect*, July, 1908.

The original design of this first speculative house for Mrs.
Josephine van Rossem in 1903 was so changed by the addition
of the porch structure, the expressed timbers, the massive
boulder and clinker brick wall, the pergola across the brick-
paved drive and the conversion to the natural shingle (from
horizontal clapboard siding) that the house was thereafter
published as the Neill house.

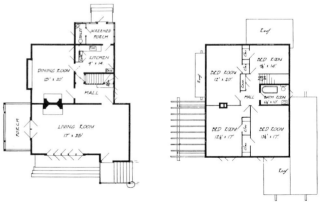

The additions and alterations commissioned by James W. Neill for the second van Rossem house were so extensive that the original character of the three year old structure was virtually eliminated.[20] Shingles were placed over the original clapboard siding, the side entry porch was incorporated into the living room, a new porch was placed on the front, and the bay window seat was removed from the living room to facilitate access to the newly developed front terrace which was created by the clinker brick and boulder wall along the front of the property. Because of the pergola built across the driveway to the west and the sheltered terrace added off the living room to the east, the front elevation took on a new horizontality which was accentuated by the bold front wall, the horizontal bands of casement windows and the strong line of the planter box at the second floor level.

Interior detail.
Marvin Rand photograph.

20. Following major additions and alterations the second van Rossem house is hereafter identified as the James W. Neill house.

Detail of narrow gate.
The Architect, December, 1915.

Prospect Park Tract Development, 1908.
Photograph courtesy of Pasadena Historical Society.

John Bentz and his partners enhanced their tract by planting
trees in response to the vast arid site along the Arroyo.
The Bentz house is the third from the left.

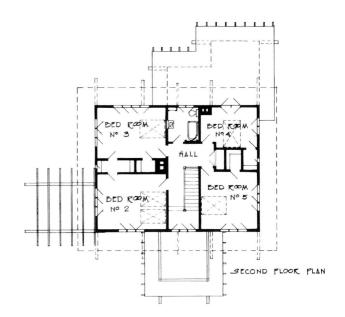

SECOND FLOOR PLAN

John C. Bentz house, 657 Prospect Square, Pasadena, 1906.
Photograph courtesy of Greene and Greene Library.

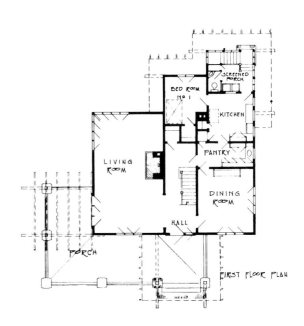

FIRST FLOOR PLAN

The Bentz house was originally designed as a model to
encourage the further development of the tract. Today it is one
of the most beautiful sites in the neighborhood and shares

the beauty of the ravine to the side with its distinguished
neighbor "La Minatura," the Frank Lloyd Wright concrete
block house for Mrs. George Madison Millard.

Meanwhile John C. Bentz, the longtime friend and client of the Greenes, joined with Nylles Eaton and J. C. Brainard in the purchase of the old Cooley tract, 32 acres located two blocks north of Arroyo View Drive where so much of the Greenes' work was attracting attention. Bentz and his associates developed the tract as "Prospect Park," and Mr. and Mrs. Bentz called upon the Greenes to design their home. It served somewhat as a model home demonstrating then as today the quality of design set for the entire area. The Bentz house is a classic example of the basic concepts of the Greenes' simple two-story shingle clad bungalow. Modest in scale, its features covered the spectrum of the Arts and Crafts philosophies and, though constructed of simple materials, it remains a testimony that the Greenes' talents could bring great dignity to every facet of their architecture.

The origin of the house was described by Mrs. Bentz:

It was decided that we build on the least expensive lot there. Mr. Greene was called on to draw the plans and specifications—Henry Greene being the engineer. He thought he wouldn't possibly be able to do so for he was so very busy with five big jobs in Pasadena at the time, but considering our friendship he did as we wanted, a very simple one. My mind was quite set upon the Swiss Chalet type of house of which he approved heartily saying square or nearly square houses give the most room and are more economical—he also advised the use of hallways for the same reason.[21]

Wood finishes were hand-rubbed and careful attention was given to every detail. Ironically, the Bentz house, set on what may have been initially the least desirable site, has matured into the most lovely of the subdivision and shares honors with its next door neighbor, Frank Lloyd Wright's famed "La Miniatura" Millard house. Together these two landmarks, along with the other houses along the street, helped provide Pasadena with one of the finest examples of good neighborhood planning and development.

Mr. and Mrs. Bentz were friends of Mr. and Mrs. F. W. Hawks whose project earlier in the year had been scrapped. According to Mrs. Bentz:

The Hawks were anxious for plans also at this time—and seeing those for us—had ours copied with some alterations suitable to their own needs.[22]

 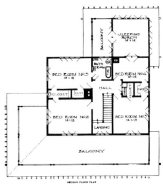

F. W. Hawks house, 408 Arroyo View Drive, Pasadena, 1906.
The Western Architect, July, 1908.
Plan, *The Craftsman*, August, 1912.

Discarding the exciting but more costly first design, the Hawks, who were close friends of the Bentzes, proceeded with a version of the Bentz design modified by the retention of the broad covered porch from the earlier project.

21. Letter to the author from Mrs. John C. Bentz, dated November 30, 1958.

22. *Ibid.*

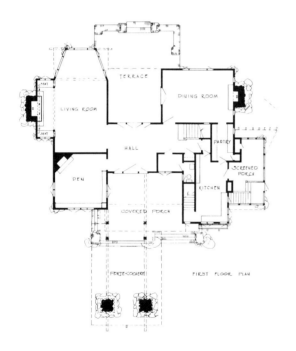

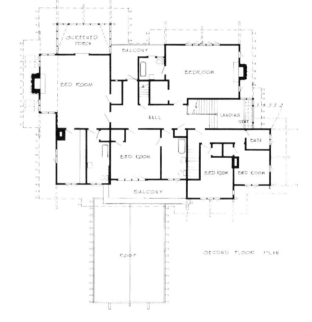

John A. Cole house, 2 Westmoreland Place, Pasadena, 1906. *Architect and Engineer*, June, 1910.

The Cole design represents the first use by Greene and Greene of the great timbered porte cochere on the front elevation of the house. The porte cochere became the major element affecting the central axis of the plan arrangement, and the entry hall bridged the two side wings allowing a view to the rear garden terrace.

The basic difference between the Hawks and Bentz houses was the full covered porch across the front of the house, a concept retained from the original Hawks project. The Hawks house was thus more simple and less costly than the earlier project. Nevertheless, it was distinguished by its broad covered promenade and roof deck which encouraged outdoor living in the front yard with its panorama of the San Gabriel Mountains and the upper valley of the Arroyo Seco.

It was a busy year. While construction was underway on the Hawks house, the Greenes were also building the John A. Cole house at No. 2 Westmoreland Place across from the Hawks house. This was the first house to incorporate the extended porte cochere as the dominant feature of the front elevation. The strong central axis which it created was the key to the plan. The great boulder chimneys also gave distinction to the house. The overall scale and the magnitude of the granite boulders were immense but as they related to the structure and the landscape testified that they were the product of master sculptors. Unfortunately their positioning on the sides of the house hid them from sight until the recent removal of neighboring buildings revealed their sculptural beauty.

Detail of chimney, Marvin Rand photograph.

Rear view, Lloyd Yost photograph.

By 1907 much of the Greenes' work was concentrated in Pasadena and, consequently, they moved their offices into the Boston Building just behind their earlier Kinney-Kendall building. The office staff had been steadily growing and early in 1907 the name of Mary L. Ranney appeared as designer on certain drawings. Hitherto Charles and Henry had maintained control over the entire operation from initial conception through the design, working drawings and supervision. However the flood of work, the moving of the offices back to Pasadena, and the fact that the first design by Miss Ranney was for her own home probably influenced the brothers' unwonted permissiveness.

The Mary L. Ranney house was next door to the Willetts bungalow and at the end of the string of houses along Arroyo View Drive. Although a small two-story structure, it was well composed and through the simplicity of its landscaping and the carefully handled clinker-brick entry wall the transition between structure and site was most beautifully developed. Possibly because of Miss Ranney's performance on her own house she was given the opportunity to design the bunkhouse for the Charles W. Leffingwell ranch in Whittier, California. On this occasion her name was listed on the drawings as designer. Aside from draftsmen affixing their initials to their drawings this was the only occasion where the Greenes are known to have relaxed their absolute control.

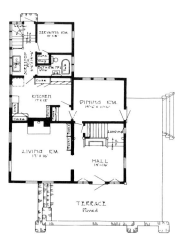

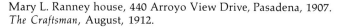

Mary L. Ranney house, 440 Arroyo View Drive, Pasadena, 1907. *The Craftsman,* August, 1912.

Mary Ranney was a draftsman in the Greene office and was given the opportunity to develop much of the design for her own house.

FRONT (EAST) ELEVATION

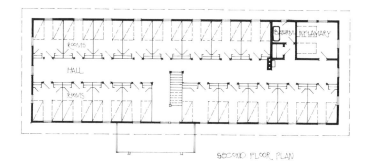

SECOND FLOOR PLAN

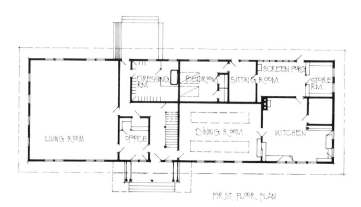

FIRST FLOOR PLAN

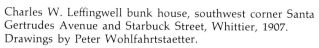

Charles W. Leffingwell bunk house, southwest corner Santa Gertrudes Avenue and Starbuck Street, Whittier, 1907. Drawings by Peter Wohlfahrtstaetter.

Unprecedentedly, the drawings for this commission were allowed to be inscribed: Designed by Mary L. Ranney in Office of Greene and Greene, Archts.

Although work in the Greene office was extremely heavy due to the major large commissions, a small design was produced for Fred Stahlhuth, the mason who was most responsible for interpreting the Greenes' designs for boulder and clinker brick masonry work which was rapidly becoming popular among builders who referred to it as "the peanut brittle style."

Fred Stahlhuth house, 380 S. Pasadena Avenue, Pasadena, 1907. Marvin Rand photograph.

The first significant national architectural publication to review the work of Greene and Greene was *The Architectural Record*. In the October issue of 1906 there was a ten page article entitled "An Architect of Bungalows in California." It was written by Arthur C. David and commented upon nine Greene and Greene houses with thirteen photographic illustrations. Mr. David spent considerable time discussing the origins of the bungalow and its appropriateness to specific areas of the United States, and evaluated the Greenes' work both in regard to the bungalow and creative architecture.

> The houses are highly successful, largely because they so frankly meet the economic, domestic and practical conditions which they are intended to satisfy. All of their chief characteristics—their lowness, their big overhanging roofs, their shingled or clapboarded walls, the absence of architectural ornament, the mixture which they afford of simple means with, in some instances, almost a spectacular effect —all these characteristics can be traced to some good reason in the actual purpose which this sort of house is intended to meet. Of course, in addition thereto Messrs. Greene and Greene must be credited with a happy and unusual gift for architectural design. Their work is genuinely original, and if anything like as good has been done with cheap little houses elsewhere in this country, it has not been our good fortune to come across it.[23]

Though somewhat of a backhanded compliment, Mr. David recognized what has often been neglected or overlooked by later observers who have concentrated their attention on the large elaborate commissions which were to follow. The Greenes were doing excellent and original work with the small and inexpensive bungalow—the "cheap little house."

David also credited the Greenes with not falling into the trap of "affectation and rusticity" in their handling of the bungalow with the one exception of the use of boulders in their chimney and foundation design. He stated that "large heavy boulders,...are ugly in themselves, and are entirely out of keeping with their surroundings and with the service they perform. The use of such uncouth and heavy masonry is a mere affectation."[24] Others saw a natural beauty in them, however. Whatever Mr. David's feeling about their being unrefined, there is little question that in the hands of the Greenes their effect was astonishingly successful. On this point the Greenes were much more in tune with the overall concepts of the Arts and Crafts Movement and it is possible that Mr. David was not sufficiently familiar with California to appreciate the beauty in the materials of the natural arroyos. Charles Greene's own article of 1905 clearly defined the Greenes' feelings on the subject:

> Furnace fires have ceased to be a necessity, but the hearth is not forgotten. Recourse once again to the fieldstones brings nature indoors and we have a simple but generous shelter for the great back log and glowing embers.[25]

Mr. David's concluding analysis was very interesting:

> One additional comment on the work of Messrs. Greene and Greene deserves to be made, which is that their methods of design are not so well adapted to large as to small houses. It is the low, one and a half or two story dwellings in which they excel, and when they come to design a building that is higher, bigger and more expensive, they do not sufficiently adapt their technical machinery to the modified conditions. Take, for instance, the house at 665 South Orange Avenue, in Pasadena [the Libby house]. In this larger and higher building the simple roof does not make any effect at all in proportion to its expanse, and the whole effect, instead of being light, graceful and picturesque, is awkward and inept. It looks like an overgrown boy who has clung to his pinafores.[26]

The great commissions of the next few years unquestionably controverted David's opinion that the Greenes' methods of design were not as well adapted to large as they were to smaller residences. The architectural world was amazed by the exquisite work that soon came off the Greene and Greene drawing boards, and the world continues to applaud the brothers' masterful creations of the next three years. It is with the Gamble, Blacker and other houses of that period that the Greenes' reputation has come to be established. And, in a sense, rightly so. In fact, however, the brothers had already exhibited a talent for large house

23. Arthur C. David, "An Architect of Bungalows in California," *The Architectural Record*, October, 1906, pp. 311-12.

24. *Ibid.*, p. 312.

25. Charles Sumner Greene, "California Home Making," Tournament of Roses Edition, *Pasadena Daily News*, January 1, 1905, p. 27.

26. David, *op. cit.*, p. 315.

design. It seems obvious that Mr. David was not acquainted with the Robinson house (under construction) nor considered the Pitcairn house. However, he was a competent observer. The Libby house was not a masterpiece. It bears witness to the Greenes' development and reveals that great architecture is not usually created—unlike Aphrodite —without labor and experimentation. This large design also suffered from a limited budget which precluded the total design embellishments that were soon to become a hallmark of the Greenes.

The important point to realize, however, is one that David expressed very well:

> Whatever deductions we may make, however, in considering the work of Greene and Greene, it remains true that they have imparted as much architectural propriety and a more positive charm to the design of inexpensive bungalows as have any architects in this country.[27]

The brothers Greene had already created an architecture and claim to fame which was not dependent upon large budgets and expensive luxuries. They had given a grace and dignity to the inexpensive house and a new direction to domestic architecture. It was this spirit and quality of their architecture which attracted the wealthy; but additional budgets merely allowed a full and marvelous blossoming of the artistry which had now begun to manifest itself. Historians generally focus on the large commissions of 1907 through 1909, but the excitement and vigor of the four years from 1903 through 1906 were truly creative years in which Charles and Henry Greene began developing, experimenting with and refining those ideas which inspired their great masterpieces.

27. *Ibid.*

IV

The Ultimate Bungalows 1907-1909

During the brief period between 1907 and 1909, Greene and Greene created seven designs which reached such a high level of craftsmanship and design sophistication that they have rarely been equalled. As a result, these houses, among the finest examples of the Arts and Crafts Movement in America, may properly be identified as the "ultimate bungalows."

The first of these masterpieces was the Robert R. Blacker house (1907) which was built on the most prestigious site of Pasadena's Oak Knoll subdivision.[1] Here the Greenes demonstrated that the fundamental concepts of their bungalow philosophy—the provision of shade and shelter in a hot climate, free cross-circulation of air, and an open relationship between house and landscape—applied just as well to large estates as to the "small and cheap wooden bungalows" to which Arthur C. David had referred.

The Greenes, however, were not the first architects to work on designs for the Blacker house. Initially, this commission had gone to Myron Hunt and Elmer Grey. But the San Francisco earthquake of 1906 had raised questions in Robert Blacker's mind about the footings and substructure. When he expressed his concern to Hunt and Grey, he was unsatisfied with their response and promptly dismissed them from the project.[2] Almost immediately, it seems, he turned to Greene and Greene.

The Blackers liked the Hunt and Grey floor plan, however, and it was probably at their insistence that Greene and Greene used virtually the same basic plan. Apart from this, there is very little similarity between the two designs. Hunt and Grey had placed a two-story stucco structure in the center of the five-and-a-half acre property. A perspective drawing from the rear corner of the site makes it appear that their primary interest was in the creation of extensive formal gardens which emphasized the formality of the floor plan, yet seemed to stifle the three-dimensional quality of the design so that the house appeared almost incidental to the general scheme.[3]

The Greenes, on the other hand, moved the house toward a corner of the property and thus allowed for a freer, more natural garden setting reminiscent of the Japanese. To break even further from the formality of the original Hunt and Grey plan, they designed an enormous, heavily timbered porte cochere which angled out from the central entry to rest on a clinker brick pillar beside a circular drive which swung in from the corner. The long bridge timbers necessary for the construction of the porte cochere were personally selected by Henry Greene who made special trips to the northern lumber areas to study the grain structures of the timbers. This porte cochere became the dominate feature of the overall design and served to relate the large two-story shingled house to the surrounding grounds. In order to provide easy access to the rolling gardens, the living room wall was bent and opened onto the tiled veranda overlooking the pond and pergola across the garden. The central court patio at the rear in the Hunt and Grey design was de-emphasized by the Greenes who instead developed a large terrace off the living room. This terrace

1. Because of the lengthy period of careful maintenance and restoration by the present owners, Mr. and Mrs. Max Hill, the structure has, in recent years, been frequenty identified as the Blacker-Hill house.

2. Interview conducted by the author with Mr. Donald McLain. He was acquainted with Mr. Blacker prior to the Hunt and Grey incident and recalled Mr. Blacker's story of their dismissal.

3. Herbert Croly, "Some Houses by Myron Hunt and Elmer Grey," *Architectural Record*, October, 1906.

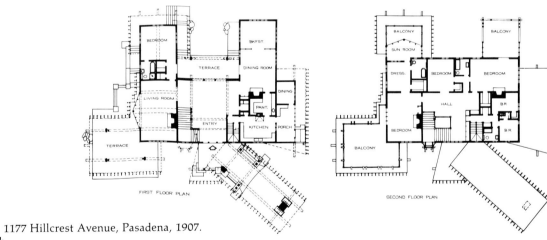

FIRST FLOOR PLAN

SECOND FLOOR PLAN

1177 Hillcrest Avenue, Pasadena, 1907.
Marvin Rand photograph.

A tremendous expression of the American Arts and Crafts
Movement and of the California bungalow, the Blacker house
was the largest, most elaborate and subtly detailed of the
Greenes' bungalow designs.

View of the side and rear gardens.
Photograph courtesy of Greene and Greene Library.

By gently sculpting the terrain, the basement billiard room opened directly out upon the rolling informal gardens of the original six acre site.

was sheltered by the expressed timber structure of the sleeping deck of the upstairs bedroom. In silhouette, the projection of the articulated wooden beams, rafters and roof lines blended gracefully into the landscape.

The Blacker house, comprising more than 12,000 square feet exclusive of the full basement, billiard room, terraces and attic, was the largest and most lavish commission which the Greenes developed in their bungalow style. In addition to the house and gardens, they also designed a garage, a gardener's cottage, a greenhouse and pergola.[4] Their attention to detail and craftsmanship in each of these designs lent unity to the whole estate.

4. In recent years, under interim ownership, the major portion of the Blacker property was sold off for subdivision, the pergola and pond demolished, and the garage and gardener's cottage remodeled into separate residences.

Rear view of east wing.
Marvin Rand photograph.

Left:
Detail of timber joinery.

Below Left:
Detail of porte cochere.

Below Right:
Detail of corner brace.
Marvin Rand photographs.

Inspired in part by their fascination with the Orient, the structure and detailing of the Blacker house transcends function and becomes an art form itself.

The foundations of the house were built of clinker brick and grouted with a black mortar. The basic structure and large beams were of Oregon Pine. The split shakes used for the walls were dipped in dark green creosote base stain for long life, and the roofs were of malthoid, a composition material largely made up of asbestos with a flexibility which allowed for the soft roll of the gutters at the roof edge.[5] The eaves extended far beyond the walls to protect the house from the hot rays of the noonday sun, and the extensive attic, completely floored and larger than most residences, was fully cross-ventilated and helped shield the interior of the house from the summer heat.

The "U" shaped plan afforded direct access to the central court. By placing the outside terrace off the living room and positioning the house on the corner of the site, the Greenes were able to merge the living area visually and physically with the gardens, pools, pergola and lawns to the east; by fitting the exterior of the structure into the rolling contours of the site, they were able to relate the billiard room in the basement to the rear garden to the south. It was in just such subtle arrangements that the Greenes' understanding and skill separated them from many of their contemporaries.

The living room of the Blacker house is distinctive among Greene and Greene works. Subtle patterns of lily pads were done in relief in the ceiling construction, and the entire ceiling was then covered with gold leaf which reflected a soft warm glow from the indirect lighting. Tiffany glass fixtures were also designed with similar patterns inspired by the planting of the pond outside. In this house more than in any other the Greenes' playfulness was revealed in the stained glass windows where plant motifs even went so far as to suggest the landscaping in the gardens outside.

The dining room, which was 35 feet in length, could be opened to include another 15 feet by folding back the wall of glass doors. Furthermore, in the event of larger banquets,

Dining room and breakfast room. Leroy Hulbert photograph, courtesy of Greene and Greene Library.

the table of the all-glazed breakfast room was built to fit the end of the dining table. Great banks of casement windows and french doors opened to the outdoors, allowing cool breezes to flow through the house when desired and permitting freedom of movement to and from the gardens.

The interior panelling and wood detailing were in teak and mahogany and the peg detailing in ebony and mahogany. Switch plates for the lighting fixtures were of the same woods as the wall panelling and the push buttons were ebony. The lighting fixtures were wood and Tiffany glass. Doors to closets, storage or service areas were all concealed in the panelling of the major spaces and were opened by the touch of an electric button. The design of the billiard room particularly exhibited the extent of the Greenes' careful planning. Overhead heating ducts were carried out in wood chases with handsome wood grills. The floor was a ground and polished terrazzo and the walls and ceiling panelled in soft redwood brushed to bring out the grain and toned with a faint stain. In one corner, which Mr. Blacker had designated as a serious card-playing area, a standing urinal was concealed in the wall panelling. All of the furnishings were designed for the house, and oriental carpets and auxiliary accessories were personally selected by the Greenes in close association with Mr. and Mrs. Blacker.

5. In later years the olive shingle exterior was stained a dark brown, then eventually was reshingled by Mr. and Mrs. Max Hill who had the original shingles perfectly matched. They omitted the stain, however, allowing the weathered aging of the wood to give natural color to the exterior surfaces. The original malthoid composition roofing has long since been replaced with a wood shake roof.

Above: Detail of entry stairwell.

Right: Entry hall and stairway.
Marvin Rand photographs.

Structurally, the Blacker house reflects a greater influence of the Orient—particularly in the heavy timber work, the joinery, porch railings and interior lanterns—than any other Greene and Greene building with the possible exception of the Tichenor house. Publications of that period paid considerable attention to the touches of Oriental or Swiss architecture found in this house, sometimes with a degree of exaggeration. One such article was entitled "A Southern California House in Japanese Style." Another likened it to a Swiss Chalet with traces of the California bungalow. More accurately, however, the design of the Blacker house evolved from the deep convictions of Charles and Henry Greene, who had for years been seeking an architectural vocabulary which would be appropriate to California life. Here they demonstrated clearly that their principles were as applicable to the large estate as to the small bungalow. The flowing, graceful plan, the expressed structural system, the concern for unified design were all here. The large budget merely facilitated their more complete and luxurious expression. Building costs of the Blacker house were over $100,000. This allowed exquisite and detailed workmanship and design features never before possible for the brothers.

Robert R. Blacker guest house.
Lloyd Yost photograph.

The guest house, although of vastly different scale, harmonizes with the main house of the Blacker estate.

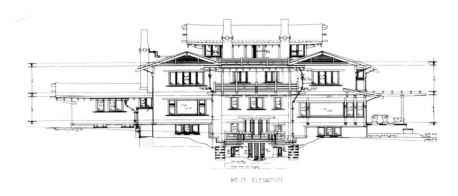

WEST ELEVATION

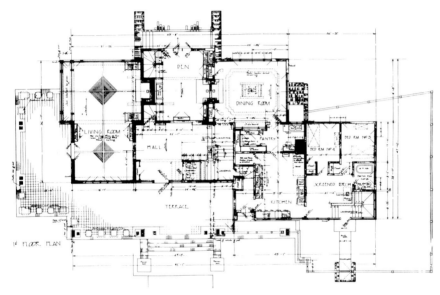

1ST FLOOR PLAN

Freeman A. Ford house project, Pasadena.
Courtesy of Greene and Greene Library.

Strong emphasis on the use of the horizontal line of the side
pergola, the kitchen wing, the bold balcony and the third
level roof was a deliberate attempt to gracefully relate the
large house to the landscape.

During the construction of the Blacker house, Greene and Greene were also working on two separate schemes for Freeman A. Ford. Both of these designs were completed through the final stages of ink and linen working drawings and were ready for construction. The first scheme was dated May 16, 1907 and the second July 9, 1907. The timing is unusually close and suggests that both designs were in the planning stage at the same time, although why they both should have been carried through the costly process of linen working drawings is not clear.

A careful study of these drawings reveals that the Greenes were exploring the relationship between large structures and their sites through the strong emphasis of the horizonal line. Even in the Blacker house the great side terrace and the angled porte cochere were not fully sufficient to counter the bulk of the main house. In the Ford project the Greenes were more successful. By stretching the kitchen service wing laterally out to the north as a one-story element and balancing this with the pergola off to the south, the breadth of the entire project in relation to its height was doubled. In a further emphasis on the horizontal, the second level projected forward over the entry terrace. By the use of broad, heavy-timbered structural elements, balcony railings, a front central low splayed roof, wide groupings of casement windows, a break between the siding and the venting of the gable-roofed portions, and the floating of the narrower third level roof as a separate element, the Greenes countered the basic rectangular box which housed the living spaces. Unfortunately, the first design was never built. The excitement of the high-ceilinged den with its stairway and loft across one end and the strength of the vertical thrust of the arroyo elevation were lost forever. Nevertheless, many new elements of the Greenes' architectural vocabulary appearing in this design were refined in the David B. Gamble house a year later.

Freeman A. Ford house, 215 S. Grand Avenue, Pasadena, 1907.
Photograph courtesy of Documents Collection,
College of Environmental Design, UCB.

Freeman A. Ford house.
View of living room.
Photograph courtesy of Documents Collection,
College of Environmental Design, UCB.

The Freeman A. Ford house finally built was the second concept, essentially a single-story courtyard design. Here the Greenes brought the entry through the central court to the front door. While the previous use of the "U" plan seemed to exhibit more of Henry Greene's influence, the undulating lines of the exterior of this house danced in and out, creating pockets and islands of space suggesting the hand of Charles.

Here, as in their other major works, the Greenes were in full control of the landscaping, the lighting, the distinctive furniture, and the leaded glass designs. The entry was placed opposite the formal pond in the central courtyard and reflected the excitement of the previous design by incorporating an open stair and balcony around the perimeter of the two-story entry. Aside from the axial formality of the entry, the plan was relaxed. In the front of the sleeping wing a second level rose upward as additional quarters and

roof terrace. The remaining structure was single-story and rambled casually around the formal, tiled courtyard.

The long drive in from the street through the orange trees swung into a circular motor court leading off the broad stairway to the central courtyard. To the right, the garage was tucked low and to one side. Between the service wing of the house and the garage the roll of the earth berm was raised high to screen the utility yard — an unusual touch which gave added character to the landscape design. This was a typical example of the way the Greenes' imagination and innovation turned awkward situations to their own advantage. Unfortunately, in later years the upper space and lofts of the entry were removed and the roof over the entry lowered, the expressed rafters clipped back, and a mission tile roof installed in place of the subtle rolled-edge malthoid composition roof. However, the power of the design was so strong that even with such major changes the Ford house remains an unusually appropriate California home.

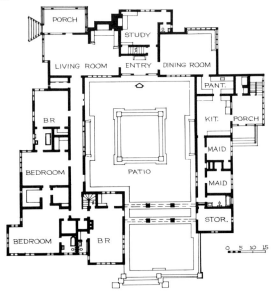

The Ford plan was the Greenes' most effective development of the "U" court plan concept and demonstrated the joint input of each of the brothers—Charles' touch on the exterior where the spaces dance in and out, and Henry's discipline giving strength and order to the random arrangement.

Central court and entry.
F. W. Martin photograph, courtesy of
Mr. and Mrs. James Marrin.

Low spreading eaves of the single-story design allowed
sunshine into the courtyard and yet shielded the walls from
the mid-day heat. Horizontal bands of casement windows
provided for both the free circulation of the breezes from the
arroyo and the entry of the cheerful morning sunlight.

The Greenes had been highly influenced by articles in the early issues of *The Craftsman*, but it was not until 1907 that Stickley began publishing illustrations of the Greenes' work in support of his own Craftsman ideals. He then became so enamoured of the Greenes' work that illustrations of Charles Greene's own home and of the Theodore Irwin house were used in Stickley's book entitled *Craftsman Homes*, published in 1909, and his articles on the Greenes appeared in June and July of 1907, January and February of 1908, and April and May of 1909. Other periodicals such as the *Ladies Home Journal, The Western Architect, Architect and Engineer*, and *House Beautiful* also printed articles on the Greenes, emphasizing the charm of the smaller bungalows.

Charles Greene also expressed his personal philosophy regarding his own work and architecture in general. Particularly revealing were his statements included in J. M. Guinn's *History of California*:

> I am an American. I want to know the American people of today and the things of today. It is my earnest endeavor to understand the lives of men and women; then perhaps I may be able to express their needs architecturally. I seek till I find what is truly useful and then I try to make it beautiful. I believe that this cannot be done by copying old works, no matter how beautiful they may seem to us now. When confronted with actual facts I have not found the man or woman who would choose to live in the architectural junk of ages gone. The Romans made Rome and the Americans — well! — they are making America. Who could live in a house of two hundred years ago and be happy if we had to conform to all the conditions of today? How in the name of reason, then, can we copy things two thousand years old? Is the Paris opera house built onto the front of a railway station or a Greek temple plastered over the entrance to an office building good art? One is apt to seize the fact for the principle today and ignore the very lesson time should teach. The old things are good, they are noble in their place; then let our perverted fingers leave them there.

> Let us begin all over again. We have got to have bricks and stone and wood and plaster; common, homely, cheap materials, every one of them. Leave them as they are—stone for stone, brick for brick, wood for wood, plaster for plaster. Why are they not better so? Why disguise them? Thought and care are all that we need, for skill we have. The noblest work of art is to make these common things beautiful for man.[6]

In July 1908, Charles wrote an article entitled "Bungalows" in *The Western Architect* in which he said:

> In the beginning there are three great things the prospective builder should know by heart:

> First—Good work costs much more than poor imitation or factory product. There is no honest way to get something for nothing.

> Second—No house however expensive can be a success unless you, the owners, give the matter time and thought enough to know what you want it for.

> By success, I mean all things necessary to your comfort and happiness in the life you are obliged to lead.

> Third—You must employ someone who is broad enough to understand and sympathize with you and your needs and yet has the ability to put them into shape from the artist's point of view...

> The style of a house should be as far as possible determined by the four conditions:
>   First—Climate
>   Second—Environment
>   Third—Kinds of materials available
>   Fourth—Habits and tastes—i.e., life of the owner

> The intelligence of the owner as well as the ability of the architect and skill of the contractor limit the perfection of the result.[7]

Certainly, these four conditions were determining factors in the design for the David B. Gamble house (1908).[8]

6. J. M. Guinn, *A History of California and an Extended History of Its Southern Counties*, 2 volumes. Historic Record Company, Los Angeles, California, 1907, pp. 540-41.

7. Charles Sumner Greene, "Bungalows," *The Western Architect*, July, 1908, p. 3.

8. The Gamble House was made a gift by the Gamble family in 1966 to the City of Pasadena in a joint agreement with the University of Southern California. It is now administered through the U.S.C. School of Architecture and Fine Arts and operated as a national architectural treasure, open to the public for tours as well as housing the Greene and Greene Library.

David B. Gamble house, 4 Westmoreland Place, Pasadena, 1908.
Marvin Rand photograph.

The Gamble house achieved its low, sensitive relationship to
the rolling site through the utilization of strong horizontals
expressed in the cantilevers, roof lines, broad bands of casement windows, sleeping porches, outdoor terraces, and
wide stairways.

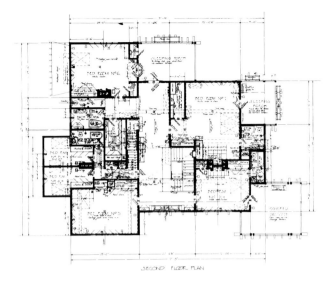

SECOND FLOOR PLAN

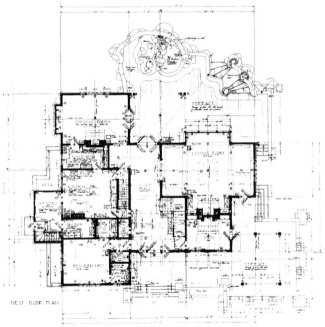

FIRST FLOOR PLAN

David B. Gamble house.
Courtesy of Greene and Greene Library.

In plan, the Gamble house is formal, strongly zoned according to function and carefully arranged about the broad central hall.

David Gamble, a second-generation member of the Proctor and Gamble Company of Cincinnati, had retired in 1895. When he and his wife Mary decided to establish permanent residence in Pasadena, they bought a property on Westmoreland Place. On the high point of the gently rolling site were two full grown eucalyptus trees measuring 26 and 32 inches in diameter. These majestic trees appealed to both the Gambles and the Greenes, and the various designs for the house evolved about them.

Rear terrace.
Leroy Hulbert photograph, courtesy of
Greene and Greene Library.

In each of the schemes for the design the two enormous eucalyptus trees were significantly incorporated into the planning of the rear terrace, and the actual structure was cut back to accomodate them.

The basic relationships of the living spaces were adopted early—from the beginning schemes of the final design of the ground floor certain elements remained throughout. The plan developed from the nature of the site, the prevailing breezes and the special living pattern established by the Gambles. It was decidedly zoned. A strong central entry and circulation area divided the living room and den from the wing composed of the dining room, pantry, kitchen, service and bedroom for non-family guests. Gone was the drama of the great porte cochere of the Blacker house. In its place the Greenes developed the graceful and light structures of the sleeping porches which contributed the same sense of horizontality to the design that had been so carefully achieved in the Freeman Ford project. Indeed, many features of the Ford project were carried right across the drawing board to the Gamble house design. Details of the leaded glass entry, the fencing and torii-structured gateway to the service yard, the splayed pattern of the roof rafters over the porches, garden pottery, and the third floor billiard room were almost identical in the two designs. The Gambles, however, had no interest in billiards. Nevertheless, the third level, renamed the "attic," remained, suggesting that the Greenes were able to convince their clients of the necessity for the visual effect which it gave to the overall composition.

A dominant characteristic of the Gamble house was the broad overhanging eave which shaded terraces, porches, and walls and cast deep shadows on the detail of the wood joinery and shingled exterior. As the day progressed, shadows from the rafter tips projecting beyond the edge of the rolled roof danced across the structure. Consequently, the house appeared to be constantly alive and changing. Heavy beams necessary for the support of the long roof overhangs also played a major role in the interior where they were left exposed. Because of their size, the beams were rounded, tapered and hand-shaped to blend into an harmonious scale with the rest of the structure.

Rear terrace.
Leroy Hulbert photograph, courtesy of
Greene and Greene Library.

In contrast to the linear formality of the front terrace, the rear terrace freely curves and the transition from structure to site is accomplished through walls of clinker brick mixed with carefully placed granite boulders.

Detail of stained glass entry doors.
Marvin Rand photograph.

The Greenes clearly believed that a wooden structure should express the integrity and identity of each of the separate parts. Each member was treated as a design element and contributed to the enrichment of the whole structural composition. This belief was as much a part of the Greenes' philosophy as their concern for craftsmanship, and was expressed by Henry Greene in his discussion of the Pitcairn house when he wrote: "The whole construction was carefully thought out, and there was a reason for every detail. The idea was to eliminate everything unnecessary to make the whole as direct and simple as possible, but always with the beautiful in mind as the final goal."[9]

In the Gamble house, no detail was left to chance. The design of furniture, lighting fixtures, carpets, picture frames and hardware blended into the overall composition. Wood panelling and trim were often fastened with brass screws covered with square pegs of ebony, mahogany or oak. The various parts of the woodwork came together in different planes. This technique helped express the identity of each contributing part. By accenting the line at the meeting of the members, the movement of joints due to expansion and contraction went unnoticed.

In the Gamble house the Greenes experimented with indirect lighting. The results expressed the architects' concern to incorporate the new developments in electric lighting into their designs. Lanterns of "Tiffany" glass in plated metal frames or mahogany were suspended from the ceilings or beams by leather straps. Matching wood wall brackets accommodated Tiffany glass shades. Door hardware, electrical outlets and switches were formed to follow the soft lines of the hand carved and rubbed wood detail and plated to the desired patina. Window rods of matching woods were equipped with folded brass clips to hold the curtains; no ordinary circular holder was acceptable in the totally controlled design. Picture frames of mahogany with ebony or brass inlay detail were suspended by leather straps from brass anchors which hooked onto the door-high horizontal wood trim.

The ground was broken on March 7, 1908 and contracts called for the completion of the house by February 1, 1909.

9. "California's Contribution to a National Architecture," *The Craftsman*, August, 1912, p. 536.

David B. Gamble house. Panorama of entry hall, stairwell and living room. Marvin Rand photograph.

The formality of the plan gives way in actuality to strong
feelings of open and interpenetrating space.

David B. Gamble house. Living room inglenook.
Marvin Rand photograph.

Structure, furniture, hardware, leaded glass, lighting, and carpets were blended into one harmonious composition, each individually beautiful while also enriching the overall design.

After signing the agreement, the Gambles expressed their complete confidence in their architects by departing for the Orient. Construction went well through the summer of 1908 and, in August when the Gamble family returned, the walls were up and the roof under construction. By January, the house was near readiness although a number of refinements were to continue in the months that followed. The first finished pieces of furniture, designed by Greene and Greene and crafted in the Peter Hall mill, were delivered on January 8, 1909 with further deliveries continuing throughout the year and into the summer of 1910.

One of the outstanding features of the Gamble house was the stained and leaded glass designed by Charles Greene and crafted by Emile Lange from carefully selected pieces from the Tiffany Studios. Lange—who had earlier been with the Tiffany Studios in New York—worked closely with Charles and meticulous care was given to the subtle coloring brought about in some areas by the laminating of the glass and emphasized by the variation of the leading process. As with Tiffany's work, each piece of glass was wrapped with copper foil and then joined one to another. In the veining of the leaves of the oak tree design, the thin lines of lead were etched as a further embellishment of the design.

Lange considered his work on the Gamble house doors his greatest triumph. He was therefore deeply hurt and disappointed when Charles expressed dissatisfaction with some of the coloring in the doors and, according to one of the draftsmen in the office, nearly broke into tears at Charles' remarks.[10] Lange was not the only one to suffer from such blunt criticism. It was not unusual for the Greenes to demand that part of the work on their structures be re-done. Although such demands were widely attributed to Charles, there is evidence suggesting that Henry Greene was equally demanding although more tactful in expressing dissatisfaction.

The Gamble house was a clear statement of the Greenes' faith in the integrity of basic units. Where the primary material was wood, these basic units were linear, as in columns, beams, rafters, railings, and drapery rods; planar as

10. Interview with Leonard W. Collins.

in wall panelling and shingles, and volumetric forms which allowed hand forming. In materials other than wood, these basic units would be the varied forms of brick, tile, boulders, formed metal, and ornamental glass. For the Greenes, each of these units contributed to the richness of the whole architectural composition and yet retained its own identity and individual function. For example, on the exterior terraces quarry tile was used where spaces were flat and open but gave way to brick where a change of level or direction occurred. The transition from one basic unit to another was achieved through a meticulous attention to detail.

Detail of rear terrace, air vents and sleeping porches.
Marvin Rand photograph.

By 1909, the work of Greene and Greene was gaining recognition not only from American critics outside of California but also from contemporaries abroad. In his *Memoirs*, the distinguished English craftsman and historian, Charles Robert Ashbee wrote:

I think C. Sumner Greene's work beautiful; among the best there is in this country. Like Lloyd Wright the spell of Japan is on him, he feels the beauty and makes magic out of the horizontal line, but there is in his work more tenderness, more subtlety, more self-effacement than in Wright's work. It is more refined and has more repose. Perhaps it loses in strength, perhaps it is California that speaks rather than Illinois, anyway as work it is, so far as the interiors go, more sympathetic to me....

Charles Greene then took us to his workshop where they were making without exception the best and most characteristic furniture I have seen in this country....Here things are really alive—and the arts and crafts that all the others were screaming and hustling about, are here actually being produced by a young architect, this quiet, dreamy, nervous, tenacious little man, fighting single handed until recently against tremendous odds.[11]

11. Charles Robert Ashbee, *Memoirs*, Victoria and Albert Museum, London, recently brought to my attention by Professor Robert W. Winter.

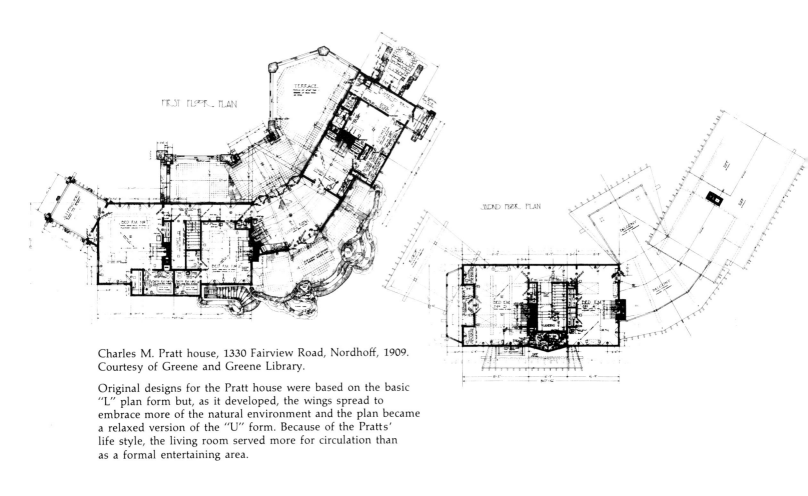

Charles M. Pratt house, 1330 Fairview Road, Nordhoff, 1909. Courtesy of Greene and Greene Library.

Original designs for the Pratt house were based on the basic "L" plan form but, as it developed, the wings spread to embrace more of the natural environment and the plan became a relaxed version of the "U" form. Because of the Pratts' life style, the living room served more for circulation than as a formal entertaining area.

The Greenes' concern with the desires of their clients prompted them to design a house for Mr. and Mrs. Charles M. Pratt which was quite different from their other bungalows. Unlike the Blacker, Ford and Gamble houses of Pasadena, this Ojai Valley residence, named "Casa Barranca," was built primarily as a winter home. Mr. Pratt was a large shareholder in the Ojai Improvement Company which owned the Foothills Hotel. Consequently, he and his wife usually entertained at the hotel rather than at home. Therefore, the Greenes placed less emphasis on a formal entry and spacious living and dining areas. Instead, the entry door opened directly into the modestly scaled living room which, except for the corner fireside inglenook, served more as the central circulation area about which the "V"

formed plan revolved. Directly opposite the entry, the entire rear wall of the living area opened directly to the covered rear terrace and the view of the natural rocky terrain of the foothills. Despite the informality however, every detail of the Pratt design was given the Greenes' strict attention. In the interior of the dining room, they were able to carry out concepts of high-ceilinged space that had been such an exciting—although seldom employed—feature in earlier designs. Wood expressed the space, and matching graining of the panelling of the upper portion of the high walls accentuated the vertical. The hanging wood-framed Tiffany glass lighting fixture was suspended by leather straps and cast a light pattern the size of the dining table below which the Greenes also designed.

The Pratt design was the most casual of the "ultimate bungalows." The multi-gabled design of the roofs seemed to emulate the graceful mountains behind.
Marvin Rand photograph.

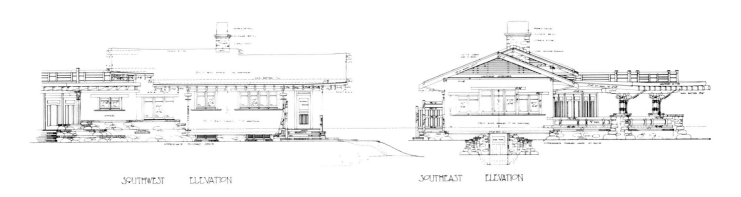

SOUTHWEST ELEVATION   SOUTHEAST ELEVATION

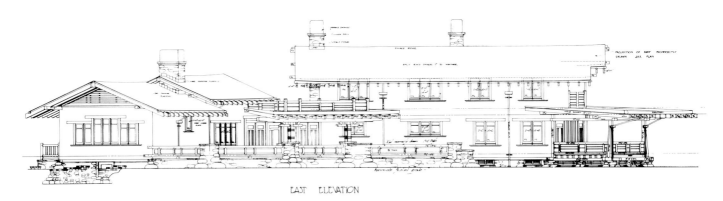

EAST ELEVATION

Charles M. Pratt house. Elevation drawings.
Courtesy of Greene and Greene Library.

In developing the 14 acres of property, the architects simply planted fruit trees among the indigenous chaparrals. Natural rock outlined the entry and defined the circular drive leading up to the house.

In his notes of an interview with Mr. Thaddeus S. Timms, caretaker of the Pratt property for 27 years, Professor Robert Judson Clark recorded:

> The Pratts spared little expense in keeping the property in perfect order. Henry Greene came up every 4 or 5 years to supervise the rejuvenation of the exterior and interior of the house. It took a whole crew of men six to eight weeks to do the job and they lived on the property for the duration. Anything that Henry Greene did or said was okay and the rule, as far as the Pratts were concerned.[12]

The caretaker also pointed out that special shutters were made to cover the windows and doors when the Pratts were away, each specially numbered and stored in the basement. In addition special coverings were made for each piece of furniture.

12. Interview by Robert Judson Clark with Thaddeus S. Timms, caretaker at the Pratt estate for 27 years. The author is deeply grateful for the privilege to have access to Professor Clark's private notes.

Detail of timber joinery of rear terrace.

French doors leading to the rear terrace.
Marvin Rand photographs.

The beautiful linear composition of the french doors, designed by Henry following Charles' departure for England, is one example of many in the Pratt design where the brothers' individual influences can be readily discerned.

Charles M. Pratt house. Dining room.

In contrast to the rambling floor plan, the
dining room is almost square and is
accentuated by the extraordinarily high
ceiling panelled in woods with matching
grains finished in faint stains to express
the board and batt detail. The geometry
of the space is further emphasized by the
octagonal form of the lighting fixture
designed of leaded "Tiffany" glass (with
inserts of jade) within the intricately detailed
mahogany lantern frame.
Marvin Rand photograph.

Detail of living room mantle and fireplace curio cabinet.
Marvin Rand photograph.

Detail of a corner of an upstairs bedroom.
Marvin Rand photograph.

William R. Thorsen house, 2307 Piedmont Avenue, Berkeley,
1909. Courtesy of Documents Collection,
College of Environmental Design, UCB.

The Thorsen house is the most significant example of the
Greenes' "ultimate bungalow" style in the Bay Area, and is
an excellent response to the site and the living pattern of the
clients.

Entry stair, foundation, and structural detail.
Marvin Rand photograph.

In response to the slope of the site, the wood structure rested upon massive clinker brick foundation walls which allowed for the development of the basement spaces for storage and a large ballroom.

In each of the large bungalows of 1907-09, the Greenes exploited all opportunites to stretch the plan forms out onto the site to envelop portions of the outdoor spaces. While the characteristics of each site influenced the character of the plan forms, the brothers were apparently intent on breaking from the compactness of the tight box plan form whenever the client and budget would allow. The "U" form was fully developed in the Freeman Ford house and again in a more restrained manner in the Dr. S. S. Crow house. But the form which seems to have answered more of the demands of the clients, the site, and the architects was the "L" plan which allowed for variations in which the vistas and gardens could be controlled by the designer. This was used in the plans for the Thorsen and Anthony houses, both of which were built on inner city lots.

The William R. Thorsen house in Berkeley presented the Greenes with a new challenge. The climate differed from that of Southern California, and the site was a city lot which sloped sharply to the street and had a commanding view of the Bay Area. Because of the spectacular view, the architects broke away from their customary multiple casement windows and used larger sheets of plate glass in the major windows. The dining room was thrust forward with the polygonal frontal portion entirely in glass. Because of the steep slope up and away from the front street, the main floor sat high on the foundation and the main portion of the structure followed the sloping street to the left of the site, virtually cradling the small interior rear garden and shielding it from the noise of surrounding traffic. To compensate for the height of the house, the elevation along the north side street property line was coupled to the garage by a richly detailed timber bridge and elaborate fence and gate design—a treatment which elongated the horizontal lines.

Here, contrary to most of the Greenes' work, little emphasis was placed on the advantages of outdoor living. This may have been the result of the client's wishes, climatic conditions, site constraint, or a combination of all three. There was, in fact, almost a pointed effort to divorce the living room from the garden by the large scale and placement of the fireplace. The plan did not encourage free movement in and out of the house. The relationships of

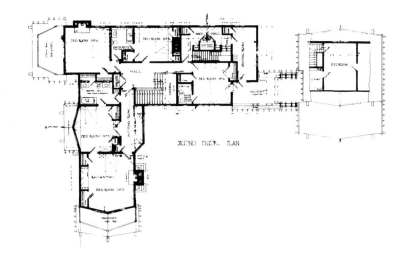

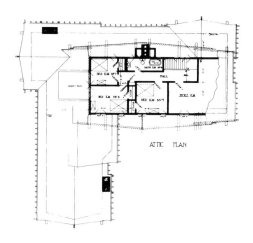

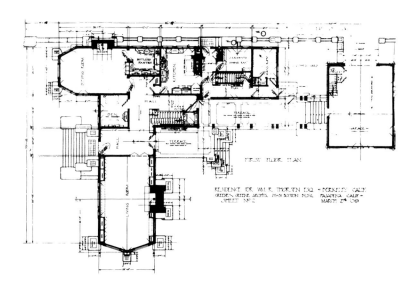

William R. Thorsen house.

The plan followed the street lines and cradled the inner garden, providing a high degree of privacy.

Right:
Side elevation detail.
Marvin Rand photograph.

Interior arrangements are subtly expressed on the carefully composed exterior design which contributes to the human scale realized in even the large bungalows.

the plan and spaces within the house reflect a more formal life style than the bungalows of Southern California. In fact, the Thorsen house is identified as a bungalow only because of the materials, the detailing, and characteristics of the Greenes' design. To point out the degree of formality in the living pattern, with the exception of a pass-through, there was no direct access between the kitchen and butlers' pantry which served the dining room. Such an arrangement required the employment of additional help.

On the second level, both the front and side wings of the plan provide sleeping quarters. The primary bedrooms were placed along the front although only one of the three was given a significant advantage of the view; unlike the living room below, the master bedroom was cloistered with only a few casement windows to the south and small windows to the rear. Upon close study, the entire plan of the Thorsen house shows clearly that the Greenes worked very closely to interpret the Thorsen's living pattern in a very personal and individual manner. Because of the sharp slope of the property, the basement allowed for a grand ballroom, the "Jolly Room," beneath the living room, complete with a massive fireplace, and an entry hall with a richly panelled and intricately detailed ceiling. The furniture, especially designed for the house, was actually made in a lower room. Perhaps Peter Hall's mill was so busy that he sent some of his craftsman north to work on the Thorsen furniture.

The climate in Berkeley, so different from that of Southern California, called for different designs. The glass areas were more open and the roof overhangs were cut back as there was no need to shield the house from a hot, dry sun. The Greenes flared the roof out as it reached toward the ridge and, in so doing, dramatically softened the lines of the elevations, compensated for the three-story height of the north wing, and introduced a somewhat Swiss feeling to the design. The result is sensitive and pleasing.

Gentle shaping of the columns and the wrought iron metal straps combine to take the necessities of building beyond normal standards. They are functional, they are bold, and they are beautiful.
Marvin Rand photograph.

In the exterior detail there was the same bold expression of hand-shaped timbers as in the bungalows of Southern California. In the posts of the rear colonnade the timbers were strapped together and secured with the familiar driven wedge. The natural expression of the changing interior functions as revealed on the exterior elevations was extraordinarily successful. The use of different materials marked the transition between the wooden structure of the house and the masonry foundation wall of the basement which was handled with a sculptor's care. Here again, the transitions between conditions, elements, or materials exemplified the Greenes' art. The use of wrought iron in the landscaping was particularly successful. In arched supports over the gateways and for the hanging lanterns, and in the gates themselves, the Greenes displayed their sensitivity to the nature of the material, and produced some of their best abstract compositions.

On the interior, the use of woods, joinery and detail was quite similar to that in the Blacker, Ford, Gamble and Pratt houses. However, there was a dramatic change in the character of the overhead lighting. Mr. Thorsen disliked the lighting fixtures in the Blacker house which were suspended by wood or leather supports and specifically requested that no such elements appear in his design. As a result, the Greenes developed leaded Tiffany glass designs recessed and flush into the ceiling.

The William R. Thorsen house remains the most significant example of the Greenes' bungalow architecture in the northern part of California and is one of the finest examples of the Arts and Crafts Movement in the Bay Area.[13]

William R. Thorsen house. Gate.
Marvin Rand photograph.

13. The Thorsen house, in later years, has become the home of the Sigma Phi Fraternity at Berkeley. Fortunately the members and alumni of the fraternity are proud and astutely aware of the values inherent in preserving such a national treasure and are taking steps to insure the future of the landmark structure.

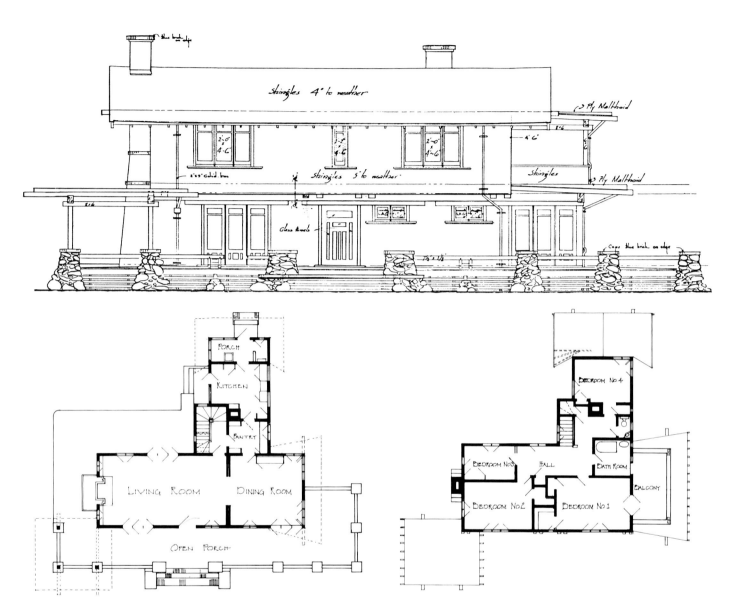

In addition to the masterworks of the years 1907-1909, a few other commissions were handled by the office during those three years. East of Pasadena, on the slopes of the foothills of Sierra Madre, the 1908 home for William J. Lawless contained furniture designed by the Greenes which is worthy of note.

William J. Lawless house, 585 Central Avenue, Sierra Madre, 1908. (Demolished) Courtesy of Avery Architectural Library. Plans by Philip Enquist.

The most modest house built by the Greenes during the years of the "ultimate bungalows," the Lawless design made use of the cobblestones of the Sierra Madre foothills, thus helping to relate the small two-story house to the surrounding environs.

179

Early in 1909, construction began on a simple and compact bungalow for Judge William W. Spinks. The plan was a basic rectangle with minor variations and the two-story design was grouped mostly under one simple broad gable. The outstanding feature of the Spinks house was the elegant simplicity of the site development. Situated just down the vista from the Blacker house, the Spinks house rested serenely in the midst of broad expanses of open green space in both the front and rear yards. To the rear, the site dropped rapidly into a large valley and presented a handsome view of the mountains in the background.

The plan was compact. The interiors were left without elaborate detail and thus provided more opportunity for the occupant to express his own personality. There was, of course, the Greenes' usual sensitive treatment in the stair detail and in the wood trim about all of the spaces. However, the restraint exercised throughout, coupled with the elegant composition of the skylight and the beauty and simplicity of the overall design, suggests the dominant influence of Henry Greene.

Work in the Greene and Greene office had been heavy since 1903. More and more discerning clients were turning to the young and progressive brothers. Many former clients requested additions or changes to former designs in order to accommodate their growing families. Alterations were preferred to the alternative of moving to another house. The widespread acceptance of their work not only put greater demands upon the firm but also provided greater challenges to both Charles and Henry. As the business expanded, it demanded a greater degree of organization within the office. Henry, by necessity, had become the business man of the firm without relinquishing his own hand in the planning, organization, and structural concerns as well as exercising a restraint to Charles' imagination. Henry directed the entire operation of the office, saw to the orderly preparation of the ink and linen working drawings, kept relations between the firm, the clients and the contractors running smoothly and, in general, made it possible for the firm to produce the great amount of high quality work in such a short span of time.

Charles was no less pressed; he felt compelled to put in the same personalized efforts for each client until he was spending long days, evenings and weekends working in

William W. Spinks house, 1344 Hillcrest Avenue, Pasadena, 1907. Marvin Rand photograph. Peter Wohlfahrtstaetter drawings.

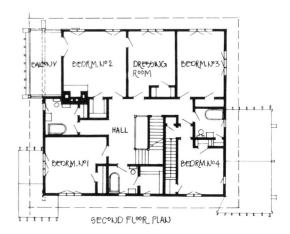

SECOND FLOOR PLAN

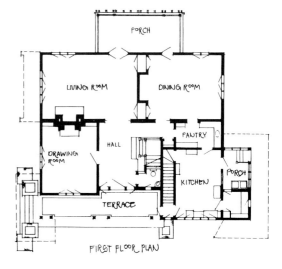

FIRST FLOOR PLAN

180

his studio on the third level of his own home. His appearances in the office were infrequent. The draftsmen had little opportunity to know him personally and generally felt in awe of him. Leonard W. Collins, recalled that he was somewhat afraid of Charles who at times exhibited an actor's temperament. Collins remembered that both the Greenes, though totally different, were quiet men who never raised their voices. The brothers' personal offices reflected their personalities and the very nature of the tasks which the growth of the practice had brought about. Charles' office was complete with oriental rugs, a beautiful cabinet designed for art objects and his many books on art and architecture. In contrast, Henry's office was very practical, containing product catalogues, drawing boards, and filing cabinets.

At the peak of their success Charles' temperament could no longer tolerate the pace and the pressure of the work of the firm. Thus, early in 1909 he went to London, rented a home near Kensington Garden, and remained there with his family until almost the end of the year. His faith and trust in Henry and his high regard for Peter Hall made possible his departure at such a crucial period. Henry, with the help of his father, who had joined the firm to handle the book work, calmly supervised the construction of the ultimate bungalows. He even managed to take on a few new clients for whom he handled the entire design work. During the months Charles was away, Henry had the undivided and full support of all who worked in the office. The design for the Dr. S. S. Crow house (1909) in Pasadena captured the hearts of the entire staff.[14] Not only was it an expression of Henry's own talent but also, because of its smaller scale, it had a personal quality about its design with which each of the office members identified. It was one of the most graceful compositions ever created by the firm. Here was exhibited a restraint which lent a genuine dignity to the design. There was a linearity about the plan composition, the low, horizontal roof lines, and the window and door

14. The design for the Crow house is also identified with Edward S. Crocker, who purchased the house in January of 1911 and who has often been identified as the initial client. The records are clear, however, that Henry Greene designed the beautiful bungalow for Dr. Crow while Charles was in England.

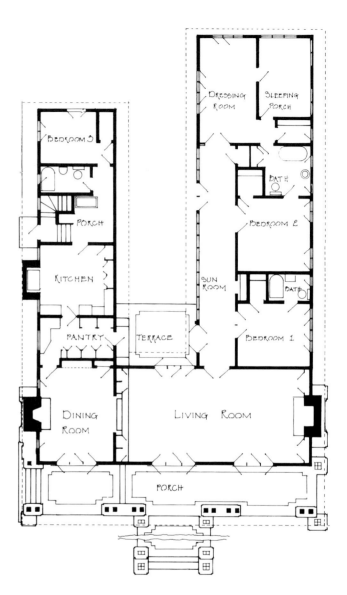

Dr. S. S. Crow house. Drawing by Philip Enquist.

Dr. S. S. Crow house, 979 El Molino Avenue, Pasadena, 1909.
Marvin Rand photograph.
Drawing by Peter Wohlfahrtstaetter.

Designed by Henry Greene while Charles was in England, the
scale, proportions and subtle restraint of this house establish
it as one of the most significant designs ever produced by the
firm.

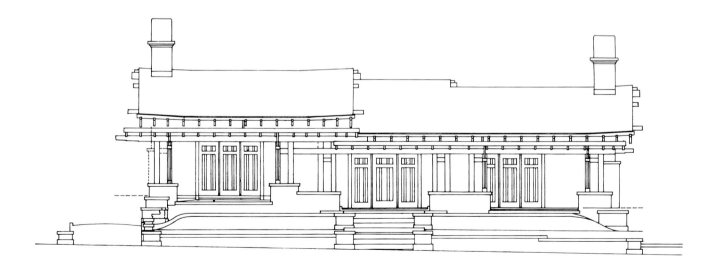

designs which was very refreshing. Clear instead of stained glass sufficed in the french doors, and seemed more appropriate. At the same time, there was just enough detail—any more would have been too much. The subtle overlapping of the front gable roof, the slight drop in the lower ridge line, the simple way in which the house eased into the low rolling landscape, suggested a very special kind of architectural composer. The plan was so direct as to appear almost unthought. It returned to the simple straight lines of Henry's earlier designs, but because of the careful composition lent a high degree of individuality to each interior space. Henry's development of a floating "torii" inspired archway as a transition from the living to the dining area was intriguing. The flowing ceiling contributed to the spaciousness of the two rooms. The major circulation artery was a wide hall fully glazed to the central garden with additional light from the skylighted ceiling. Here again Henry exhibited his mastery of the linear abstract composition. The scale and forms of stained glass in the skylight have a beautiful relationship with the structural members. It was subtle, and exemplified the Greenes' efforts to "try and find what is truly necessary and then try to make it beautiful."

Detail of sun room skylight.
Marvin Rand photograph.

The skylight is one of the most beautiful elements of the design and it is greatly enriched by the sensitive blending of the major structural members with the minor struts supporting the stained glass.

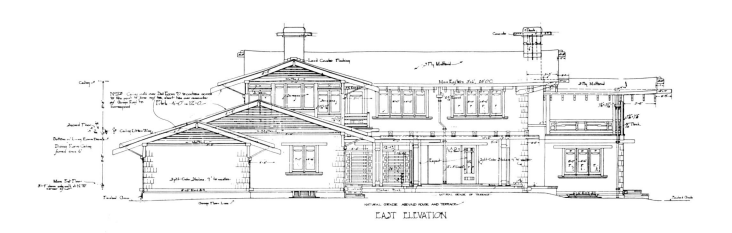

EAST ELEVATION

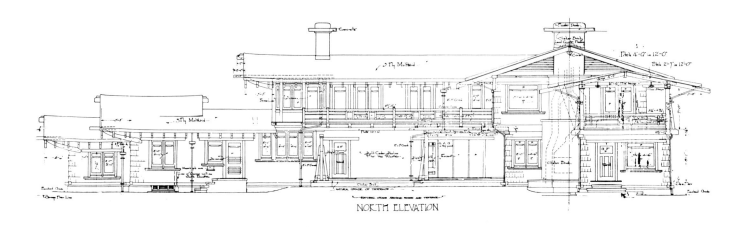

NORTH ELEVATION

Earle C. Anthony house, 910 N. Bedford Drive, Beverly Hills, 1909. Courtesy of Avery Architectural Library.

The house was moved from its original location at 666 S. Berendo Street, Los Angeles, in 1923.

The last of the masterworks of these years was the bungalow for Earle C. Anthony, the only major house of the period to be built by the firm in Los Angeles. Anthony, whose interests were in automobile sales and radio, had selected a site on the corner of Wilshire Boulevard and Berendo Street. However, the rapid change of the development along the Wilshire Boulevard "miracle mile" made the life of the area as single family residential property short, and in 1923 the house was moved to Beverly Hills.[15]

The plan for the Anthony house again followed the "L" form, but somewhat more casually than in the Thorsen plan. The interior arrangements flowed with greater ease and there was more attention given to relating the interiors to the rear gardens. Balancing the side wing of the house, which screened the oriental garden from the neighboring property, a long pergola embraced the street side of the garden and solid walls provided privacy.

The Anthony house related more to the larger ultimate bungalows and was more complex in its exterior configuration and in its detail and roof lines than the Crow-Crocker house; but, unlike the other ultimate bungalows, its interior room arrangements are much more in line with Henry's interpretation of the relaxed nature of California life. However, he misjudged Mrs. Anthony in developing such an earthy, wooden bungalow. Not long after the house was finished, she began to be disenchanted with the dim interiors, the abundance of wooden expression, and the bungalow character of the house. In 1913 the Greenes were brought back to modify the upstairs sitting room and to make other alterations which included painting portions of the wooden detail to lighten the interior.

15. In 1923 film star Norman Kerry purchased the Anthony house and had it moved in three sections to its present location in Beverly Hills. He engaged Henry Greene to handle the resiting and the garden development.

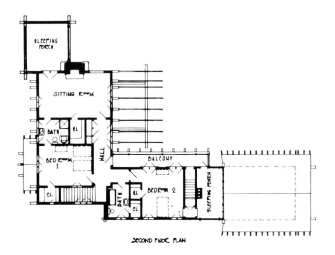

SECOND FLOOR PLAN

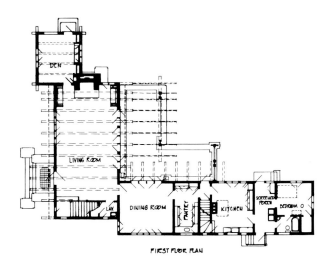

FIRST FLOOR PLAN

The plan is more direct than that of the Thorsen house—circulation is well organized, and the major spaces are larger, simpler, more open and less formal.

The Anthony house was the last of the masterworks of 1909. Mrs. Anthony's reaction to the natural quality of the design was an early indication that public taste was turning from the principles of the Arts and Crafts Movement to traditional designs which had previously been identified with affluence. But the Greenes were too busy to see or acknowledge this change. Their own feeling about their talents and their place in the spectrum of the architectural profession at the time was revealed in a letter to Mr. Pratt in which Charles voiced more of his inner thoughts about his work, his art, his profession and his relation to his "patron" than in any other single writing:

> In some cases I made corrections in the work done when I was not on the ground. Of course this could have been done cheaper in the common way and by sending a man from the office instead of myself. But does not the result justify the expense?
>
> Art reduced to a commodity of course can not argue so, for investment seeks fixed financial return. But living art never can be so reduced. It must have become a curio in the hands of a dealer before it can be bartered without injury to the art. This is one good reason why living art scarcely ever can compete with the old. Once exploited it ceases to be art.
>
> You say that you have never before paid so high a price for this kind of work; to which I reply that I believe you mis-judge the character of mine. In other words, is the comparison fair? Knowing what I do of the architectural practice of today I can not be very far wrong. Furthermore there is no one to my knowledge who has the temerity to limit the number of commissions to a personal supervision.
>
> It is too much to expect that anyone may see the excellence of this kind of thing in a few days. The work itself took months to execute and the best years of my life went to develop this style. I realize that you are concerned in affairs much more weighty than a little country home in the Ojai, but trivial as it may seem to you my effort was for the best. My plea is not so much for the fact as for the principle— not so much for the artist as that art may find expression.
>
> I do not claim for my management the strictest economy. Art and commerce are divided and must ever be.... If one can afford to have these things, does it not argue as well for you as for art that one should have them. I do not speak on my own authority alone as to the intrinsic art value of my work, though I could never have produced it without knowing that ...

Into your busy life I have sought to bring what lay in my power of the best that I could do for art and for you. How I wish I had the power to look into your soul to more fully understand not what you think but what you feel. I doubt not for a moment your power of appreciation, but I should know better what to say without arguing.

> I have known many people that love the beautiful but it is beyond their reach. For you all these things are possible and, believe me, I have given what I could personally because I thought you would like it and because I felt sure that you would, in the end, appreciate.

> C. Sumner Greene[16]

Whether there was a realization in the firm in 1909 that this would be an end to an entire era in the work of Greene and Greene is doubtful. Nevertheless, one thing is certain. The Greenes were creative artists who had found a particular architectural vocabulary with which to express their own particular art form, and they were confident that this art form was the ultimate expression of the bungalow style.

True, they had been spoiled by wealthy clients who made it easy for them to demand only the best in materials and workmanship. They were spoiled too by the opportunity to be very selective in accepting commissions. And, by 1909, there was still so much work remaining on both the structures and their furnishings that there was little time to analyze or even notice the changing tastes of the public. The Greenes were still at the peak of their careers and that momentum was strong enough to carry them through the next few years before the effect of changing tastes and economics would affect the very substance of their extremely specialized practice.

16. From a handwritten draft of the letter which we do not know assuredly was ever sent. Documents Collection, Greene and Greene Library, The Gamble House.

Armenian Pilgrims Church project, Fresno, 1908.
Courtesy of Documents Collection,
College of Environmental Design, UCB.

Numerous schemes were developed for the church, and this
design most closely conveyed the spirit of earlier Greene and
Greene work.

Shelter for Viewlovers, Monks Hill, Pasadena, 1907.
(Demolished) Courtesy of Pasadena Historical Society.

V

Convictions in Conflict with Change   1910-1922

In 1910, when Charles returned from England, the firm of Greene and Greene entered into its third and final phase. The first major departure from the wooden, shingle-clad character of the ultimate bungalows was an elaborate project for John Lambert designed in 1910 for a large corner site in Pasadena. The house was planned with a stucco or gunite exterior. In response to the plasticity of the material, the overall design was softer, more sculptured, and less linear than the Greenes' earlier work. However, the roof construction and the use of major timbers in the porch design was unmistakably reminiscent of their previous work. A very large house accentuated by drawing the plan out to provide a buffer for the rear gardens was designed. Vast terraces flanked the dining and living rooms to the rear and great retaining walls and planter areas reached out from the structure into the gardens. No expense was spared. Interior spaces were large and extensive attention was devoted to the service wing. It was one of the firm's most expensive designs, which was probably the reason why the project was never built. The Lamberts, in fact, turned to other architects and built a much more modest two-story, tile-roofed Spanish Revival house on the same site.

Perhaps the Greenes had gone too far, had expected too much, had refined their art to such a high level that costs had become prohibitive. The Lambert design was only the first of several projects which were never carried into construction. In fact, the first three commissions of 1910 never progressed beyond the design stages. By 1910 the Greenes were reputed to be very slow and very costly. Fewer and fewer commissions came their way and they were no longer able to pick and choose among wealthy clients. However, there was still much activity in the office—the completion of the ultimate bungalows with their furnishings and new work on the drawing boards; but only three new works—the Ernest W. Smith bungalow, the Sam L. Merrill house, and the Keith Spalding bunk house — were built during this year.

There is little to suggest that Charles had much to do with these three designs. With few exceptions, Charles had little to do after 1909 with any of the smaller bungalows. His conception and practice of art had resolved itself to exquisite but expensive "total" design. He did not compromise those ideals.

Whatever the changing tastes of the general public at this time, a considerable amount of attention was given to the Greenes by many periodicals. In late 1910, there were major articles in *Architect and Engineer* on the Ford, Gamble, Cole, and Blacker houses.[1] But, the accolades of the press did little to bring in new work for the firm.

---

1. "The Bungalow," *The Architect and Engineer*, Vol. XXI, No. 2, June, 1910, pp. 55-65; A. W. Alley, "A Southern California House in Japanese Style," *The Architect and Engineer*, Vol. XXI, No. 3, July, 1910, pp. 62-63.

FRONT — WEST ELEVATION

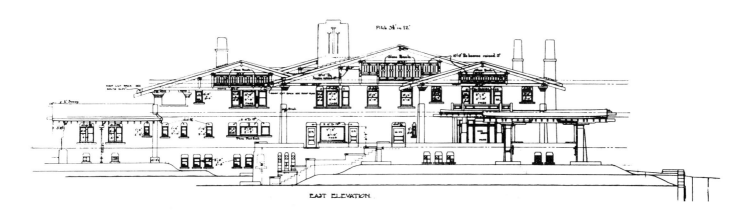

EAST ELEVATION

Project: John Lambert house, Pasadena, 1910.
Courtesy of Avery Architectural Library.

Of the several major projects of 1910, the Lambert design demonstrated that the Greenes could adapt to changing attitudes and break from the wooden bungalow. However, the scale of this project and the Greenes' criteria for craftsmanship made it too costly and the clients turned to other architects for a more modest design.

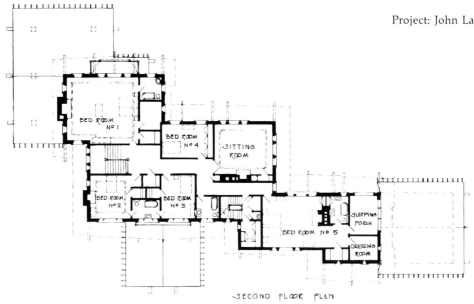

SECOND FLOOR PLAN

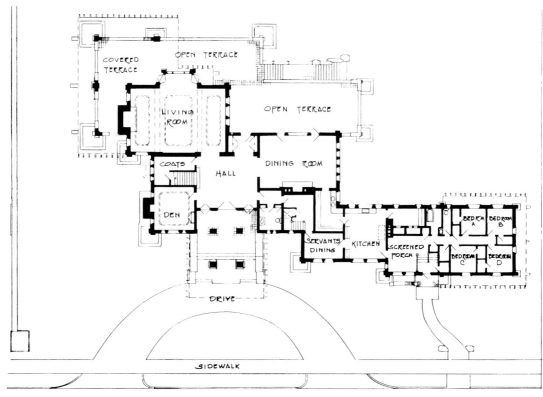

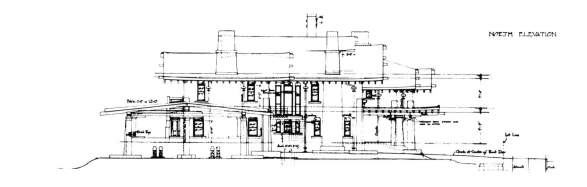

NORTH ELEVATION

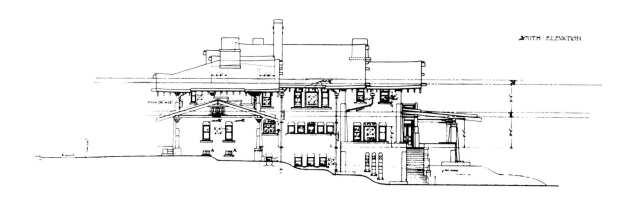

SOUTH ELEVATION

Project: John Lambert house.
Side elevation drawings.
Courtesy of Avery Architectural Library.

Ernest W. Smith house,
272 Los Robles Avenue,
Pasadena, 1910.
Side elevation and chimney,
Marvin Rand photograph.

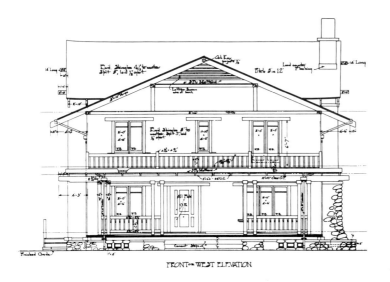

FRONT OR WEST ELEVATION

Elevation drawing, courtesy of Avery Architectural Library.

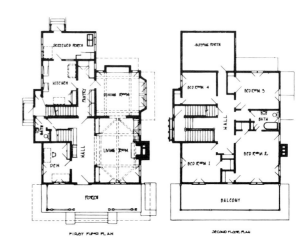

FIRST FLOOR PLAN   SECOND FLOOR PLAN

Like the early work of 1903-1906, the clean straightforward order of the Smith plan and the charm of its restrained interior illustrates the flexibility of the Greenes' architectural vocabulary.

Sam L. Merrill house, 1285 N. Summit Avenue, Pasadena, 1910. Marvin Rand photograph.

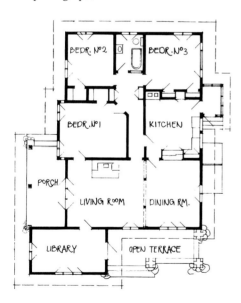

By carefully positioning the library, the added gable roof lent character to the exterior composition and provided privacy for the side porch.
Drawing by Peter Wohlfahrtstaetter.

The brothers' work was well represented in numerous articles in the 1911 edition of the special New Year's supplement periodical of the *Pasadena Daily News*. A major article in this issue was entitled "Pasadena Portico of Paradise — The Trend of Architectural Development in Pasadena." Despite its attention to the Greenes, however, the real significance of the article lay in the comments on changing architectural directions:

> Our forests are rapidly going. Wooden buildings, even wooden roofs are things of the present.... The development of the new mode of building in reinforced concrete has grown in Southern California with leaps and bounds. There is good reason for this local development. We have material at our door everywhere which makes cement. We have sand and gravel by the square mile. It is a certainty that when the day of wood is gone by, the day of concrete will be here to remain.

Equally important was the fact that because of the poor use of wood, and design quality in some builders' bungalows, public taste was turning now to the use of plaster and stucco. In his own writing, Charles Greene opposed the use of white as a building color in the bright California sunlight, and the Greenes constantly expressed the natural color of the aggregates when using stucco and plaster.

During this phase of their careers, the year 1911 was the most productive and diverse. Elements from the wooden years were blended with the more plastic opportunities to be found in stucco and gunite. Again, several projects were completely developed, but only on paper.

Charles was rapidly moving toward an establishment of his own individual identity. In the 1911 exhibition of the Los Angeles Architectural Club and in the accompanying "Yearbook" an entry appeared which was entitled "Sketch of a Dwelling Place—by Chas. Sumner Greene, Architect, Pasadena — for W. B. T. Esq. near Pasadena." He had changed directions upon his return from England. Times had changed and good woods were hard to get. His interest in the missions revived. Furthermore, Charles refused to sacrifice his principles and beliefs in order to compete for work. With the coming of income tax he saw the end of quality construction and believed that clients would not pay for his kind of quality. Coupled with these feelings, Charles and Henry were dismayed by the bad imitations

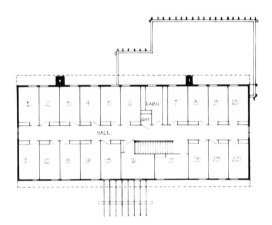

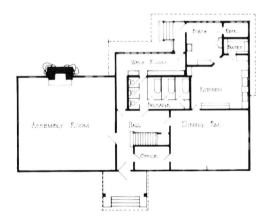

Keith Spalding bunk house for Sespe Ranch,
2896 W. Telegraph Road, Fillmore, 1910.
Drawings by Philip Enquist.

of their bungalows. Their own work was being published alongside mundane plans in the bungalow books and both builders and the public were identifying Greene and Greene with these inferior houses. There were, of course, a few architectural contemporaries who competently emulated the Greenes. Among these Walker and Vawter, Arthur and Alfred Heineman, G. Lawrence Stimson, and Arthur Kelly produced the most commendable results. In Australia, James Peddle (who lived in Pasadena from 1911 to 1914) designed various works in and around Killara near Sydney which closely related to the Greenes' work in Southern California.

Among his architectural contemporaries and about town, Henry Greene had become highly respected as a dedicated professional of unquestionable ethics who demanded the highest standards in his work and associations. He was appointed in 1911 by Pasadena Mayor William Thum, along with fellow architects Myron Hunt, Elmer Grey, and Frederick L. Roehrig, to formulate the first city "code of building procedure," a document which later was adopted as the formal building law of Pasadena.

In 1911 the Greenes began work on the Mortimer Fleishhacker house, which was situated high in the hills of Woodside, California in the midst of a large estate of virgin, mountainous terrain north of Palo Alto. Over the years, numerous additional projects, structures, landscape, and garden developments were built which kept Charles busy at times when he had no other work on the drawing boards. Mortimer Fleishhacker, President of the Great Western Paper Company, at Woodside, California and active in the business world of San Francisco, was most influential. He is purported to have offered the brothers a million dollars in commercial building if they would work in the Bay Area. The Greenes, however, refused the offer.[2]

The Fleishhackers had looked about for some time for an architect. Although they did not like the work of the Greenes in Pasadena, particularly the Japanese influence, they did meet with Charles Greene and shortly thereafter awarded their work to the firm. Robert Judson Clark records that "the Fleishhackers had seen many houses in the East with thatched roofs and they requested an English house,

2. Interview by the author with Nathaniel Patrickson Greene.

Mortimer Fleishhacker house, 329 Albion Avenue, Woodside,
1911. Marvin Rand photograph.

The largest of all Greene and Greene designs, the Fleishhacker
estate concept developed vast, formal gardens to contrast
with the natural chaparral of the rolling, mountainous site.

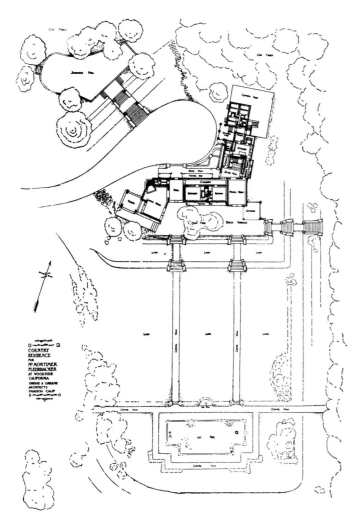

Mortimer Fleishhacker house. Partial site plan.
The Architectural Record, 1916.

Primarily the work of Charles Greene, the design reflects his and the clients' interest in the English country house. Considerable attention was given to the gardens which were a dramatic departure from the informality of earlier Greene landscape designs.

with thatched roof, if possible. Mr. Greene agreed."[3] But Charles was very slow about giving them any idea of his intentions for the house. "He would sit on the little hill for hours and contemplate the scene and situation." It was finally decided to build around a large oak tree prominent in the center of an open portion of the site.

The Fleishhacker's interest in the English country house and Charles' recent return from nearly a year in England appear to have been timed prefectly. Charles felt that he had done all he could with wood and, if he was to continue with architecture, would need to reach out to other forms. Furthermore, the overall scale of the site, house and gardens offered a challenge. The opportunity to work in the northern part of California was also a welcome change, for Charles was beginning to complain of the "stale air" in and around Pasadena. The overall size of the Fleishhacker house also allowed for the kind of variation and freedom in the development of the plan form which Charles liked. Here he could break from the linear or the box form and strike out on an angle as in the Pratt house. Now he was working with a scale the like of which he had never before encountered. By comparison, the Blacker estate was small. The vastness of the mountainous site offered the opportunity to develop the transition between a man-made environment and the natural chaparral of the hillsides and valleys. The final solution to the gardens, however, was not developed until the late 1920s.

The degree of attention paid to the development of the overall form of the house and the vast garden was not felt on the interiors to the extent that was customary with the Greenes. The large rooms were shockingly simple by comparison with those in the ultimate bungalows. The use of wood was minimal and, in this case, painted. There was the typical Greene touch of the one-by-six inch wood trim band around the rooms at door height and a half-timbered ceiling in the gallery. But nowhere were the fittings for lighting fixtures designed by the brothers, nor was the

3. The author is grateful to Robert Judson Clark for access to his personal interview notes with members of the Fleishhacker family and for his authorization to include quotations therefrom.

View of rear terrace.
Photograph courtesy of Documents Collection,
College of Environmental Design, UCB.

furniture made for the house. Both the client's desires and Charles' preoccupation with the vast site development curtailed such attention to detail. Despite the lack of the Greenes' usual elaborate interiors, however, careful examination makes it clear here that the restraint was calculated and richly successful.

The most significant feature of the construction was the external skin of "gunite," a thin layer of extremely fine quality concrete placed by blowing the ingredients at a high pressure through a hose and mixing the correct amount of moisture at the nozzle. The end result was a surface material far more durable than stucco and plaster and highly fire retardant, a paramount concern due to the mountainous terrain of the Fleishhacker site.

Throughout the following years, the Greenes made various additions and alterations for the Fleishhacker estate; many major elements, including the dairy house and the water garden, were not to appear until the twenties when Charles Greene was working independently at his studio in Carmel.

Nathan Bentz house, 1741 Prospect Avenue (originally
addressed as 1708 Olive Avenue), Santa Barbara, 1911.
View of original front elevation, Roy Flamm photograph.

This was the last of the large, shingle-clad bungalows executed by the firm. The masonry, arched foundations, pergola,
and stairway formed a bold transition to the rocky hillside
site which Bentz developed into an elaborate oriental garden.

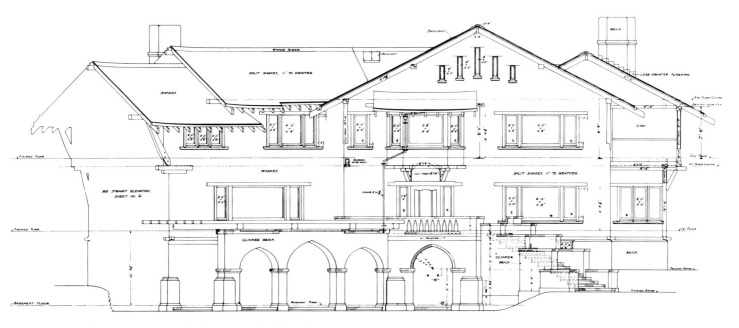

Elevation drawing, courtesy of Mrs. Lorton L. Clough.

When Nathan Bentz decided to build a home in Santa Barbara to house his fine art collection, he turned to Greene and Greene. He personally knew of their work through his brother and was well aware of the Greenes' serious interest in Oriental art. But the association was much deeper and more basic than a simple relationship between architect and client. Both the Greenes and the Bentz brothers were devoted to the finest in whatever they approached. The association between the Greenes and Nathan Bentz had begun some years before Bentz decided to build his own home and this may account for the design which related more closely to the Greenes' work of 1907 through 1909. The Nathan Bentz house (1911) was the last of the large bungalows, but the use of steel I-beams and the plaster, sculptured living room ceiling were totally new for the firm.

The irregular and sloping hillside site helped provide unique characteristics for the Bentz house. The major leg of the basic "L" form was bent to embrace the entry terrace and soften the high scale of the western elevation as well as to respond to the configuration of the site and the com-manding view of the Pacific Ocean and the Channel Islands. Because of the slope, the lower level (which housed the art collection) was developed in masonry and provided a dramatic transition between the wooden structure above and the rugged, rocky site.

Bold, pointed arches of the masonry understructure dominated the lower frontal elevation and indicated the Greenes' new direction with less use of wood as the major building material. However, the main floor above and the balance of the structure read right out of the recognizable Greene and Greene handbook. Changing attitudes were again evident in the interior. Walls were of simple plaster with sculptured arched openings between spaces with wood expressed only in detail at windows, openings, and the stairwell. There is restraint exhibited in the interior detail of the Bentz house but not in the size of its spaces. The home was to be open to many friends and professional associates, and the spacious interiors were a proper setting for entertaining fellow collectors.

The formal entry was from the oriental gardens developed on the lower portion of the site. A grand masonry stairway led to the main door above the den. The large main hall of the house extended through to the rear where a second entry allowed direct access from the roadway. The unusual feature here was the bridge leading from the circular drive to the structure, necessary because of the steepness of the site. The elegance of this bridge was a fine tribute by the Greenes to the Bentzes' love of the Orient.

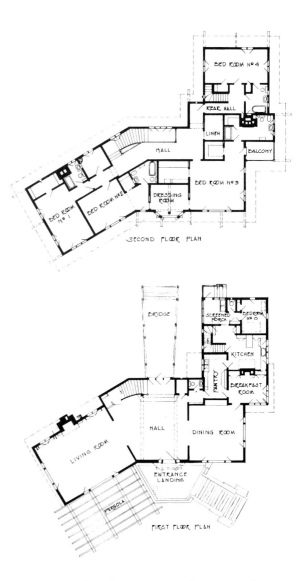

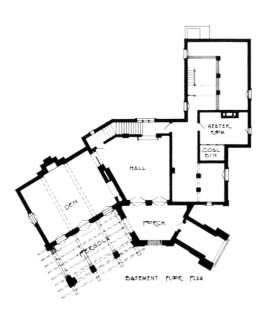

The plan steps and angles to capture the commanding view across the water to the Channel Islands.

"Oriental" bridge to original rear entrance of the house.
Roy Flamm photograph.

Earle C. Anthony turned to the large architectural firm of Parkinson and Bergstrom for the design of the basic structure of his grand automobile showroom in downtown Los Angeles, but also commissioned Greene and Greene to design the building's detail, entrance and interiors. Their contributions brought a vitality to the interior which was matched only by the later design for an addition by Bernard Maybeck.[4]

The designs for the Anthony Showroom were unprecedented and unique, expressed in molded plaster, inlaid tile, wrought iron and wood—an array of dissimilar motifs which somehow hung together in spite of their great diversity. The great octagonal columns in the center of the showroom and portions of the balcony and ceiling pattern inlay were carried out in tile, with the capitals of the columns in molded plaster—remnants of traditional scroll work. In the ceiling, executed in plaster relief and radiating from the capitals, were fan-shaped sun bursts which in some ways anticipated the Art-Deco period of the 1930s. Also, in the wooden partitions for sales personnel and in one particular wood screen the simple composition is dramatically contemporary. From the high ceilings large, heavy octagonal plaster tubs inlaid with tiles were suspended from wrought iron straps. Some five feet from the ceiling, the indirect lighting fixtures bathed it in soft light. Unfortunately, little other lighting was developed, and therefore spotlights were attached (by others) to the sides of these indirect fixtures, which destroyed their sculptured character. The wrought iron canopy over the entrance repeated the forms in the balcony railing and the sweep of the metal work of the glass doors inserted a feeling of the Art Nouveau. But in spite of this mixed palette of designs and materials, the space was fresh and elegant.

4. After the construction of the Anthony Showroom for Packard automobiles Charles' eldest son talked his father into purchasing a Hudson automobile. This drew the ire of Anthony and there developed a split between the two men which caused Anthony to turn to Bernard Maybeck for the addition to the Los Angeles showroom. In 1924, after the reorganization of the firm of Greene and Greene, Anthony came back to Henry Greene for the design of the house for his mother-in-law, Mrs. Kate A. Kelley (1924). The Greene and Greene portion of the Anthony Showroom in Los Angeles was demolished in 1963; however, the Maybeck portion remains.

Earle C. Anthony automobile showroom interior, 1000 S. Hope Street, Los Angeles, 1911. (Demolished) Photograph by R. L. Makinson.

Anticipating Art-Deco era, the Greenes combined specially designed tiles with wrought iron forms, plaster scroll work and an interesting relief design in the plaster ceiling.

Wrought iron stairwell screen detail. Photograph by Robert J. Clark.

Cordelia A. Culbertson house, 1188 Hillcrest Avenue, Pasadena, 1911. Marvin Rand photograph.

The Culbertson house is the most subtle and misinterpreted of all Greene and Greene works. The development was so complete and integrated that every minor part was a necessary element of its sculptured design. Although now altered, it remains a unique architectural statement which must be intimately experienced to be fully appreciated.

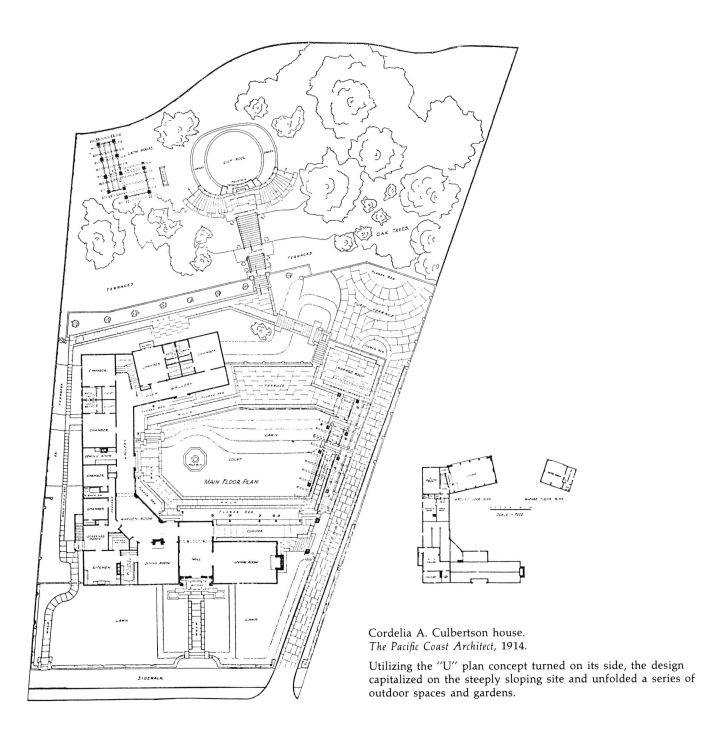

Cordelia A. Culbertson house.
The Pacific Coast Architect, 1914.

Utilizing the "U" plan concept turned on its side, the design capitalized on the steeply sloping site and unfolded a series of outdoor spaces and gardens.

A most significant house was that designed in 1911 for the three maiden sisters of James A. Culbertson. It was built directly across the street from the Blacker house. Identified as the Cordelia A. Culbertson house, this design was one of the most subtle and costly ever built by the Greenes. Modest in initial appearance, the house utilized the "U" plan, and, in scale and rear two-story development, belies its modest frontal elevation. The Greenes turned the "U" form on its side and the entrance was from one of the legs rather than the end or the pocket. More important, though, was the fact that this design was almost totally developed outside of the wooden vernacular. Only in the roof overhangs, terrace roofs and the garden pergolas did the Greenes cling to their former motifs. The plasticity of plaster and gunite was exploited on both the exterior and interior; linearity and joinery formerly identified with the Greenes gave way to a sense of sculpture brought out and accentuated by Charles Greene's sensitive but subtle handling of the undulating variation of the soft plaster. Even in the trim detail, where wood has been painted as though it were the multi-lacquered finish of a Rolls Royce, the columns were carefully sanded to reflect the undulating character of the plaster frieze. The close participation of the sisters influenced selection of the interior fittings for the large house. The special furnishings Charles designed for the house exhibited more fussiness in detail than ever before found in Greene and Greene furniture.

Possibly the better descriptive comment on this event in the Greenes' work was an article published in the *Pacific Coast Architect*, March, 1914.

> The problem to be solved in designing this dwelling place was different from the average. The owners, three maiden ladies, chose the plot of ground themselves. It was their wish to have all rooms on one level, but they objected to bedrooms on the ground floor. By placing the north wing of the building beyond the edge of the steep slope, the bedrooms are about 16 to 20 feet above the ground.

> The south wing from the front of the building contains the living room, entrance hall, dining room and kitchen. The western portion connecting these two wings contains servants' rooms, guest rooms, etc. The enclosed court, protected on the east by the pergola, is thus given the necessary privacy, no matter what may be built upon the adjacent property.

View of the lily pond in the lower rear garden.
Courtesy of Documents Collection,
College of Environmental Design, UCB.

Casual stepping stones contrast with the "Italian" influenced formal lily pond.

An extensive description of the furnishings followed.

By early 1917, the sisters, alarmed by the cost of the total project, decided that the house was too large for their needs and placed the property on the market.[5] In recent years, time has taken a toll on this, one of the most sensitively developed and minutely detailed houses ever produced in this country.

5. The Culbertson sisters, after contemplating the construction of a smaller house, purchased the Dr. William T. Bolton house (1906) in 1917, engaging Henry Greene for alterations shortly thereafter.

Henry W. Longfellow School, 1065 Washington Street, Pasadena, 1911.
Front elevation (now totally altered through remodelings).
Courtesy of Greene and Greene Library.

The only school built by the firm possessed classical characteristics but was reputed to be the most advanced design of its day because of its lighting, safety and fireproof construction.

In 1911 the Greenes were also commissioned by the Pasadena School District to design what came to be named the Longfellow School. There was little to distinguish this design or ever to identify it with Greene and Greene. The simple rectangular structure was built of reinforced concrete and adorned with semi-classical detail quite unusual for the Greenes. However, the news release describing its character suggested the progressive concepts of the firm. The structure was lauded as the first absolutely fireproof school building in the city, and was equipped with the most advanced heating and ventilation system of any such school on the Coast. The classrooms were so arranged that one side of each room was entirely fitted with windows which provided considerable natural lighting.

On May 15, 1911, a smaller news item announced that Greene and Greene had been selected to design the new Polytechnic High School. However nothing more was heard of the proposal. The commission was turned over to Myron Hunt who was highly praised for the progressive nature of his open patio plan concept for the school. Hunt was a neighbor of Charles Greene and one of the brothers' major competitors. His ability to move about comfortably in Pasadena society gained him many clients, whereas Charles Greene's nature prevented him from seeking clients through social connections. At one time Charles joined the fashionable Annandale Country Club but never attended a single event and at the end of the year let his membership lapse.

The final months of 1911 were devoted to working on the major projects for Fleishhacker, Bentz, Anthony, Culbertson, and the School District, plus three modest bungalows. These were for Charles G. Brown, Charles P. Wilcox, and Joseph K. Huston; and each was typical of the Greenes' designs of earlier years and probably moved rapidly through the office.

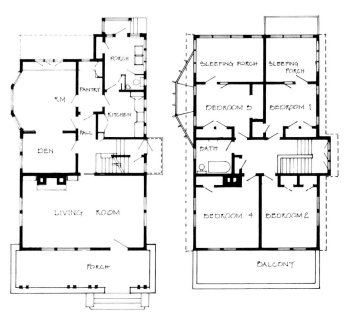

Charles G. Brown house, 665 N. Marengo Avenue, Pasadena, 1911. (Demolished) Courtesy of Dorothy Brown Herbert. Drawings by Philip Enquist.

In a final effort with the shingle bungalow, the firm produced the Charles P. Wilcox, Charles G. Brown and Joseph K. Huston designs which were all built on the same block.

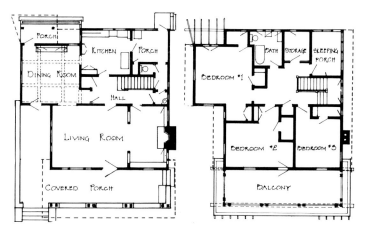

Joseph K. Huston house, 605 N. Marengo Avenue, Pasadena, 1911.
Drawings by Philip Enquist.

In 1912, new work in the office dropped off considerably. The major commission—and challenge—was the Herkimer Arms Apartment House for Mrs. Parker Earle. There was a surge of interest in apartment quarters in Pasadena during this period and the Herkimer Arms became the fashionable place for overflow crowds from the nearby resort hotels. The Greenes' first move was to relocate the existing wood frame apartment building to the rear of the lot and then to develop the new structure which was attached to the older structure. Their efforts were so effective that from the interior it was difficult to determine which portion of the unit was original and which was new.

The plan was rectangular and the compostition cubistic. Exterior walls projected above the roof line. The long overhangs of earlier Greene work were gone. The design was bold and straightforward. The uneven plaster softened the overall formality of the front elevation. The Greenes let the soft tone of the sand aggregate give natural color to the surface which was accented only by the wood timbers of the pergolas and the delicate soft greens of the oriental tiles.

The interiors, however, were much more traditional. Trim and wood detail were similar to earlier works. There was novelty in the built-in furnishings, such as beds which slid out from beneath the closets. Short steps in the entry led up to the closet, thus allowing the bed below. Here again the Greenes designed the basic furniture, although much more modestly than for their other clients. Each apartment received the same complement of special furnishings. This was as close as the Greenes ever came to any kind of production-line furniture. Over the years, street widening has altered the entry stairs and paint has obscured the original sand finish of the exterior. But little has been changed on the interior and it retains its relaxed charm.

A series of alterations and additions kept some of the office staff busy, but new work no longer dominated the activity of the office. Were it not for the jobs that former

Parker A. Earle apartment house, 527 Union (formerly Herkimer) Street, Pasadena, 1912. *California Southland*, 1918. Drawings by Peter Wohlfahrtstaetter.

The bold, cubistic exterior of the Earle apartments marked a major change in the work of the firm although their imprint is easily recognized in the interiors, the side pergolas and the use of oriental tiles. The original wooden structure was moved to the rear of the site and the new design was carefully developed so that the transition is hardly discernable on the interior.

clients brought to the Greenes, their future would have looked very bleak. Robert Blacker, for example, had brought his two sisters and a brother out to Pasadena and planned to purchase and settle them in the Greenes' house built for Dr. S. S. Crow. His relatives preferred a location on Madison Avenue nearer their nephew, however. Consequently, Mr. Blacker commissioned Greene and Greene to design what came to be called the Annie Blacker house (1912) in the earlier wooden bungalow style. The plan differed from previous work of the Greenes and was dominated by a long central hallway which was the core of both the first and second floor plans. The treatments were modest throughout and although the costs were kept down, the design possessed great grace and charm.

Apparently, the Annie Blacker house was primarily the work of Henry Greene. The unique interior touch of former years was found only in the tile detail of the den and in the built-in cabinets of the dining room. Here Henry's hand was evident in the linear composition of both the clear and the stained glass treatments of the china cabinetwork. In order to keep costs down commercial lighting fixtures were selected and the interior walls were plaster. Because of Robert Blacker's lumber interests, however, fine materials were selected for the house, as can be seen in the special woods chosen for the dining room and in the interior door panels.

Following the Annie Blacker house was a small four room bungalow for Edward S. Crocker on the rear of the property he had purchased from Dr. S. S. Crow the year before.

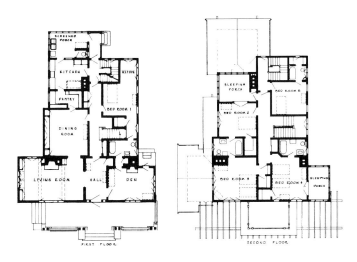

Annie Blacker house, 675 S. Madison Avenue, Pasadena, 1912. Lloyd Yost photograph.

For relatives brought to Pasadena to handle his hotel interests, Robert Blacker built this bungalow designed by Henry Greene.

Michael Kew house, 3224 Park Avenue, San Diego, 1912.
(Demolished) Photograph courtesy of Mary K. van der Pas.
Drawings by Peter Wohlfahrtstaetter.

Inspired by the clients' fascination with the English thatched-
roof house, the Greenes' design composed the combinations
of shingle, half-timber, stucco, stonework, and leaded windows
about a basically bilaterally symmetrical plan.

The major residence of this period was the Michael Kew
house (1912) in San Diego — another departure from the
Greenes' previous work. Here they combined various treatments which reflected earlier designs. The plan was asymmetrical but with a strong central axis about the entry hall
and stairwell. Major spaces were balanced on each side and
ancillary functions were handled in a side wing. Mr. Kew's
own strong interests in the English style influenced the
development of the design throughout. Except for the light
patio timbers of the rear terrace, there was none of the
obvious Greene treatment. The interiors were extensively
panelled in a Japanese oak complemented by a careful
selection of lighting fixtures and draperies to harmonize
with the Kew's antiques.

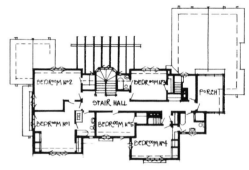

SECOND FLOOR PLAN

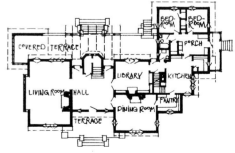

FIRST FLOOR PLAN

Shortly afterwards, the Greenes designed the Henry A. Ware house (1913) in Pasadena. Here, too, they held firmly to English traditions. Furthermore, Henry Ware insisted that the design resemble his former home in the East. Like the Kew house, the upper portion of the house was shingle with the ground floor of plaster. The plan was much more compact than the Kew design—the central hall and stairwell forming the core of the circulation pattern. In interior detail the English character was strongest in the dining room and stairwell, but in the living room the Greenes successfully introduced other forms.

A request for an indirect lighting system was a stimulus to the architects. Because of Mrs. Ware's poor eyesight, wall sconces were disturbing. Consequently, Henry Greene developed the room in redwood detail with a sculptured indirect light trough which encircled the entire space. The soft roll of the wood light shield was then repeated in the transitions to the beamed ceiling detail and in the soft graceful lines of the brushed redwood mantel treatment. The balance of the space was finished in light colored plaster with ample natural light from the banks of windows. Overall, the living room design was quiet but expressed a strong sense of unity enhanced by the natural finish of the redwood.

SECOND FLOOR PLAN

FIRST FLOOR PLAN

Henry A. Ware house, 460 Bellefontaine Street, Pasadena, 1913.
Marvin Rand photograph.
Drawings by Peter Wohlfahrtstaetter.

Strong demands by the client were influential in this design although close inspection recalls the integrity of earlier work.

211

The Greenes were moving away from the bungalow style and branching out in new directions; but in the August 1912 issue of *The Craftsman*, when the spirit of the bungalow was all but gone, Gustav Stickley devoted thirteen pages of text as well as many plans and photographs to the significance of the work of Greene and Greene as leaders of "California's Contribution to a National Architecture." The article proceeded to state that:

> The significance, moreover, of this Western accomplishment arises chiefly from the sincerity of spirit in which it is being undertaken. The type of home that abounds today in California—a type in which practical comfort and art are skillfully wedded—is no architectural pose, no temporary style. It is a vital product of a time, place and people, with roots deep in geographical and human needs. It has a definite relation to the kind of climate and soil, the habits of the people, and their ways of looking at civilization and nature.

The entire article is a rich resource for Greene and Greene scholars and a well-documented presentation of their significant influence upon American domestic architecture. But its timing suggests Stickley's own anxiety lest his Craftsman ideals become simply a part of history. Within a few years *The Craftsman* folded and his shops closed.

The Craftsman article in 1912 and numerous other articles about the Greenes which appeared frequently over the next ten years did little to encourage new clientele; the brothers' reputation was too closely identified with the wooden bungalow and colored by the spiralling construction costs which resulted from their high standards of quality and craftsmanship. Nevertheless, their reputation among professional contemporaries grew steadily through these years. Records show personal associations with many of their progressive fellows. Frank Lloyd Wright visited Charles Greene in Pasadena on several occasions and is known to have stated, "Mr. Greene, I do not know how you do it"—a reference to the high standards of craftsmanship achieved.[6] There was also the close friendship with John Galen Howard, notes of meetings with Ernest Coxhead, and of

the mutual regard between Bernard Maybeck and the Greenes.[7] Also, writers whose travels and literary works were of ever increasing influence helped make the works of Greene and Greene known throughout the world. The remarks of Ralph Adams Cram in his preface to the book, *American Country Houses of Today*, published in 1913, are as relevant today as they were when written. He said of the Greenes, Maybeck and of the California style:

> One must see the real and revolutionary thing in its native haunts of Berkeley and Pasadena to appreciate it in all its varied charm and its striking beauty. Where it comes from heaven alone knows, but we are glad it arrived, for it gives a new zest to life, a new object for admiration. There are things in it Japanese; things that are Scandinavian; things that hint at Sikkim, Bhutan, and the fastness of Tibet, and yet it all hangs together, it is beautiful, it is contemporary, and for some reason or other it seems to fit California. Structurally it is a blessing; only too often the exigencies of our assumed precedents lead us into the wide and easy road of structural duplicity, but in this sort of thing there is only an honesty that is sometimes almost brazen. It is a wooden style built woodenly, and it has the force and the integrity of Japanese architecture. Added to this is the elusive element of charm that comes only from the personality of the creator, and charm in a degree hardly matched in other modern work.

After the English traditional forms required in the Michael Kew and Henry Ware houses, the Greenes returned to their earlier bungalow vocabulary for the simple ranch house for William M. Ladd in Ojai, California. The Ladd house was a straightforward linear design composed of basic materials, well built and very appropriate for the site and its clients. Modest in budget, the design was elongated with the ground floor bedrooms separated by a bath, a staircase and a long hall along the side which served as both circulation core and entry. The living room slid off the major axis of the bedroom wing to capture and help define the outdoor terrace. On the second level, one bedroom and bath over the center of the plan gave vertical dimension in contrast to the strong horizontality of the exterior elevations. On the

6. Interviews by the author with Mrs. Charles Greene, September, 1955 and Nathaniel Patrickson Greene, March 5, 1975.

7. Interviews with Nathaniel Patrickson Greene and related documents in Documents Collection, College of Environmental Design, UCB.

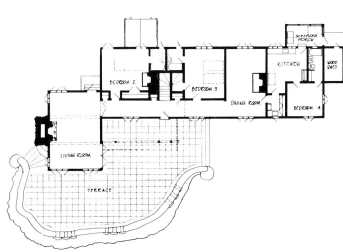

William M. Ladd house, 818 N. Foothill Road, Ojai (formerly
Fairview Road, Nordhoff), 1913.
Marvin Rand photograph.

The straightforward development of the design for the Ladd
house is one of the firm's most appropriate solutions to
the site and the living pattern of the occupants. The restraint
in its detailing reflects the beauty and flexibility of the
Greenes' philosophies and talents.

interior, the basic Greene and Greene vocabulary was utilized in restrained and simple detail. On the exterior, the
rugged chimney reflected the spirit of the Ojai Valley. The
large grounds of the Ladd property were left in natural
landscape and related well to the crisp lines of the design.

The dramatic contrasts between the Ladd and Pratt
houses revealed the Greenes' ability to adapt themselves
and their talents to the different lifestyles of their various
clients. Each house was an excellent production for its
owner; each provided an architectural enrichment to the
Ojai Valley. The Pratt house was a superbly developed
bungalow. The Ladd house incorporated the comfortable
patterns of many designs over a period of years which had
helped change and give dignity to the broader cross section of American domestic architecture.

Although many alterations and additions went through the office between 1912 and 1915, the new commissions consisted of a bungalow for Dr. Rosa Englemann, and houses for William E. Hamlin, John T. Greene and Dr. Nathan H. Williams, each of which was apparently designed by Henry Greene. Charles, at the time, was involved with additional work on one of Mortimer Fleishhacker's houses in San Francisco and was also spending more and more time with his writing. The houses were totally different expressions and demonstrated the same kind of searching frustrations which characterized the Greenes' office just prior to the turn of the century. A two-story bungalow was designed for John T. Greene (no relation) in Sacramento, California, a lawyer and land speculator who expected his bungalow to set a standard for new development in the area. The symmetrical plan and general design could well have been handled by anyone in the office familiar with the Greenes' wooden vocabulary. The original front detail incorporated massive rock piers tapering upward to support the central porch roof, but this was abandoned for a more tailored and modest timber structural treatment.

The house for William E. Hamlin was out of character for the Greenes. The solid masonry and concrete construction, the two-story exterior elevations and tiled roof were as formal and symmetrically balanced as mirror images. On the ground floor, variation in room functions demanded some flexibility in the symmetry, but on the second floor there was almost no variation and the formal balance of the plan was complete. It seems evident that lean times had forced the firm to accept commissions it would have declined earlier.

The best of the houses, which again explored new forms and materials, was the residence of Dr. Nathan H. Williams. It made use of the gunite exterior, and here the pneumatically applied exterior skin enriched the basic box structure. In the entry and terrace posts and in the second-level railings, openings were made between the webbing of the welded wire mesh and this rhythmic pattern softened the otherwise harsh concrete exterior.

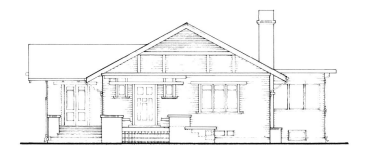

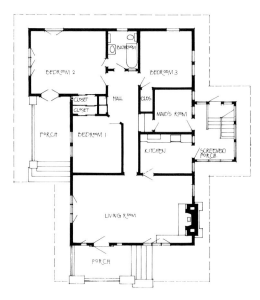

Dr. Rosa Englemann house, 1235 San Pasqual Street, Pasadena, 1914. (Demolished)
Elevation, drawing by Philip Enquist.
Plan, drawing by Peter Wohlfahrtstaetter.

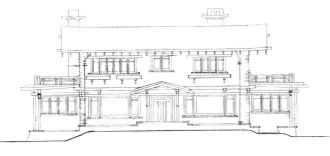

FRONT ELEVATION

SECOND FLOOR PLAN

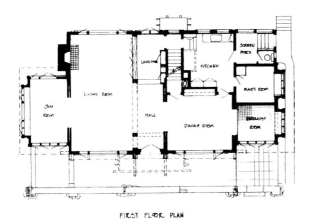

FIRST FLOOR PLAN

John T. Greene house, 3200 H. Street, Sacramento, 1915.

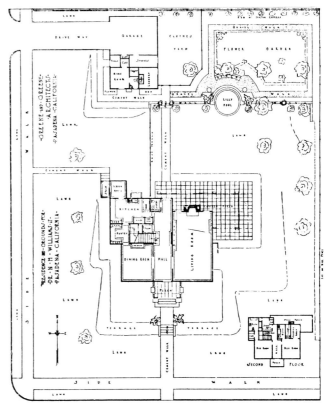

Dr. Nathan H. Williams house, 1145 Sonama Drive, Altadena, 1915. Rear view, photograph courtesy of Documents Collection, College of Environmental Design, UCB.

The pneumatically placed concrete of the exterior gave rise to Henry's decorative patterns in the columns and railings. This lightened both the weight of the structure and its visual character. Site and floor plans. *American Country Houses of Today*, 1917.

Meanwhile Charles, who had never been fully satisfied with his own buildings, turned to writing as a way of expressing his feelings about architecture. In both fiction and non-fiction he attempted to set down on paper the various ideas which had guided him throughout his architectural career.

In an unpublished novel, *Thais Thayer*, Charles developed a melodramatic plot involving an architectural student at MIT who is mistaken for the most brilliant in the class and is kidnapped and whisked away to an island in the South Pacific. There he is ordered to build a magnificent house for Thais Thayer, a beautiful singer who had lost her voice and therefore isolated herself from the rest of the world. Despite constant hardship and danger and the malice of another architect on the island, the young student builds the house. In the course of the novel Charles expounded his views on art and architecture. However, the writing was often confused and confusing, and presently lapsed into a form of bitterness.

> "What style do you like best?"
> "Anything you choose, that is, I mean I have a theory."
> "Yes, but your own feelings must lead you to some field of special interest to yourself."
> "Oh but, I try not to allow it to. You see, I must learn to do anything anybody may need. Only I must so direct the design of it that it may be consistent with the style we follow..."
>
> "Artists don't have a chance. The educated public wants skill, not soul. It can't judge because it can't feel. It only knows what it has learned. There isn't any culture. The other public is too ignorant to know what it really does want, and too busy money making to try to find out. It takes to fads, discards the old for the new!..."
>
> I've been so busy with the carvers. It's so hard to get the feeling I want — they are so stupid — it's easy to make a beautiful drawing, but to get the building beautiful, one must give one's life blood!"[8]

The first of his serious articles, "Impressions of Some Bungalows and Gardens," was for *The Architect* magazine and appeared in the December, 1915 issue. His brief discussion set forth clearly some of his most pertinent opinions

8. Documents Collection, Greene and Greene Library, The Gamble House.

and came down hard on commercialism. The article began with a discussion of California's natural beauties and of its architectural opportunities. However, the "haste of speculation and sordidness of commercialism" was responsible for the worst of California architecture. "Building bungalows is not a crime in itself, it is the quality of the product that may justify the practice or condemn it." In speaking of the term bungalow, Charles continued, "It has been the catchword of promotionists and the headline of building company advertisement.... In fact, between the automobile mania and the bungalow bias, there seems to be a psychic affinity." He went on to be even more critical: "Bungalow books are worse than architects' pictures inasmuch as they offer a selection degrading to the art." Further, when discussing the bungalow courts which had become so popular, he wrote:

> The bungalow court idea is to be regretted. Born of the ever-persistent speculator, it not only has the tendency to increase unnecessarily the cost of the land, but it never admits of home building.

It is ironic that over the years the popular bungalow courts have often been attributed to the Greenes or considered highly influenced by them, when in fact Greene and Greene were never involved with a court development. However, he went on to state the "in spite of all this there has been good work done," and bluntly referred to his own work as fine art.

His confidence was also revealed in another part of the article. He criticized the use of preliminary pictures by architects stating that "nothing should be put upon paper for them to see at the time... once the design of a bungalow is fixed by means of a picture, it is very hard to change it. Properly, no perspective for the owner of a bungalow should be made till after the plans are ready for bids; otherwise many a valuable opportunity may be lost to the betterment of the work." This is art for the artist, not for the client whose wishes and concerns can become even more an annoyance than secondary. He discussed the rights of the owner in the design of his or her own home:

> Not long since I heard an owner say, in regard to decorating and furnishing a room about which I happened to know the facts, "I would not think of asking my architect about that. It wouldn't be my room." However, this same owner

had no hesitation in visiting a department store decorator, who showed her the latest consignment and made a very good bill. The owner herself honestly believed she had made her own selection, but it was entirely the cleverness of the sales man that did the trick, and he had never seen the room which, needless to say, became extraneous to the whole scheme of the house.

Thus far he argued convicingly in his own favor. As he continued, however, he began to tread upon sensitive ground:

> Some queer things have happened to the houses, that never appeared in the designs of them, and many owners still insist on having their own way, when the training and better judgment of the architect should prevail.

On the whole, this article was Charles' most frank writing and was an appropriate parting comment to his career in Southern California. His last work in the Pasadena office was on the preliminary sketches for a project for H. T. Proctor, which was never developed, and designs for the development of Westmoreland Place for David Gamble.

David Gamble and his five neighbors along Westmoreland Place had become increasingly concerned with the

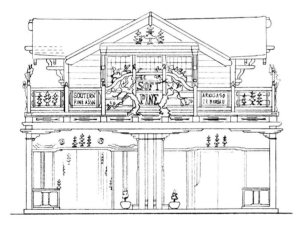

Project: Southern Pine Association exhibition pavilion, New Orleans, 1916. Courtesy of Documents Collection, College of Environmental Design, UCB.

In this project are characteristics out of the Greenes' past combined with sculptured wood forms which appear to be influenced by their work with more plastic materials.

amount of traffic shortcutting through their private roadway. Consequently, Mr. Gamble, in concert with his neighbors, had the Greenes develop handsome wrought iron gates and boulder piers at the north end and design the carefully formed split entry and landscaping of the entry at Arroyo View Drive (now Arroyo Terrace). To this were added boulder markers and handsome signs which identified the private Westmoreland Place.

During his work for Mortimer Fleishhacker, Charles had become acquainted with the Carmel artists' colony south of Monterey, California. As the years passed, he became increasingly attracted by the intellectual stimulation he had found there. Consequently, in June of 1916, he left Pasadena for a new life among the artists around Carmel. Clay Lancaster, in his account of his interview with Charles Greene in Carmel, states that the move was "partially motivated by a desire to delve into the profundities of Buddhist philosophy."[9] Uppermost in Charles' mind, however, was his desire to become a serious writer. On February 16, 1917 he wrote to his father:

> I am beginning to get my article together for *The Architect* (magazine), but so far I have done no other writing. I have been reading lately some books on Art and am beginning to feel as if I must start soon at my serious work.

His father's letter, dated March 10, 1917, revealed much about Charles' feelings:

> Well! You folks do seem to be having the times of your lives and I am glad of it and I do hope the pleasant intercourse with people who appreciate you will be beneficial to both of you and end in good friendships which will endure.... In Pasadena you saw a class of suddenly rich and another of regular creeky fanatics that you did not like and neither do I.

9. Clay Lancaster, "My Interviews with Greene and Greene," *Journal of the American Institute of Architects*, XXVIII, July, 1957, p. 204.

On March 27, 1917 Charles replied:

> Alice is giving another dinner tonight. The people here are much more simple and direct and nearly all are interested in something in contrast to people there.

In his second article for *The Architect*, entitled "Architecture As a Fine Art," Charles rambled on about the current state of architecture, predicted a pessimistic future for the architect and revealed his own frustrations when he attempted to point out the distinction between commercial architecture and the art of architecture. He then continued:

> The education of the architect and the practice of architecture as they stand today are pitted against a fast prevailing economic contingent—the concentration of capital that seeks to control the entire field of building operation, combining real estate, building and investment. The outlook is not pleasant to contemplate....We may expect that this monopolistic extension to the field of architecture will only divide the sheep from the goats, or the building commodity will heighten the distinction between itself and Architecture as a Fine Art; that it will absorb the architect so-called, but the real architect will remain sans pareil.[10]

He saw domestic building as the only evidence of architecture as an art; and described the plight of the serious architect with somewhat personal undertones:

> His case seems hopeless; his egotism, finding no means of outward expression, strikes back upon itself. But that is his personal affair. He may complain, he may be discouraged utterly; but that is as it should be, or must be under the existing condition; and though the truth of this be hard to bear, the architect must further submit to the condemnation of the businessman whose indifference can but give place to a momentary impatient contempt, for the dreamer who follows his ideal.

This second article may well have been too blunt and emotional for *The Architect*. The editors of the magazine remained courteous but, on the grounds of a restricted budget, firmly rejected any plans for future articles.

Charles, on the other hand, felt his writing was going well. On April 12, 1917 he wrote:

> Allison seemed delighted with my article and says, "Go on as long as you can keep up steam" which is encouraging especially as it will pay me $15.00 for each number. To be sure, that is not much pay for the work I have to do but

I'm glad to get it all the same. It may lead to something better in more prominent magazines. It is very encouraging to know that the best men want to hear from me.

> I am thinking very seriously of writing several articles to submit to such periodicals as the *Atlantic Monthly* and *Harper's*.[11]

In spite of his optimism, however, the second article in *The Architect* was his last publication. For a time he worked on a proposal for a major book to be entitled *Truth in Building: A Plea for an American Democratic Style*. His ideas were clearly outlined in correspondence with the Southern Pine Association which was interested in supporting the project.

> This rich field of common opportunity, ignored never the less, by the Public and the average architect, is simply this: that good and beautiful houses...are not dependent upon costly material; but the most common and easily worked material the market affords may be used to attain the greatest achievable beauty and perfection of craftsmanship. The secret of failure, if anything such openly apparent may be called a secret, is that we waste our energy and inventiveness in trying to conceal what Nature provided to our advantage.

> It must be plain that if we would solve our building problems correctly we must solve them ourselves and in accord with the general condition set by availability of material and cost. First of all we must be honest with ourselves.

That Charles was highly optimistic about the success of the book was illustrated by the terms he suggested for the project:

> $1000 down to bargain, $2500 when work is approved and ready for press. In addition as issued, shall be paid to me a royalty of ten cents a copy for the first five hundred thousand copies, and two and one half cents per copy for further issue.[12]

The anticipation of five hundred thousand copies represented an extraordinary miscalculation of public interest.

10. C. Sumner Greene, "Architecture As A Fine Art," *The Architect*, Vol. XIII, No. 4, April, 1917, pp. 217-218.

11. Documents Collection, College of Environmental Design, UCB.

12. Letter by Charles Greene to F. V. Dunham, Acting Manager, Southern Pine Assn., December 27, 1916. Documents Collection, College of Environmental Design, UCB.

The book never progressed beyond the initial outline. In later years, he completed a manuscript for a book on furniture design. This too was never published, and he burned the entire manuscript in the fireplace of his Carmel studio.

The mid-teen years were a period of adjustment and uncertainty for Charles. He had turned away from architecture but was not sure what to do in its place. His restlessness was revealed in a letter in which he wrote:

> The new work will make Hal very busy, I suppose, but it will not be as hard as waiting for something to turn up...Just now I am studying anarchism as explained by scientific writers of the nineteenth century—am surpised to find how little I knew about it and what a wrong impression I had of it. Scientifically explained, it has many good points if one could only find a way to bring it about.[13]

Charles had made no definite plans when he left Pasadena, and, until he decided whether the move to Carmel was to be temporary or permanent, the maintenance of the Greene and Greene operations was left intact under Henry's supervision. During 1917 there were several new commissions that progressed only as far as the drawings. Only two new commissions were built that year and each was solely the work of Henry. His designs reflected a careful and considered restraint. He was demanding in quality, determined in his quest for proper building procedures and dogmatic with regard to adherence to his specifications and desired craftsmanship.

The Charles S. Witbeck house, the first new major commission since the Williams house of 1915, received Henry's close attention. Various schemes were developed and Henry now had the time to do perspective renderings of the designs. The final design was quiet, straightforward and reflected some of the English country house character of certain earlier Greene and Greene work; but it was more restrained and lacked the dramatic impact of the firm's earlier work.

13. Letter by Charles Greene to his father, April 17, 1917. Documents Collection, College of Environmental Design, UCB.

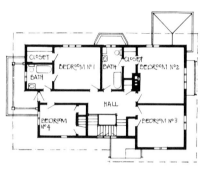

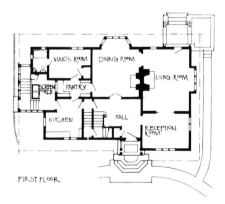

Charles S. Witbeck house, 226 Palisades Avenue, Santa Monica, 1917. Front elevation drawing courtesy of Avery Architectural Library.
Plans, drawings by Peter Wohlfahrtstaetter.

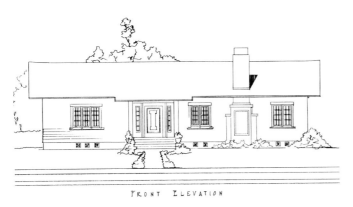

FRONT ELEVATION

• PROPOSED RESIDENCE AT FRESNO CALIFORNIA •
GREENE & GREENE ARCHITECTS, PASADENA
(372)

While the Witbeck house was compact in its two-story design and represented the conservative desires of the clients, a parallel commission allowed Henry more latitude. In designing the Howard Mundorff house in Fresno, California, he returned to the "U" form for the basic plan of the modest single-story residence. However, all references to the former bungalow image seemed to have been intentionally omitted. Instead, the exterior horizontal wood siding was painted and the detail was extremely conservative. Only the abstract massing of the chimney and the design of the entry door recalled the Greenes' earlier work. In the interior, which was carried out primarily in plaster with painted wood detail, Henry injected an inventive touch in the molded plaster indirect lighting sconces around the living room.

Howard F. Mundorff house, 3753 Balch Street, Fresno, 1917. Front elevation drawing courtesy of Greene and Greene Library. Plan, drawing by Philip Enquist.

The noisy corner site prompted Henry to return to the "U" form plan to provide quiet and privacy for this modest, cleanly designed house.

D. L. James house, Route 1, Carmel Highlands, 1918.
Photograph courtesy of Documents Collection,
College of Environmental Design, UCB.

"Beyond Carmel Greene and Greene have built on the rocks
by the sea one of the most beautiful pictures of our time.
By such work we know them."
Bernard Ralph Maybeck

The dramatic angular plans that had failed to progress beyond the drawing boards in recent years finally took form with the design and construction of the D. L. James house (1918) at Carmel Highlands, California. The most creative and ambitious work of Charles Greene's late career and the most significant structure outside of the Greenes' wooden bungalows, the James house is a monument unique in this country. The stone structure seems to have grown out of its site atop the rocky cliffs south of Carmel. At places it is difficult to ascertain just where nature's rock has ended and man's masonry genius has begun.

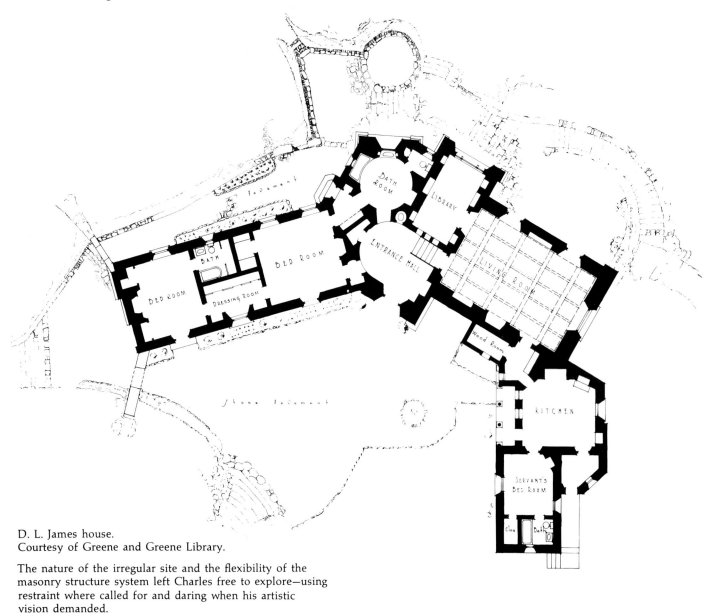

D. L. James house.
Courtesy of Greene and Greene Library.

The nature of the irregular site and the flexibility of the masonry structure system left Charles free to explore—using restraint where called for and daring when his artistic vision demanded.

Entry view. Photograph courtesy of Documents Collection,
College of Environmental Design, UCB.

Although situated only a few yards from California Highway 1, the majestic house is buffered from the world of rushing men and machines by the natural landscape it so wondrously compliments. In form, there are strong recollections of the California missions as well as the stone ruins of Tintagel, England, but they are so blended that the dignity and antiquity of man and his dreams seems here embodied as a harmonious outgrowth of nature itself.

Mr. James was a wealthy retailer of fine china from Kansas City, Missouri. He and his wife first visited Carmel in 1914, and from then on spent the summers there. In 1918 they purchased the rocky cliff three miles below Carmel. Shortly thereafter they met Charles Greene and invited him to see their new building site. Two days later Charles showed them his sketches for a building on the spectacular site. Mr. James immediately authorized him to proceed with the design which was to be both a summer home as well as a permanent home for later retirement. The basic plan of the house was a double "U" form which developed from the combination of Charles Greene's recent exploration in rambling non-linear plan concepts and the strongly irregular configuration of the rocky site, whose craggy cliffs dropped sharply, almost vertically, to the crashing surf below.

From the outset, Charles chose quarried stone as his building material. The early plans indicate the walls varying from two to three feet in thickness. Because of the nature of his handling of the stone construction, the elevational drawings served only as a rudimentary suggestion of the end result. Charles explained this:

> Ordinarily, when plans are made for a house, after careful study they are practically final, and the specifications minutely exact. These are turned over to a contractor who by contract produces the completed product. Whether he does the work by percentage or a stated sum doesn't matter, he directs the work. Now the James house was not built that way. The architect hired the men and directed the work personally; except for plumbing, electric wiring and tiling, there were no contracts.
>
> Here is the difference; prevailing custom is a system of administration by recorded instruction; mine is not *any* system, but personal direction on the job. The first is fixed, the second is elastic, yielding to contingencies, open to inspiration.[14]

The stone selected for the basic construction was quarried from a site at Yankee Point, three-quarters of a mile south. The quarried rock was sharp and more golden in color than the weathered gray of the natural site although essentially of the same material composition. The soft sandstone used for detail was selected from the beaches of Point Lobos, and for interior treatment Charles chose a limestone from the Carmel Valley. From there he also selected the lichen-encrusted rock paving for the terrace overlooking the sea.

Charles sought to express the sharpness of the quarried rock by laying it with its broken face exposed, and was able to achieve an overall softness through the magnitude of the surfaces thus constructed. For the primary stonemason Charles selected Fred Coleman who built a small cottage on the edge of the site and lived there throughout the several years of construction.

In the composition of the stonework itself Charles directed that the courses begin and end at random, creating varying horizontal levels. He was at the site every day. So intent was his concern for the exact effect he desired that he virtually stood directly over the masons throughout the construction. On several occasions when he had to travel to San Francisco to direct the marble carving he would return and have whole sections of the wall torn out and done over. Coleman must have thought Charles something of a madman, and there was a continuing battle between them over the masonry work.

14. Elmer Grey, "Some Country House Architecture in the Far West," *The Architectural Record*, Vol. LII, No. 289, October, 1922.

Watercolor sketch of arched ruins at Tintagel, England, painted by Charles Greene in 1909.
Courtesy of Mr. and Mrs. Thomas Gordon Greene.

D. L. James house. Detail of masonry arch.
Marvin Rand photograph.

As though he had been waiting over a decade to produce his watercolor in stone, Charles' design for the garden arch allowed for a similar view of the sea as his watercolor of Tintagel.

This carefully sculpted stone work, however, prompted the distinguished architectural contemporary of the Greenes, Elmer Grey, to write in 1922:

The long narrow pieces of this stone have been cut into horizontal fissures by very deeply struck joints of uneven width. This gives the same general worn-by-age appearance as that of the cliffs. The color aspect of the stonework is saved from the sameness by a tile roof of a delightfully faded old rose color—and the tiles are distributed around in just the right proportions, some on top of the chimneys and other bits elsewhere, so as to form a proper color balance. They were not laid in geometrical lines either vertically or horizontally. Nine architects out of ten would have laid them that way, but this is an instance where not only were the rules forgotten but where the architect went out of his way to violate them.

The ridge rolls up and down with delightful waywardness, and the vertical lines of the tile appear and disappear as their usual course has been intentionally broken. The way some of the main lines of the building grow out of the rock and huge boulders upon which they are built, their foundations often beginning many feet below and gradually working upward in sympathetic conjunction with the native cliff rock, has been managed so skillfully that it is impossible in some cases to tell where the one ends and the other begins. This kind of work is not architecture as now commonly known—it savors of a more plastic art, of the building of a home in thorough keeping with its rugged site.[15]

Although not a part of his original concept, Charles determined at the time of initial construction that all footings rise from bedrock. At one point there were two rock faces with a chase between them just at a major point needed for support. Instead of arching between the two faces, Charles made the decision to go some forty-five feet down the cliff and build up from solid footing which resulted in the dramatic manner in which the structure appears to grasp onto the rugged site.

The James family remembers Charles Greene as a tiny man with a sharp nose, little glasses, and a carefully curled pageboy haircut. He spoke very little and only in short sentences; his voice was so soft that the listener had to lean forward to hear him. However, his small stature and nervous laugh belied a will of iron which enabled him to battle successfully with the various craftsmen on the job.

D. L. James was a man who normally never lost his composure. However, after numerous incidents which prolonged construction, he would occasionally express his angry frustration over the delays or added costs. He was also torn between his inability to cope with the rising costs and his sensitivity towards Charles. Mrs. James' reactions complicated the situation even further for she was not as enthusiastic about the house, which was essentially the dream of Mr. James and Charles.[16]

In some areas it is uncertain whether Mr. James' or Charles Greene's influence dominated the design. For instance, there was the contrast between the free form of the exterior and the orderly bilateral symmetry of the interior rooms. Mr. James had a passion for symmetry and this may very well have exerted a degree of discipline upon Charles similar to that which Henry had exercised in earlier years.

In dramatic contrast to the exterior, the soft and gentle treatment of the plaster interior offered a sophisticated contrast to the rugged coastal cliff and the harsh weather. Special beach sands were selected according to their color, and the plaster with which they were mixed was left natural and unpainted. Because of the plasticity of the material, Charles gave subtle sculptural form to the transitions between roof and wall and to the fireplaces and windows and door openings. He took great pains to avoid straight lines by achieving an irregularity in the plaster walls, a characteristic most noticeable when the rooms were illuminated by candlelight. The high ceiling of the living room was constructed of redwood timber carefully carved and joined into the walls above chiseled stone blocks which provided a transition between planes and materials. Elements of the sea served as inspiration for the marble relief carving throughout the house.

The furniture which had been a part of Charles' plan was never built. As the construction ran into the fifth year and the costs ran far in excess of the estimated $30,000 the Jameses began to feel that Charles wanted to work on the house forever. Consequently, in 1922, Mr. James insisted that Charles modify his concepts and bring the construction to a point where they could move into the house. As a result, certain interior details of the lighting were hastily fitted for temporary use and thoughts of furniture were forgotten.

15. *Ibid.*

16. Interview with Daniel and Lilith James, April 30, 1975.

D. L. James house, Entrance court.
Marvin Rand photograph.

Careful attention was given to the
laying of the stonework, and large
stones were carved to serve as
scuppers to carry rain from the
tiled roof.

Detail of living room.
Marvin Rand photograph.

Interiors throughout the house were
finished in natural-color, sand-
aggregate plaster. Marble carving
contrasted with the simple, unadorned walls, and special attention
was given to the transition between
redwood ceiling timbers and the
plaster/stone wall structure.

In spite of the continuing mutual respect and high regard between Mr. James and Charles Greene, they saw very little of one another following the intense period of the construction. Charles' cash book indicates no further work between 1925 and 1937 when Mr. James decided to add the library to the house. Although circumstances did not permit Charles to continue work on the house as long as he would have wished, Mr. James was clearly aware from the beginning that he was a party to a unique experience of architectural creativity. Without question the D. L. James house is a singular art form, individual in all aspects, beyond the guidelines of standard practices. It is indeed an American architectural monument of extraordinary subtlety and artistic genius.

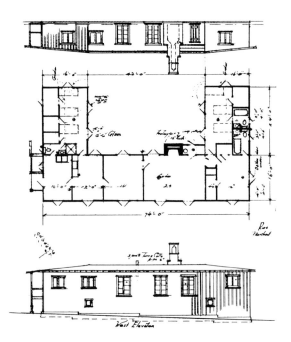

Charles S. Greene house, Lincoln Avenue at Thirteenth Street, Carmel, 1920. (Demolished) Courtesy of Documents Collection, College of Environmental Design, UCB.

Charles declared that this was as close as he ever came to repeating the Bandini house both in construction technique and form, and claimed that it was the least costly house he had built.

Since Charles had moved to Carmel, the family had lived in two rental houses. The first, a fairly large house near the ocean, had such poor wiring that Charles refused to have the power connected during their entire three years there. In 1919 they rented another house in Carmel across the street from the noted artist, George Bellows, with whom Charles became good friends.

It was while living in this second rented house that Charles purchased the property in Carmel on Thirteenth Street near Lincoln Street. Here, in 1920, he built a small one-story redwood bungalow for himself. He often stated that this was the most inexpensive house he had ever built. The simple structure closely followed the ideas of the Bandini house of 1903. The plan was "U" shaped with a series of interconnected rooms about a central court. The exterior was redwood with board and batten siding detail over a light wood frame which was never finished on the interior. Charles had planned to cover the exposed light timbers of the roof trusses and wall structure with wood paneling, but he devoted most of his efforts to his later studio and never got around to enhancing the basic comforts of the house. However, his demand for better building principles resulted in the concrete foundation for the little structure, a feature unusual in the Carmel area which attracted much attention from local builders. Because of the climate and to conserve costs, the roof was a simple, extremely low shed with virtually no overhang except for the low edge at the drip line.

Meanwhile, in 1919, while Charles was engrossed with the James house, Henry was carrying on with the slim practice coming into the Pasadena office. His major concerns were yet another scheme for John H. Poole and an elaborate project, a large two-story Spanish Colonial Revival house, for Hubert F. Krantz. Neither was built. From 1920 through 1922 there was almost no new work for the firm of Greene and Greene. Except for a smaller house for their parents, the Thomas S. Greene house (1921), on the lower part of Charles' Carmel property, there was nothing whatsoever to support the formerly active architects.

With the building of his own house in Carmel, Charles gave up all thought of returning to Southern California. The geographical distance between the brothers, coupled with the lack of work, prompted them to recognize their now differing goals and take the formal steps of reorganizing the firm. The following statement, published in the April, 1922 issue of *Architect and Engineer*, officially signalled the end of the third major phase of the work of Greene and Greene:

> Henry M. Greene, formerly of the architectural firm of Greene and Greene, 216 Boston Building, Pasadena, through office reorganization, has assumed entire charge of the business which will be continued at the same address under his name alone.

In spite of the dissolution of the partnership, neither Henry nor Charles had any thought of retirement. Each continued to seek commissions and each independently contributed a few more designs during the next two decades which expressed their unusual qualities and their highly diverse talents and personalities.

Project: John H. Poole house, Pasadena, 1917.
Drawing courtesy of Avery Architectural Library.

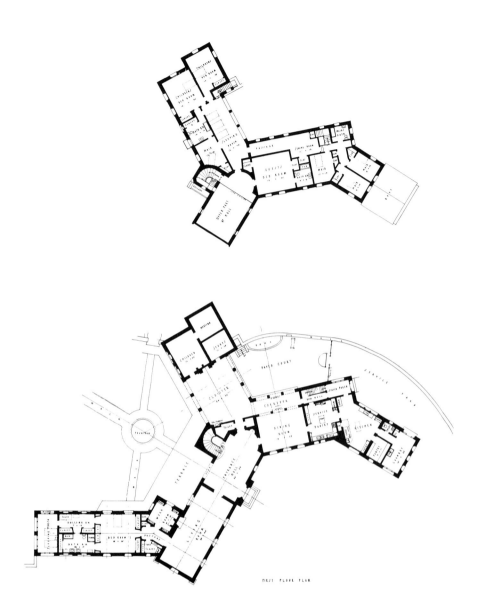

Project: John H. Poole house.
Plans courtesy of Avery Architectural Library.

Predating the James house, this first of several designs for
Poole shows Charles' interest in masonry construction forms
and freedom in plan variation.

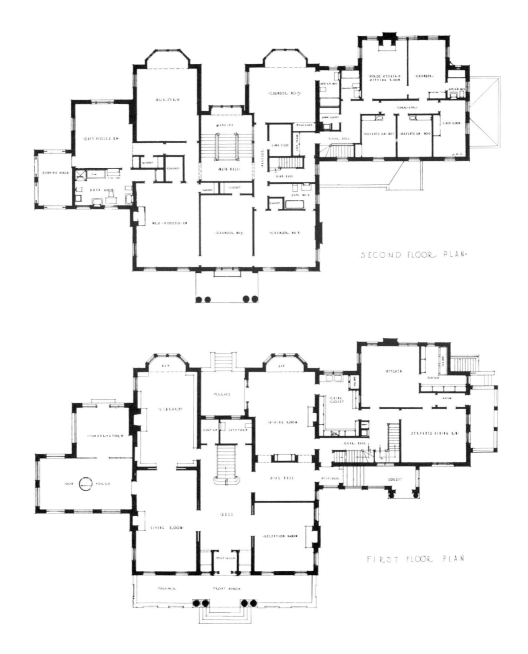

Plans courtesy of Avery Architectural Library.

A later design for the Poole house by Henry was a formal, rectilinear composition.

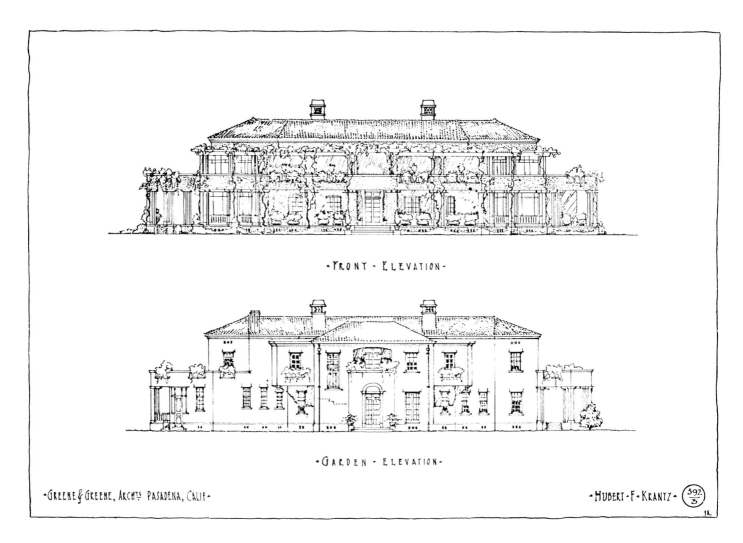

·FRONT·ELEVATION·

·GARDEN·ELEVATION·

·GREENE & GREENE, ARCH.TS PASADENA, CALIF·   ·HUBERT·F·KRANTZ· 392/3

Project: Hubert F. Krantz house, Prospect Park, Palm Beach,
Florida, 1919.
Drawings courtesy of Avery Architectural Library.

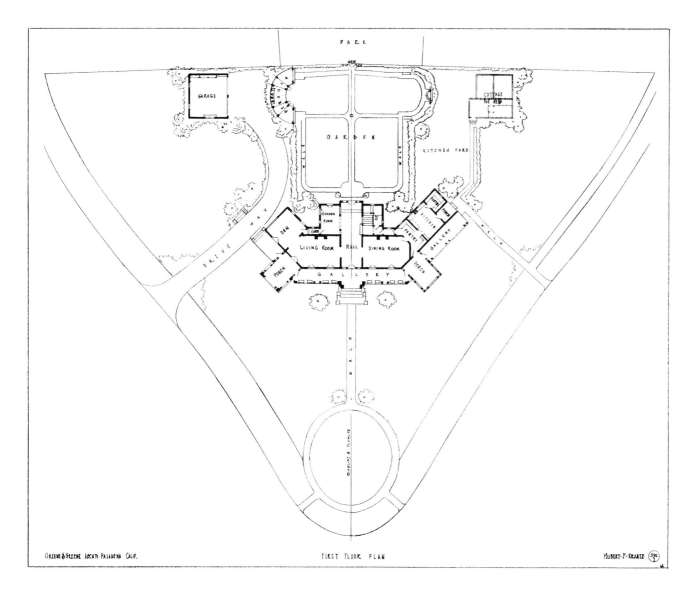

Site plan. Courtesy of Avery Architectural Library.

VI

Separate Work, Retirement and Recognition
1923-1968

The official reorganization of the firm of Greene and Greene was more a statement of fact than a change in policy. Ever since Charles had returned from England in 1909 the two brothers had recognized the growing difference in their personal interests—a difference which had prompted them to work more and more as individuals. By 1922 it was clear that Henry would continue to practice from the Pasadena office and that Charles would remain in Carmel. Although the formal partnership was dissolved at this time, very little was actually changed. Their close lines of communication remained; their association on work for clients continued; and they consulted each other frequently on a variety of subjects.

In this final period between 1922 and the 1950s, however, commissions were scarce. During the 1920s Charles executed only five new works—the Robert Tolmie studio (1922), the Carmel War Memorial (1922), his own studio (1923), a stable for Mrs. Willis Walker (1926), and a house and studio for John L. Howard (1929). Henry completed ten—the Thomas Gould, Jr. house (1924), the Kate A. Kelley house (1924), the Arthur Savage duplex (1924-25), the Samuel Z. Mardian store and flat building (1925), the Lloyd E. Morrison house (1925), the California Institute of Technology building (1925), the William Thum house (1925), the Mrs. James E. Saunders house (1926), the Mrs. Edward Strasburg house (1929), and the Walter L. Richardson house (1929).

At the time of the firm's reorganization, Charles was busy on a modest studio for the pianist, Robert Tolmie, in Piedmont, California. The design evolved from Tolmie's concern for acoustics, which dictated the size, height, form and materials of the interior. This was so important that Charles and the carpenters kept experimenting with the height and form of the studio ceiling and actually changed it three times before construction was finished. The result was a ceiling two-stories high at one end of the 20' x 40' studio and one-story at the other.

The plan of the rustic, shingle-clad structure was simple and compact. On the ground floor the entry, kitchen and stairwell related to the lower end of the studio. Above the kitchen and entry the two bedrooms and bath opened onto the balcony which projected into the high-ceilinged major studio space.

The interiors reflected Charles' interest in molding the plaster as well as his concern for its affect on sound. The details of the balcony supports and railings exhibit the Greenes' long standing and easily identifiable forms. In addition, Charles included in the carved design of the railing the date and his initialed signature, an eccentricity of his later years. Thoughtful and meticulous attention to detail was apparent in the modest sculptural treatment over the fireplace in the studio and in the redwood rain gutters. Exterior forms expressed interior planning.

Meanwhile Professor and Mrs. Rudolph Schevill, friends of Frank Lloyd Wright, visited Carmel. There they admired the D. L. James house and met Charles. As a result, they called on him to add a spacious music studio to their David and Jesse Holms designed bungalow in the Berkeley Hills. Here, as in the Tolmie studio, the acoustics were of primary importance. Charles capitalized on the slope of the site which allowed for a two-story height and split levels to the south of the original structure. The addition opened onto

Robert Tolmie house, 250 Scenic Avenue, Piedmont, 1922.
Photograph courtesy of Robert Judson Clark.
Drawings by Philip Enquist.

Charles' casual handling of the Tolmie design allowed the
form of the house to emerge freely from the internal require-
ments. The primary concern was the music studio, with all
other elements secondary.

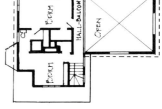

FIRST FLOOR PLAN   SECOND FLOOR PLAN

235

Rudolph Schevill music studio, 77 Tamalpais Road, Berkeley, 1922. Marvin Rand photograph.

Charles carefully developed the two-story addition to blend harmoniously with the original bungalow designed by David and Jesse Holms.

Detail of interior stairway and balcony.
Marvin Rand photograph.

As with the Tolmie studio, acoustics were the primary design determinant. Wood was used minimally in the door and window trim, the book cabinets, and for the railing of the balcony—the entrance from the main house.

an upper level balcony from which one could look out over the entire studio. The stairway was tucked to the right and turned at the foot to enter the high volume of the main space. At the far end high windows with french doors, placed to frame the trees, opened to the garden. To the side, french doors also opened to a small shingle-railed balcony, the most handsome detail of the exterior elevations. Directly below the upper level balcony was a small kitchen and a bathroom with an elaborate oval sunken tub. Both the kitchen and the bathroom were screened from the main studio by built-in bookcases. Overhead an enormous solid pine beam supported the balcony. This beam, the railing, the bookcases and the window and door trim were the only elements of natural wood. Elsewhere sand plaster was sculpted to forms which satisfied both aesthetic and acoustical demands.

At this time Charles was also working on the Carmel War Memorial (1922) for the center strip of the main

Carmel War Memorial, Ocean Boulevard at San Carlos Avenue, Carmel, 1922.
Marvin Rand photograph.

The uniformity of the stone work was out of character for Charles Greene. However, his handling of the heavy redwood beam for the bronze bell was reminiscent of his earlier work.

Charles S. Greene studio, Lincoln Avenue at Thirteenth Street, Carmel, 1923.
Marvin Rand photograph.

Embraced by majestic trees which border the road, Charles' studio has a quiet and graceful air of permanence and appropriateness. Unlike the unfinished redwood bungalow behind, it was carefully detailed, well-built, and exemplified his attempts to create beauty from the most modest materials—in this case used brick which he had acquired from the demolition of a nearby hotel.

237

Charles S. Greene studio, Detail of entry closet window.
Marvin Rand photograph.

thoroughfare of Ocean Boulevard at San Carlos Avenue. This was a simple arch constructed of stone. For some unknown reason this stone was cut to such precise form that it lost its natural character and was more suggestive of a concrete imitation. Equally uncharacteristic of Charles' earlier work were the forced shapes of the stone at the top of the arch which seemed to strain in order to accommodate the curve. The only portion of the design which really expressed the Greene "touch" was the familiar shaping of the wood timber within the arch from which hung the bronze bell.

The following year Charles was involved with three ventures. The first was a minor addition to the Mortimer Fleishhacker house; the second was a proposal that Charles design the Carmel Public Library, but this commission was awarded to Bernard Maybeck after the sudden death of the major donor to the library, who was a close personal friend of Charles; the third was the design and construction of his own studio.

The studio fronted directly on Lincoln Avenue and was situated forward and to the side of the wooden bungalow he had built in 1920. The studio was constructed of brick which Charles had purchased in 1919 from the demolition of a hotel in nearby Pacific Grove. He had always had a work place of his own, separate from the rest of the family, and when he bought the used brick he probably had this studio in mind. But it was not until he sold some property

Wood block stamps which Charles carved for pressing patterns in the soft plaster interior.
Courtesy of Mr. and Mrs. Thomas Gordon Greene.
Marvin Rand photograph.

Interior of studio.
Courtesy of Greene and Greene Library.

The plaster interior was intentionally allowed to undulate and thus express a more sculptured feeling.

Detail of ceiling timber support.
Marvin Rand photograph.

he had owned for several years that he was able to start construction in 1923.

Because of the hardwood he had used in his Northern California work, the White Lumber Company of San Francisco provided him, free of charge, the oak flooring and the teakwood for the carved doors. And, as he was able to do some of the work himself, the costs of the studio were kept down to approximately $2500.

Charles' interest in the California missions had grown with the years. It was not surprising, therefore, that when he designed his own studio, the nature of the brick masonry led to the use of the arch and of mission tiles for the roof. A lack of funds at the time, however, necessitated the substitution for part of the roof of a more modest composition roofing intended as only a temporary roof. It remained throughout his life and was completed by his youngest son.

On the north, a twelve-panel skylight dominated the open gabled ceiling of the main space which was finished in natural sand aggregate plaster and formed to provide excellent accoustics. The sand for the plaster was taken from the ground directly in front of the studio, and resulted in a subtle variation in the soft plaster colors which contributed to the artistry of the interior. Further delicate detail was added by pressing small wooden blocks, which Charles had carved, into the wet plaster. The open gabled roof was supported by beams specially cut at a mill in Palo Colorado Canyon and carefully carved by Charles before being lifted into place.

View of entry from main studio.
Marvin Rand photograph.

The linear composition of the interior of the arched entry door was a dramatic contrast to the richly carved pattern of its exterior face.

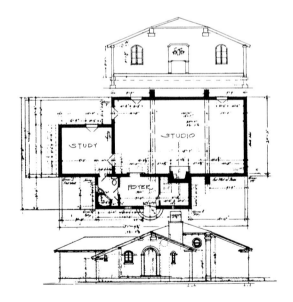

Plan and elevation drawings.
Courtesy of Documents Collection,
College of Environmental Design, UCB.

The plan was simple. There was a large main studio, a side study or bedroom where Charles did much of his writing, and a bath and entry hall facing the street. Most of the teakwood doors were carved in patterns reflecting the variety of Charles' interests and moods—realistic ship scenes, plant life and abstract geometric compositions. The entry door was particularly interesting with its arched top and elaborately carved exterior depicting pots with plants growing vertically up each side and joining in the arch. In sharp contrast, the interior of the door revealed one of Charles' rare linear abstract designs.

The oriental rugs, furniture, screens and *objets d'art*, and even the great Steinway grand piano which had been acquired for daughter Anne were moved from the unfinished bungalow into the studio along with examples of Charles' own chair designs and the ebonized book cabinet which he designed and had built for his private office in Pasadena.[1] The studio was not only the archive of its artist-architect but a showcase in Carmel where musical recitals were given and philosophical groups gathered. Nevertheless, Charles was now to enter a lean period and had no further work of any substance until 1927.

Although Charles had been kept busy since the reorganization of the firm, Henry had little to do in Pasadena until 1923. He then turned his attention to a commission which had been in the project state for four years. As early as 1911 Mrs. Thomas Gould, Jr., a subscriber to *The Craftsman*, had become enamoured with the Greene and Greene bungalows illustrated in that magazine. She was determined to own a Greene and Greene house. But it was 1920 before the Goulds could seriously consider building, and when she first consulted Henry, Mrs. Gould had already drawn up a general floor plan. While he was still working on this design, however, the Goulds purchased a farm on the outskirts of South Ventura which had a commanding view of the ocean. Consequently, they discarded the initial project in favor of a more modest scheme which Henry proposed and which was constructed in 1924.

1. A detailed description of the interior and of the art objects is discussed by Clay Lancaster in his article "My Interviews with Greene Greene," *Journal of The American Institute of Architects*, XXVIII, July, 1957, pp. 202-206.

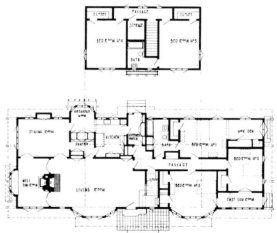

Thomas Gould, Jr. house, 402 Lynn Drive (formerly addressed as 3441 Gale Way), Ventura, 1924.
Marvin Rand photograph.

Considerably more simple than the earlier project for the Goulds, Henry's linear design was more ordered while offering nearly as much space, although much more economically.

This new plan was a narrow, symmetrical rectangle with a partial second-story over the center portion. Henry suggested a Spanish Colonial Revival form, but Mrs. Gould was still determined on a Greene and Greene bungalow. Henry deferred to her wishes but confined the elaborate detail of previous years to the post and beam construction adjacent to the entry and to the windows boxes and the projecting beams in the open gabled roof. The exterior remained wood, but he now accentuated the horizontality of the design by the use of clapboard siding.

The interior walls were primarily plaster. But wherever he did use wood Henry handled it with the same care demanded earlier in the "ultimate bungalows." Despite the Gould's fear that he would be too gentle to cope with the builders, they soon discovered that once construction began, Henry exercised absolute control. In fact he was so demanding that the sanders working on the finish of the interior woods frequently had to take time off to allow their fingers to heal.[2]

Modest and straightforward as the Gould house was, Henry's design of the leaded glass for the dining room revealed personal talents which in the past had often been overshadowed by Charles' activities. In these particular cabinet windows the refined linear composition was interwoven with a lyrical flow of line in the handling of floral elements and birds in flight.

Meanwhile Earle C. Anthony had broken his interim allegiance to Bernard Maybeck and returned to Henry for the design of his mother-in-law's home, the Kate A. Kelley house (1924), which was built in the Los Feliz district of Los Angeles. Again Henry turned to popular Spanish Revival forms and materials. He was obviously willing to accomodate to current taste in order to survive, which led to the curious development of him becoming less "true" to his own architectural development and distinction than were the few remaining ardent admirers of Greene and Greene work. The Kelley house echoed very little of the Greenes' vocabulary except for the use of the bold metal straps and wedges in the timbered truss of the high ceiling in the living room and in the design of a few small stained glass windows.

2. Interview by the author with Thomas Gould, Jr. January 12, 1973.

Back in Pasadena, Henry retained the stucco and tiled roof in his modest design for the Arthur Savage duplex (1924-25). The plan was absolutely symmetrical and fraught with the usual problems of a duplex of narrow linear form on a standard city lot.

At this time the original Earle C. Anthony house (1909) was set for demolition to allow for the construction of a multi-story apartment building when it was rescued by the distinguished actor of the silent screen, Norman Kerry. He and his wife had the house moved in three sections to Beverly Hills and engaged Henry Greene to handle the resiting and rejoining of the structure and to design the grounds and gardens. In dramatic contrast to the tight, rectangular original site, the new lot was larger, somewhat triangular in shape and offered opportunity for a more spacious landscape development.

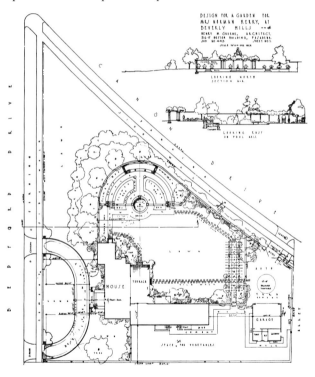

Plot plan for resiting of Earle C. Anthony house, 910 N. Bedford Drive, Beverly Hills, 1925. Courtesy of Avery Architectural Library.

The new owners of the Anthony house engaged Henry Greene
to relocate the house on its new site, and his designs for
the gardens, although still formal, are much more free, open
and relaxed than the tight, linear scheme of the original site.
Marvin Rand photographs.

William Thum house, 1507 Mountain Street, Pasadena, 1925.
Marvin Rand photograph.

Security and concern for fire gave direction to this design
which Henry developed around the concrete vault of the
library and enveloped with a dense gunite exterior surface and
tile roof.

Detail of side porch columns and railing.
Marvin Rand photograph.

To bring unity to the exterior, Henry returned to concepts he
had developed for the Williams house of 1915 and took
advantage of the flexibility of wet gunite.

Throughout this period Henry was busy with numerous alterations and additions to earlier structures which helped to keep the office going but provided little opportunity for creative expression. Along with these minor works, four new commissions in 1925 made this the most active year of Henry's practice after the reorganization of the firm. A two-story store and flat building for Samuel Z. Mardian, the Lloyd E. Morrison house and a small structure identified as "The Dugout" for the California Institute of Technology were not outstanding. The William Thum house, however, was particularly interesting.

William Thum, a former mayor of Pasadena, insisted that the security, fire protection and acoustics of the library be of primary concern. The general plan was a basic rectangle. The house was built around the library, a reinforced concrete fire-and-sound-proof room with the rough character of the concrete ceiling structure expressed internally. The total design was carried out very simply, the interior was finished plaster with a minimum of natural wood trim and sculptural detail. Today the exterior remains untouched. The natural color sand aggregate stucco finish has aged to a soft warm gray-brown accented only by the rhythm and color of the tile roof. To the side of the house, the continuity of materials was carried out in the porch posts and railings. These were constructed of stucco applied over a pipe-and-wire-mesh skeleton which allowed for a pattern of cut-out holes.

The Thum house does not reflect the Greenes' earlier style; neither does it embrace the prevailing Spanish Colonial Revival nor acknowledge the modern movement. Instead, the overall statement is a gentle expression of Henry's ability to adapt his own convictions to what he felt were the desires and best interests of the client.

The following year, Henry designed and built a house next door to his own home for Mrs. James E. Saunders. While its shingled exterior design returned to some of the wooden vocabulary of the earlier years, its steep roof and clipped overhangs separated it from the bungalow era. But remnants of the Craftsman tradition appeared in the handling of the timbers of the entry, as well as in the portico, hardware design, downspouts and the small leaded glass detail in the front door.

Mrs. James E. Saunders house, 130 Bellefontaine Street, Pasadena, 1926. (Demolished) Front elevation drawing courtesy of Greene and Greene Library.

Although there was a distinct attempt to divorce the house from the bungalow idea, the Saunders design still possessed characteristics of the Arts and Crafts Movement, particularly in the entry and door details.

245

Walter L. Richardson house, 27349 Avenue 138, Porterville, 1929.
Marvin Rand photograph.

Devoid of stylistic pretensions, Henry Greene's last major
architectural commission was so well handled that its continued
function as residence and center of the vast Richardson ranch
remains as fresh and appropriate in its rugged environment
today as when constructed.

In 1927 Henry designed a second-story addition to the front wing of the Crow-Crocker house. Fortunately this did not progress beyond the planning stage and the graceful lines of the original house were left intact. He was also involved in moving the Jennie A. Reeve house to its third site next to the country club and golf course in Long Beach. He designed a major addition to the rear of the structure, landscaped the grounds, and supplemented the original Greene and Greene furniture with several pieces of his own creation.[3] The following year he designed the Mrs. Edward Strassburg house (1929) in Covina, giving it a slightly English quality as requested by the client.

His last major work was the Walter L. Richardson house in Porterville, California. Richardson had done some building in Pasadena and was well acquainted with the Greenes' work although he had never had any direct association with them. In 1917 he purchased a ranch in Porterville and built a small house there for his family. In 1929, when he suggested that they either build a swimming pool or a larger house, the family voted unanimously for the larger house, to be situated on the brow of a hillside in the midst of vast orange groves and to be called "Tenalu" after an Indian camp formerly located on the site. He had already roughed out the plan when he met with Henry. It was a simple "U" form embracing an intimate garden in contrast to the vast, rolling hillside. Henry was delighted with the rough drawing and intrigued by Richardson's request that the house be built of adobe made on the site from the natural materials found there. The two men agreed that Richardson would act as his own contractor and that Henry would handle the supervision by mail with occasional trips north to Porterville when necessary.[4]

In order to start building before the winter rains, Richardson broke ground as soon as Henry had worked out the basic concepts of the entire design and from then on, throughout the construction, Henry kept sending on page after page of more detailed drawings and instructions which constituted almost day to day specifications.

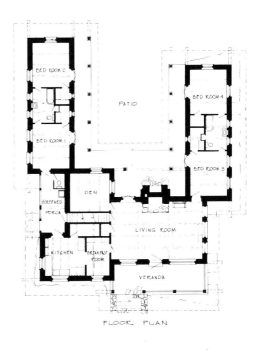

Richardson's desire for a "U" plan form to embrace a small inner garden amidst the vast terrain was met with obvious approval by Henry who had championed the concept throughout his career.

3. Unfortunately, substantial alterations have removed much of the most significant interior character from the Reeve house although the exterior remains in excellent condition.

4. Interviews by the author with Mr. and Mrs. William B. Richardson, son and daughter-in-law of Walter L. Richardson, May, 1974. The house has remained continually in the Richardson family and, with the minor exception of the relocation of the living room entry, is in nearly original condition.

Walter L. Richardson house. Detail of side elevation.
Marvin Rand photograph.

The construction combined stone with adobe bricks made
from material found on the ranch, integrated with reinforced
concrete headers and a bold, wood-timbered roof system.

The high foundation walls of the basement were composed of natural stone which supported the adobe walls and roof of rough timber. Although much of the detail and some materials were new to him, Henry insisted on exercising firm control. As he wrote to Richardson:

> In doing work this way there is always a tendency of both workmen and Owner to start changing the plans. But remember that the Architect works out the things "on paper" in advance, and often when a change is made without consulting him, things don't work out and discrepancies occur which would not have happened if the plans had been followed, or his instructions asked for. This may make some delay or trouble, but it is the only way to do. You must take somebody's advice, as you have employed me to do that architectural work, and I have thought things out, please at least, give me the opportunity to speak before you take action.[5]

In the design of the house, Henry attempted to relate the various elements to the rugged site. The natural adobe was expressed on the exterior and the heavy timbers left with adze marks. The interior was plastered with muted earth color aggregates and the timbers were waxed with soft colors. Detail and door woods were sandblasted or brushed with a stiff wire brush. The hardware, hinges, lighting fixtures and door plates were made on the site and echo forms from the Greenes' earlier days.

Henry was emphatic about the aesthetic aspects of his design. During one of his visits to the site he found that the test sample of the stain on the exterior beams was too dark and insisted that it be sanded off and lightened. He also noticed that there were too many carpenters at work at one time and insisted that their numbers be reduced because he felt that such an attempt to hurry the work would result in mistakes. He designed several pieces of furniture for the house. His breakfast room dining table was as sensitive and straightforward as any of the previous Greene work and its light scale, proportions and design demonstrated a talent too often ignored. He became so involved in the stitchery designs for the curtains of druid cloth that he sent color samples of the thread he had selected to Mrs. Richardson and the two girls.

5. Letter by Henry M. Greene to Walter L. Richardson, July 11, 1929. Courtesy Mr. and Mrs. William B. Richardson.

Shutter detail.
Marvin Rand photograph.

One of his letters written after the house was completed indicated his personal views at this time:

> I was glad to hear that the walnut table came out so well and that you like it. Also that the cost was so reasonable. Those "old fellows" some of them turn out fine cabinet work. There are left a few of these older men, Swedes, Germans, and English, who really learned their trade and love their work.... In my opinion, they give the work a quality which cannot be secured in any other way; modern machinery to the contrary, notwithstanding. Machines can never supply that personal human character.

He added:

> It would be fine if you could, at some later time, make up more furniture for the house and let me design it for you. This is the real way to get things done.[6]

But Henry never had another opportunity to design furniture. In fact, except for a few minor alteration commissions in Pasadena, the simple lines and natural materials of the Richardson house stand as the final statement of Henry Greene's architectural career.

6. Letter February 17, 1931.

Mortimer Fleishhacker water gardens, 329 Albion Avenue, Woodside, 1927. Marvin Rand photograph.

The addition of the reflecting pond to the Fleishhacker estate is both tranquil and breathtaking—with a suggestion of a Roman aqueduct silhouetted against the rolling hills.

Between 1923 and 1927 Charles had been involved in only two projects, one for a Mrs. Walker and another for Mrs. Jennie Crocker Whitman, both of Pebble Beach. Neither was carried out. In 1927, however, he was called upon to design the quiet but dramatic water gardens for the Mortimer Fleishhacker house. Laid out on the central axis of the formal gardens to the rear of the house, the materials and forms of the water garden softened the formality of the manicured lawns and lily pond of the original design and provided a more successful transition to the wild, mountainous terrain of the surrounding area.

The water gardens were developed on a separate and lower plateau and thus required considerable stairway transitions leading down to the shallow reflecting pond. From the terrace of the house only the stone arches at the far end of the water garden were visible, arousing curiosity and enticing the observer along the raked gravel paths to the brow of the hill. Here the view as a whole was impressive. The transition from the upper formal gardens was handled with such ease that the lower water gardens appeared to be an integral part of the original landscaping construction. The dramatic change of material was countered by the symmetry of the design. Stone was the basic material—with different types selected for different functions. Large uniform slabs were employed for the paving and stairways, whereas texture and color became more important in the wall construction. Every detail was carefully planned to draw the visitor down to the very edge of the reflecting pool, along its entire length, around the arcaded end structure which was reminiscent of the great Roman aqueducts, and back along the side.

The following year the Fleishhackers commissioned a small stone dairy house on the edge of a ravine across the road. Mrs. Fleishhacker had "envisioned serving tea there every afternoon." Charles, eager for new projects, developed the two-story stone structure in forms closely related to the water gardens. This dairy house, however, was too far from the house, little if ever used, and eventually came to be regarded as "Greene's Folly."[7]

7. Interview with Mrs. Mortimer Fleishhacker, Sr. Notes courtesy Robert Judson Clark.

View through arcade toward formal upper gardens and house. Marvin Rand photograph.

Mortimer Fleishhacker water
gardens. Detail of retaining
wall and stone planter pots.
Marvin Rand photograph.

Each facet of the water garden was developed in a differing type of stone, each contributing color and textural enrichment to the overall composition. Marvin Rand photograph.

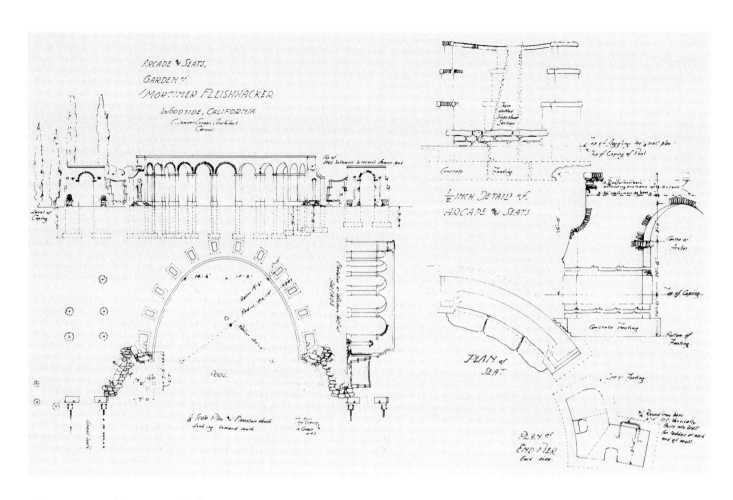

Plan, courtesy of Documents Collection,
College of Environmental Design, UCB.

At this time and well into 1930 Charles was also wrestling with various schemes for a gothic room addition to the Fleishhacker's San Francisco house. Apparently he confided some of his problems to Henry for on May 11, 1930 Henry wrote:

> You spoke about finishing the working drawings for the gothic room for Mr. Fleishhacker....I am not doing anything myself and wondered if I could help you finish them if I came up....It would be rather interesting to work on some gothic as I have never done anything in that style myself.[8]

8. Documents Collection, College of Environmental Design, UCB.

Mortimer Fleishhacker dairy house, 329 Albion Avenue, Woodside, 1928. Marvin Rand photograph.

Ultimately nicknamed "Greene's Folly," the dairy house had been the idea of Mrs. Fleishhacker who had envisioned serving afternoon tea there. However, the structure was too distant from the house and was little if ever used.

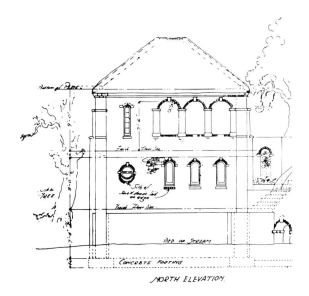

NORTH ELEVATION.

Courtesy of Greene and Greene Library.

Martin Flavin garden walls, Spindrift Road, Carmel Highlands,
1928. Detail of entrance gate and masonry wall.
Marvin Rand photograph.

Interior stairway and balcony.
Marvin Rand photograph.

Above the carved french doors leading to Flavin's private
library, wrought iron stairs and balcony were added for access
to an upstairs bedroom.

Martin Flavin house. Detail of stairway.
Marvin Rand photograph.

Detail of wrought-iron balcony.
Marvin Rand photograph.

Evidently he did not join Charles on the project as Charles wrote him on December 1, 1930:

> Mr. Fleishhacker's plans are not done yet, but I think I am getting it worked out. It has been the hardest work I have ever done, but I hope to make a success of it if he has the patience to wait for me.[9]

Perhaps he did not. The gothic room was never built.

In this same year Charles began work on a major alteration to the Martin Flavin house, "Spindrift," near Carmel. Flavin's home had been built on a rocky point at Carmel Highlands in 1922 by Charles H. Gottschalk, but shortly thereafter its continuing development became the work of Charles Greene. As Martin Flavin wrote: "Charles Greene was not the architect, but over a long period of years he contributed to it almost everything of value and distinction, both inside and out....I regard Charles Greene as its creator."[10]

By far the most exciting and significant of the alterations was the small library which Charles designed entirely in natural unfinished redwood. Each segment of the triangular pattern of ceiling paneling was carved by Charles in a different design. The effect was both dramatic and unique. Carving was also carried out in the panels of the closed cabinets to each side of the walls of bookshelves. At one end of the library he designed a built-in seat suitable for sleeping, and over this were stained glass windows with hand-blown rondels. To compensate for the relative lack of natural light and for the darkened quality of the all wooden interior, he created hand-beaten copper hanging shades suspended from scrolled wrought iron brackets, which swivelled from the wall, one at each side of the window seat and a larger version at the opposite end of the room. On each side of the two doors on the central axis of the library were similar copper lights with wooden handles and long cords, allowing them to be lifted from their wooden wall mounts and carried along the shelves in search of a particular book. The major double doors opening directly from the living room were also carved by Charles.

9. *Ibid.*

10. Letter by Martin Flavin to this writer, March 16, 1966.

Martin Flavin library, 1931.
Marvin Rand photograph.

The library is one of the most
intimate and sensuous spaces ever
designed by Charles, who was
also responsible for every facet of
the construction.

John. L. Howard house, 86 Ave Maria Road, Monterey, 1929.
Photograph courtesy of Robert Judson Clark.

Rustic shingle detailing on the exterior belies the beautiful
detailing and craftsmanship evident upon close inspection.

Some time later a large scenic carving was completed for the massive stone fireplace and considerable time was spent in the development of the stone garden walls, the major entry walls, and the large iron gates leading in from Spindrift Road. As an independent design, the Flavin library was perhaps the most significant of Charles' late work.

Charles' last complete work was the John L. Howard house and studio (1929). These two structures, both modest in scale, were developed entirely in wood on a small lot in the rugged mountain region of Monterey. Here the exterior shingle pattern rambled up and down in irregular lines. The treatment of the interior recalled the fine periods of the Greenes' early work, and the superb detail and finishes were carried out with the craftsmanship expected of Charles.

The fact that the Greenes were working in the style they had pioneered in 1903 was unfortunate. Had they embraced the modern movement with the same vigor with which they had broken from the past, their talents could have made further contributions to American architecture. But neither Charles nor Henry was comfortable with the machine age and, as a result, some of their own work from 1920 on became as dated as the styles against which they had rebelled.

Charles expressed his feelings about the modern movement when he wrote:

> Building today is engineering, not architecture. The ideal of engineering is precision and economy, the slogan of manufacturers. Both of them have a fever of facts and figures, but the public is immune from this malady. It is the merchant who molds the nation with his publicity stuff.... Careless of the quality of material and work he sets a premium on clever design that discreetly covers the engineering it can never be a part of. The real modernist architect turns with disgust from this unmeaning display to aesthetic denial of beauty.[11]

Along with their other projects during the 1920s, Charles and Henry were each involved in various additional designs for Mrs. Frances F. Prentiss who had now become as much identified with the Cordelia A. Culbertson house as the Culbertsons themselves. She had engaged Charles to design pieces of furniture, marble sculpture for the entry way, screens for the bedroom, nine carved and painted plaques for the dining room and sundry other items, all of which Henry tried desperately to coordinate from the Pasadena office. But the timing of the completed works, the high costs involved, and the client's dissatisfaction with the carved panels for the dining room required considerable renegotiation and correspondence. Henry's sense of frustration was evident in a letter to Charles regarding the panels:

> Mrs. Prentiss says not to do anything more on the panels you are making for the Dining Room. She says, quite frankly, she does not like them.... She said she thought you would do something that would just blend in with the walls, but these three panels that you have hung look spotty and disturb the harmony that she felt in the room before...she rather criticizes you for not letting her know costs and do something so she would understand a little better what was to be done before doing it. I do not know what is wrong, unless it is your method of doing things.[12]

Charles replied:

> I have settled with Mrs. Prentiss and she says the three pieces are to go in the loggia. I am thoroughly disappointed, but it can't be helped....I feel that the plaques are as good as anything I have ever done and the dining room will always seem unfinished to me.[13]

11. Letter by Charles Greene to Professor Vladimir Ulehla in Brno, Czechoslovakia, June 29, 1929. Documents Collection, Greene and Greene Library.

12. Letter by Henry Greene to Charles Greene, January 27, 1928. Documents Collection, Greene and Greene Library.

13. Letter dated March 26, 1928. Documents Collection, Greene and Greene Library.

Charles Sumner Greene in typical attire on the steps of his Carmel studio in the early 1930s.
Photograph courtesy of Greene and Greene Library.

The lean years were hard for both to adapt to but the depression years were especially difficult for Henry. For a short time into the 1930s he maintained the original offices in the Boston building in Pasadena, but in 1933 he wrote to Charles:

> Mrs. Prentiss and Mrs. Blacker have quit doing things now, as have a number of old clients so this cuts me out of the small things that helped to pay office expense so I will have to give up my uptown office....I am going to move my things home now, as I have thought of doing several times in the past few years.[14]

With the death of his wife in 1935, Henry's life changed radically. Unlike Charles, he had been very much a family man and now that his wife was gone, his children grown, and no work of substance to keep him occupied, he found the old Bellefontaine house too large and too lonely. Thus, late in 1940, he moved into the home of his eldest son, Henry, and spent part of the year in Northern California with one of his other sons, William.

Now past seventy years of age, he tried to keep busy with a few minor alterations, some engineering for Charles and two small jobs for his children, one a house project in Pittsburg, California (1944) for William Sumner Greene and his wife Harriott and another for his daughter Isabelle and her husband, Alan McElwain, in Granada Hills, California, which McElwain built himself.

Charles was somewhat more active during the 1930s. There were a few small projects for his old friend, Martin Flavin, and a brief, abortive venture with a builder, Park Abbott, who wanted very much to build something that Charles had designed. With Charles' permission, he distributed from his contracting offices in Oakland an elegant announcement in 1937 stating that "Charles Sumner Greene will act as his advisor on the designing of buildings and by special appointment, as an architect to his clients."[15] This arrangement was soon annulled as Abbott had neither the capital nor wealthy clients for work of such high quality and cost.

14. Letter dated June 12, 1933. Documents Collection, Greene and Greene Library.

15. Documents Collection, Greene and Greene Library.

Charles' last architectural work was for D. L. James, who decided in 1939 that he needed a proper library to house his collection of rare books. Charles developed several schemes, but none pleased either him or the Jameses. In the end it was James' son, Daniel, who suggested that the narrow space under the house behind the stone arches be expanded. For most of 1940 Charles worked on this design, and when he ran into problems with the fireplace construction and elements of structure and bearing, he wrote to Henry suggesting that he come up to Carmel and work with him. There were structural elements which, as in earlier years, he left for Henry's attention. Construction was begun in 1941 and moved slowly until March of 1944 when Mr. James' sudden death halted the project.[16]

16. In the 1950s Mrs. James decided to go ahead with the library on the advice and encouragment of Elizabeth Gordon, editor of *House Beautiful*. In general, Charles' design was followed except for the bathroom.

D. L. James library addition, 1940. Detail of shelving and storage units. Marvin Rand photograph.

Detail of fireplace and molded plaster columns and stone capitals.
Marvin Rand photograph.

ANNO DOMINI MCMLII

ARCHITECTS MUCH HONORED IN YOUR HOMELAND
FOR GREAT CONTRIBUTIONS TO DESIGN, SENSITIVE
AND KNOWING BUILDERS WHO REFLECTED WITH
GRACE AND CRAFTSMANSHIP EMERGING VALUES
IN MODERN LIVING IN THE WESTERN STATES, FORMU
LATORS OF A NEW AND NATIVE ARCHITECTURE

THE AMERICAN INSTITUTE OF ARCHITECTS

NOW HAILS AND HONORS YOU

HENRY MATHER GREENE

AND

CHARLES SUMNER GREENE

FOR YOUR CONTRIBUTIONS TO THE DESIGN OF THE AMERICAN
HOME. YOUR GIFTS HAVE NOW MULTIPLIED AND SPREAD TO ALL
PARTS OF THE NATION, AND ARE RECOGNIZED THROUGHOUT THE
WORLD, INFLUENCING AND IMPROVING THE DESIGN OF SMALL AS WELL
AS GREAT HOUSES. YOU ENRICH THE LIVES OF THE PEOPLE. YOU
HAVE MADE THE NAME OF CALIFORNIA SYNONYMOUS WITH SIMP·
LER, FREER AND MORE ABUNDANT LIVING. YOU HAVE HELPED SHAPE
OUR DISTINCTIVELY NATIONAL ARCHITECTURE. AND IN GIVING TAN·
GIBLE FORM TO THE IDEALS OF OUR PEOPLE, YOUR NAMES WILL BE
FOREVER REMEMBERED AMONG THE GREAT CREATIVE AMERICANS.

SECRETARY   PRESIDENT

Citation presented to Charles Sumner Greene and Henry
Mather Greene by the national organization of The American
Institute of Architects in 1952.
Courtesy of Greene and Greene Library.

Although work was scarce, Charles was leading an active life in Carmel. In 1936 he was appointed to the local committee for the Federal Art Project, but more important to him were his personal studies. After the move to Carmel, Charles and Alice Greene became involved with a small philosophical group absorbed in the work of Ouspensky and Gurdjieff, which met periodically, often in Charles' studio. People moved in and out of this group but a small nucleus including Charles and Alice remained constant. Charles was considered by the group a profound student of Buddhism,

> not only from an intellectual standpoint but from a human and living one . . . so much so that he agreed to give private readings to two of his friends. . . . We met regularly in his beautiful studio for a long time and read and studied *A Buddhist Bible* by Dwight Goddard. . . . [Charles] was really deeply steeped in the whole Buddhist approach to life, and he lived it. He had a quiet way of keeping us to the center of his teaching trying always to expound to us its meaning and transcendental beauty.[17]

This study of oriental philosophy not only appealed to Charles' inner feelings but provided him with a positive outlook on life at a time when he was withdrawing more and more from the crass realities of the commercialism which he had long refused to accept. Group discussions were a constant stimulus and at times he would distribute voluminous sheets of handwritten observations and ideas to the other members. Some were intended for publication. One of his favorite quotations from *A Buddhist Bible* concerned what he referred to as Mind-essence:

> It is in full possession of radiant wisdom and luminosity, penetrating everything by the purity of its concepts, seeing everywhere adequately and truly, its mind innately free and unprejudiced, ever abiding in blissful peace, pure, fresh and unchangeable.[18]

17. Correspondence from Dora Mayer (formerly Hagemeyer) to the author, February 20, 1970. Dora Mayer was actively involved in these group sessions and the private sittings. Her accounts of these activities are detailed and have provided important knowledge of Charles' personal involvement with the group.

18. Dwight Goddard, *A Buddhist Bible.*

His constant search for Truth inspired him to write a friend in 1935:

> Today the rational mind dominates, it sees Nature as all inclusive and Art as Man's exclusive part of Nature. It beholds Nature and Art forever separate. You, Edward Weston, with joyous heart and modern tool in hand have reached beyond personal expression to the root of Truth, finding beauty by the way where and as you looked.[19]

Toward the end of their professional lives, little mention was made of the Greenes in academic journals or by architectural historians. Since the 1922 publication of the James house their work had virtually dropped out of print. After the close of the Second World War a new appreciation for natural materials developed. Through articles by architect L. Morgan Yost and writer Jean Murray Bangs, the work of Greene and Greene began to claim its place in the spectrum of creative American architecture. New generations soon became aware of principles and craftsmanship which were truly inspiring. On March 9, 1948 Charles and Henry Greene were honored with a Certificate of Merit presented to them by the Southern California Chapter of The American Institute of Architects.

During the 1950s more attention was focused on the Greenes' work. In his film *Architecture West*, Erven Jourdan acknowledged the significance of their work along with the work of Frank Lloyd Wright, Bernard Maybeck, and Pietro Belluschi, among others. In 1952 the Greenes were hailed as "Formulators of a New and Native Architecture" and presented with the coveted Citation from the national organization of The American Institute of Architects.

Henry fully appreciated the recognition bestowed upon him and Charles by the architectural profession and was proud that their work was the subject of considerable interest to other generations. He remained alert and physically active until he came down with pneumonia in the winter of 1953. He recovered, but his health continued to fail until his death in a Pasadena rest home on October 2, 1954 at the age of 84. He was buried in the family plot in the cemetery of the Episcopal Church of Our Savior in San Gabriel, California.

Charles Sumner Greene and Henry Mather Greene in Pasadena in the late 1940s.
Courtesy of Greene and Greene Library.

Charles, on the other hand, was not well and apparently was not fully aware of the attention and respect now accorded their work. He did not grasp the reality of Henry's death until his nephew William Sumner Greene sat down and took the time to make him understand. Then for a few fleeting moments Charles realized that Henry was gone and turned to William with tears in his eyes to say simply, "He was a good man."[20]

Three years later on June 11, 1957, at the age of 89, Charles died at his home in Carmel. Private funeral services were held at the Little Chapel by the Sea Crematorium in Pacific Grove and on July 2, 1957 his ashes were buried without a marker at the foot of his mother's grave in the El Encenal Cemetery in Monterey, California.

19. Documents Collection, Greene and Greene Library, The Gamble House.

20. Interviews by the author with William Sumner Greene and Harriott Greene.

The interest in and influence of Greene and Greene has continued to grow. The publications of Yost and Bangs were followed by additional articles by Esther McCoy and Clay Lancaster, as well as a chapter by this writer in *Five California Architects* by Esther McCoy.

After the 1948 and 1952 awards and citations, visitors from all parts of the world began to seek out the Greene and Greene buildings. The David B. Gamble house became a focus of attention as it had been preserved in its original condition and contained all of the furnishings designed with the house. In February, 1966, James N. Gamble, acting on behalf of his brothers and sisters,[21] presented the deed to his grandparents' home to the Board of Directors of the City of Pasadena in a joint agreement with the University of Southern California. Under the agreement the University, through its School of Architecture and Fine Arts and its appointed Curator, was vested with the responsibility for the restoration and preservation of the house and for the development of such appropriate programs as would maintain the Gamble home as a center for educational and cultural activities consistent with its architectural significance. Following a formal dedication on September 25, 1966 The Gamble House was opened to the public on a regular schedule.[22]

On October 12, 1968, in celebration of the one hundredth anniversary of the birth of Charles Sumner Greene, The Gamble House officially dedicated the Greene and Greene Library as permanent archives for portions of their papers and also for material dealing with their contemporaries in the Arts and Crafts Movement.[23]

Henry once observed that Greene and Greene had been fortunate to be in the right place at the right time. To this we should add that not only the place and the time, but the combination of their individual and diverse talents made possible the evolution of new forms which could be adapted equally to small as well as large structures. If they are to be associated with a particular style, then it would be to that which we call the Arts and Crafts style, with its emphasis on functional design and superb craftsmanship.

Perhaps the best statement about their work is found in the thought of William Morris which the Greenes themselves repeated throughout their long careers: they always sought to determine what was truly necessary and then tried to make that beautiful.

21. The gift of the Gamble house was made by David G. Gamble, Edwin C. Gamble, James N. Gamble, Joseph D. Messler, Mrs. Joseph W. Scherr, Jr. and Mrs. Harlan J. Swift.

22. In their support of this generous action by the Gamble family, the children and grandchildren of Charles and Henry Greene have joined the Gambles in contributing valuable drawings, photographs, letters and other original documents to the Gamble home, and as a result the Gamble House has become a center for the study of the work and lives of Greene and Greene.

23. The balance of the significant papers and drawings of Greene and Greene are housed in the rare documents collections of the Avery Architectural Library, Columbia University, and the College of Environmental Design Library, University of California, Berkeley.

Selected Bibliography

Ackerman, James S. "One Hundred Years of Significant Building, Houses Since 1907," *Architectural Record*, (February, 1957), p. 203.

Alley, A. W. "A House in Japanese Style," *House Beautiful*, (March, 1909), pp. 76, 77.

Andrews, Wayne. *Architecture, Ambition, and Americans: A Social History of American Architecture*. New York: Harper & Row, 1947.

_____. "The Impatient Evolution of the American House." *House Beautiful*, (February, 1965), pp. 90-105.

Ashbee, Charles Robert. *"Memoirs,"* typescript, London, The Victoria and Albert Museum Library, 1909.

Bangs, Jean Murray. "Greene and Greene," *Architectural Forum*. (October, 1948), pp. 80-89.

_____. "Prophet Without Honor: Greene and Greene, Architects in Pasadena," *House Beautiful*, (May, 1950), p. 138, ff.

_____. "Los Angeles—Know Thyself," *Los Angeles Times*, Home Magazine, (October 14, 1951), pp. 4, 5, 11.

_____. "A parting salute to the Fathers of the California Style," *House and Home*, (August, 1957), pp. 84-95.

(see also: Harris, Jean)

Banham, Reyner. *Architecture of the Well-Tempered Environment*. London: Architectural Press, 1969.

_____. *Los Angeles—The Architecture of Four Ecologies*. London: Penguin Press, 1971.

_____. "The Master Builders: 5," *London Times*, (August 8, 1971), pp. 19-27.

Besenger, Curtis. "How to Capture the Intangible in Permanent Form," *House Beautiful*, (April, 1958), pp. 148-151, ff.

Bitterman, Eleanor. *Art in Modern Architecture*. New York: Reinhold, 1952.

Brooks, H. Allen. "Chicago Architecture: Its Debt to the Arts and Crafts," *Journal of the Society of Architectural Historians*, Vol. XXX, No. 4, (1971), pp. 312-317.

Burchard, John and Bush-Brown, Albert. *The Architecture of America—A Social and Cultural History*. New York: Little, Brown & Co., 1961.

Byers, Charles Alma. "Some California Bungalows," *House Beautiful*, (August, 1908), pp. 59-62.

Clark, Arthur Bridgmen. *Art Principles in House, Furniture and Village Planning*. Palo Alto: Stanford University Press, 1921.

Clark, Robert Judson (ed.). *The Arts and Crafts Movement in America 1876-1916*. Princeton: Princeton University Press, 1972.

Cram, Ralph Adams. *American Country Houses of Today*. New York: Architectural Book Publishing Co., 1913.

Croly, Herbert. "Some Houses by Myron Hunt and Elmer Grey," *Architectural Record*, (October, 1906), pp. 281-295.

_____. "The Country House in California," *Architectural Record*, (December, 1913), pp. 483-499.

Current, William R. and Karen. *Greene and Greene: Architects in the Residential Style*. Fort Worth: Amon Carter Museum, 1974.

Darling, Kenneth Glendower. *My Early Life in California and My First American and European Tours, (1890-1908)*, Honnold Library, Claremont Colleges, Rare Book Room.

Darrach, James M. A. "Why Not a Bungalow?," *Country Life in America*, (October, 1906), pp. 637-640.

David, Arthur C., "An Architect of Bungalows in California," *Architectural Record*, (October, 1906), pp. 306-315.

Davidson, Marshall B. (ed.). *The American Heritage History of Notable American Homes*. New York: American Heritage, 1971.

Ellis, Harvey. "A Craftsman House Design," *The Craftsman*, (July, 1903), pp. 269-277.

_____. "An Urban House," *The Craftsman*, (August, 1903), pp. 312-327.

Embury, II, Aymar. *One Hundred Country Houses: Modern American Examples*. New York: Century, 1909.

Ferguson, Lillian. "Pools in the Garden," *Sunset Magazine*, (September, 1923), p. 64.

Fitch, James Marston. *American Building—The Historical Forces that Shaped It*. Boston: Houghton Mifflin. 1947.

Freudenheim, Leslie Mandelson and Sussman, Elizabeth Sacks. *Building with Nature: Roots of the San Francisco Bay Region Tradition*. Santa Barbara and Salt Lake City: Peregrine Smith, Inc., 1974.

Gebhard, David and Von Breton, Harriette. *Architecture in California 1868-1968*. Santa Barbara: Standard Printing, 1968.

Gebhard, David; Montgomery, Roger; Winter, Robert W.; Woodbridge, Sally and John. *A Guide to Architecture in San Francisco and Northern California*. Santa Barbara and Salt Lake City: Peregrine Smith, Inc., 1973.

Grey, Elmer. "Architecture in Southern California," *Architectural Record*, (January, 1905), pp. 1-17.
_____. "Some Country House Architecture in the Far West," *Architectural Record*, (October, 1922), pp. 308-315.

Greene, Charles Sumner. "California Home Making," Tournament of Roses Edition, *Pasadena Daily News*, (January, 1905), pp. 26, 27.
_____. "Home Making in California," *Pasadena Daily News*, 1907.
_____. "Bungalows," *The Western Architect*, (July, 1908), pp. 3-5, plates 1-9.
_____. "Impressions of Some Bungalows and Gardens," *The Architect*, (December, 1915), pp. 251, 252.
_____. "Architecture As A Fine Art," *The Architect*, (April, 1917), pp. 217-222.
_____. "Architecture and the Machine Age," *The Carmelite*, (October 30, 1930).
_____. "Symbolism," unpublished manuscript, (November, 1932), Greene and Greene Library.

Greene, Henry Mather. "The Use of Orange Trees in Formal Gardens," *California Southland*, (April, 1919), p. 8.

Guinn, J. M. *A History of California and an Extended History of Its Southern Coast Counties*. Los Angeles: Historic Record Co., 1907.

Hamlin, Talbot. *Architecture Through the Ages*. New York: G. P. Putnam Sons, 1940.

Harris, Jean. "The California Houses of Greene and Greene Redefined," *Architectural Digest*, (September-October, 1975), pp. 181, 182.
(see also Bangs, Jean Murray)

Hitchcock, Henry-Russell. *Architecture: 19th and 20th Century*. Baltimore: Penguin Books, 1958.

Hopkins, Una Nixson. "A Chalet in Pasadena," *House Beautiful*, (February, 1906), pp. 11, 12.
_____. "A Study for Homebuilders," *Good Housekeeping*, (March, 1906), pp. 259-264.
_____. "A House of Fine Detail That Conforms to the Hillside on Which It Is Built," *The Craftsman*, (June, 1907), pp. 329-335.
_____. "The Development of Domestic Architecture on the Pacific Coast," *The Craftsman*, (January, 1908), pp. 450-457.

Howard, John Galen. "Country House Architecture on the Pacific Coast," *Architectural Record*, (October, 1916), pp. 333-335.

Jodon, M. Laura. "El Hogar—A Quaint and Interesting Home in Pasadena," *Los Angeles Times*, Illustrated Weekly Magazine, (September, 1904).

Jordy, William H. *American Buildings and Their Architects. Vol. 3, Progressive and Academic Ideals at the Turn of the Twentieth Century*. Garden City: Doubleday, 1972.

Kakudzo, Okakura, *The Ho-o-den, an Illustrated Description, Chicago, 1893*. Chicago: The Worlds Columbian Exposition, 1894.

Keith, Henrietta P. "The Trail of Japanese Influence in our Modern Domestic Architecture," *The Craftsman*, (July, 1907), pp. 446-451.

Kelly, Arthur R. "California Bungalows," *Country Life in America*, (May, 1914), pp. 42-45, ff.

Kirker, Harold Clark. *California Architecture in the 19th Century: A Social History*. Berkeley: 1956.

————. *California's Architectural Frontier*. San Marino: Huntington Library, 1960.

Kornwolf, James D. *M. H. Baillie Scott and the Arts and Crafts Movement—Pioneers of Modern Design*. Baltimore and London: Johns Hopkins Press, 1972.

Lancaster, Clay. "Japanese Building in the U. S. Before 1900," *The Art Bulletin*, (September, 1953), pp. 217-225.

————. "My Interviews with Greene and Greene," *AIA Journal*, (July, 1957), pp. 202-206.

————. "The American Bungalow," *The Art Bulletin*, (September, 1958), pp. 239-253.

————. "Some Sources of Greene and Greene," *AIA Journal*, (August, 1960), pp. 39-46.

————. *The Japanese Influence in America*. New York: Walton H. Rawls, 1963.

Locke, Seymore E. "Bungalows: What They Really Are," *House and Garden*, (August, 1907), pp. 245-253.

McCoy, Esther. "Notes on Greene and Greene," *Arts and Architecture*, (July, 1953), pp. 27, ff.

————. "The California House—How It Started," *Los Angeles Times*, Home Magazine, (July 19, 1953), pp. 13-17, ff.

————. "7 Pioneers Who Showed the Way," *Los Angeles Times*, Home Magazine, (September 9, 1956).

————. "Roots of California Contemporary Architecture," *Arts and Architecture*, (September, 1956), pp. 36-39.

————. *Five California Architects*. Chapter III, "Greene and Greene," Makinson, Randell L., New York: Reinhold, 1960.

McGroarty, William G. *History of Los Angeles County*. New York: American Historical Society, 1923.

Makinson, Randell L. "Greene and Greene," Chapter III; McCoy, Esther, *Five California Architects*. New York: Reinhold, 1960.

————. "Japan's Impact on American Architecture," *This Is Japan*, No.11, (September, 1963), pp. 148-151.

————. "Greene and Greene: The Gamble House," *The Prairie School Review*, (Fourth Quarter, 1968), pp. 4-26.

————. "An Academic Paper: The Gamble House," *The Prairie School Review*, (Fourth Quarter, 1968), p. 31.

————. *A Guide to the Work of Greene and Greene*. Santa Barbara and Salt Lake City: Peregrine Smith, Inc., 1974.

————. "Special Report — Greene and Greene," with photography by Yasuhiro Ishimoto. Osaka: Kakenaka Komutin Co., Ltd., *Approach*, (Spring, 1975), pp. 10-29, ff.

Mullgardt, Louis Christian. "Country House Architecture on the Pacific Coast," *Architectural Record*, (October, 1915), pp. 422-452.

Mumford, Lewis. *Roots of Contemporary American Architecture*. New York: Reinhold, 1952.

Pehnt, Wolfgang (ed.). *Encyclopedia of Modern Architecture*. New York: Harry N. Abrams, 1964.

Saylor, Henry H. *Bungalows*. New York: McBride, Winston & Co., 1911.

Scully, Vincent. "American Houses: Thomas Jefferson to Frank Lloyd Wright," *The Rise of an American Architecture*. Kaufman, Jr., Edgar (ed.). London: Pall Mall Press, 1970.

————. *American Architecture and Urbanism*. New York: Frederick A. Praeger, 1969.

Stickley, Gustav. *Craftsman Homes*. New York: The Craftsman Publishing Co., 1909.

————. "The Value of Permanent Architecture as a Truthful Expression of National Character," *The Craftsman*, (April, 1909), pp. 80-91.

Strand, Janann. *A Greene and Greene Guide*. Pasadena, published by author, 1974.

Wenzel, Paul and Krakow, Maurice. *American Country Houses of Today*. New York: The Architectural Book Publishing Co., 1913.

Whiffen, Marcus. *American Architecture Since 1780: A Guide to the Styles.* Cambridge: MIT Press, 1969.

White, C. H. "Teakwood for Interior Decoration," *Architect and Engineer,* (March, 1911), pp. 94-97.

Wight, Peter B. "The Residential Architecture of Southern California," *Western Architect,* (September, 1920), pp. 91-96.

Winter, Robert W. "American Sheaves from 'C.R.A.'," *Journal of the Society of Architectural Historians,* (December, 1971), pp. 317-322.

Yost, L. Morgan. "Greene and Greene of Pasadena," *Journal of the Society of Architectural Historians,* (March, 1950), pp. 11-19.

(Author Unknown)

"Pasadena's Latest Building," *Pasadena Daily Evening Star,* (July 11, 1896), p. 1.

Pasadena Illustrated Souvenir Book. Pasadena Board of Trade, 1898.

Pasadena California—The City Beautiful. Pasadena Evening Star, Star Publishing Co., 1902.

Pasadena Illustrated Souvenir Book. Pasadena Board of Trade, 1903.

"American Domestic Architecture," London: *Academy Architecture,* 1903.

Tournament of Roses Edition, *Pasadena Star-News,* 1904.

Tournament of Roses Edition, *Pasadena Daily News,* 1905.

"Some California Bungalows," *Country Life in America,* (October, 1905), pp. 637-640.

Architect and Engineer, (March, 1906), pp. 56, 57.

"The California Bungalow: A Style of Architecture Which Expresses the Individuality and Freedom Characteristic of our Western Coast," *The Craftsman,* (October, 1907), pp. 68-80.

"Wooden Dwellings in California on the Lines of the Old Spanish Adobe," *The Craftsman,* (February, 1908), pp. 568-571.

Los Angeles Times, Sunday Edition, (May 10, 1908).

"Some Pasadena Homes Showing Harmony between Structure and Landscape," *The Craftsman,* (May, 1909), pp. 216-221.

"A Mountain Bungalow Whose Appearance of Crude Construction is the Result of Skillful Design," *The Craftsman,* (December, 1909), pp. 227-230.

"Pasadena, Portico of Paradise by a Los Angeles Architect," Tournament of Roses Edition, *Pasadena Daily News,* 1911.

"Coming School to be Most Modern," *The Pasadena Star,* (May 16, 1911).

"California's Contribution to a National Architecture: Its Significance as shown in the Work of Greene and Greene Architects," *The Craftsman,* (August, 1912), pp. 532-547.

"The Wonderful Things One Can Do In a Garden with Architectural Features," *The Craftsman,* (August, 1912), pp. 559-563.

"Cordelia Culbertson Residence," *Pacific Coast Architect,* (March, 1914) pp. 10, 11.

"The House Set Upon a Hill: Its Picturesque Opportunities and Architectural Problems," *The Craftsman,* (August, 1914), pp. 532-539.

"Your Own Home; Number Three: Selecting the Materials for Durability, Economy and Picturesqueness," *The Craftsman,* (February, 1915), pp. 534-546.

"Your Own Home; Number Six: The Approach to the House," *The Craftsman,* (May, 1915), pp. 202-210.

"A New Appreciation of Greene and Greene," *Architectural Record,* (May, 1948), pp. 138-140.

"Pasadena Developers of California Type Homes to be Honored," *Pasadena Star-News,* (June 1, 1952), p. 26.

"Honored by AIA," *Architectural Forum*, (June, 1952), p. 64.

"AIA Citation," *AIA Journal*, (July, 1952), pp. 4, 5, ff.

"Henry Mather Greene," obituary. *Pasadena Star-News*, (October 6, 1954).

"California: The Emergence of a Tradition," *Architectural Record*, (May, 1956), pp. 16b, ff.

"Charles Sumner Greene," biography. *The National Cyclopaedia of American Biography*. New York: James T. White & Co., 1957, Vol. 48.

"Recognizing Our Own Architectural Traditions," *House Beautiful*, (January, 1957), pp. 54-59, ff.

"The Undiscovery Beauty of Our Recent Past," *House Beautiful*, (January, 1957), pp. 48-53.

"Charles Sumner Greene," obituary. *Architectural Record*, (August, 1957), p. 24.

Index

Acknowledgements

In addition to those persons identified in the Preface, appreciation is extended to the following for their varying roles and contribution during the research for this book.

Mr. and Mrs. George A. Adamson
Thomas Ahern
Mrs. Elliott Bandini
Jerry Barclay
Mrs. B. A. Behrend
Louise Bentz
Edward Blacker
Robert R. Blacker
Mr. and Mrs. Richard W. Bland
Mary Borgerding
Edward R. Bosley, III
Mr. and Mrs. George Brumder
James Burch
Jay E. Cantor
Mrs. Frank Carpenter
Theodore Cavagnaro
Mr. and Mrs. Andrew Chute
Alson Clark
Myrtle Clark
Mrs. Lorton L. Clough
Helen Cockroft
Leonard Collins
Marjorie Townsend Conley
Mr. and Mrs. Thomas C. Cotter
Mr. and Mrs. Harley Culbert

Pauline DeWitt
Mrs. Oliver Drake
Mr. and Mrs. Donald D. Duffy
Paul Duffy
Mr. and Mrs. W. K. Dunn
Mr. and Mrs. Conrad Escalante
Mrs. S. M. Falkenborg
Margaret Fay
Roy Flamm
Martin Flavin
Mr. and Mrs. Mortimer Fleishhacker, Jr.
Ebba Fox
Mr. and Mrs. Cecil H. Gamble
Mrs. Clarence J. Gamble
Mr. and Mrs. David G. Gamble
Mr. and Mrs. Edwin C. Gamble
Mr. and Mrs. James N. Gamble
Mr. and Mrs. Sidney D. Gamble
David H. Gauntlett
Marianne Ford Gough
Thomas Gould, Jr.
Miss E. Graber
Dr. and Mrs. William R. Grant
Bettie Greene
Isabelle Greene
Mr. and Mrs. H. P. Grider
Robert Donald Hall
Harwell Hamilton Harris
Nini Richardson Hart
Mr. and Mrs. Richard F. C. Hayden
Dr. Robert A. Heebner

Dorothy Brown Herbert
Mr. and Mrs. Vincent Heublein
Mr. and Mrs. Max Hill
Mrs. Guy E. Hodgkins
Mrs. Wallace Hurff
Mr. and Mrs. Henry Hutchins
Mrs. Howard F. Isham
Dr. and Mrs. Hart Issacs
Mr. and Mrs. Daniel L. James
Margaret Cole Jarecki
Mrs. John N. Jeffers
Peggy Johnson
Betty Keith
Dorothy Koenig
LuVerne LaMotte
Mr. and Mrs. Ellwood Lankford
Rozene Kerry Lawrence
Margaret Carver Leighton
Eleanor MacInich
Donald Maclain
Mr. and Mrs. L. A. McConnell
Mr. and Mrs. Michael McKee
Mr. and Mrs. C. Burke Maino
Robert Mardian
Patricia Marks
Mr. and Mrs. James Marrin
Dora Mayer
Mr. and Mrs. Kennon Meidema
Mrs. Stephen Mengos
Margaret Meriwether
Mrs. William B. Merwin

Elizabeth Gamble Messler
Dr. and Mrs. Joseph D. Messler
Mr. and Mrs. Kinsey Miller
Elizabeth Monning
Elliott Morgan
Mr. and Mrs. Robert Morris
Mrs. George K. Mullins
The Neighborhood Church
Donald Nollar
Mr. and Mrs. Gordon O. Norman
Mr. and Mrs. Richard A. Pauloo
Penny Penha
Josephine Pletscher
John W. Poole
Mr. and Mrs. Howard W. Porter
Mr. and Mrs. Edvin Remund
Mr. and Mrs. James Richardson
Mr. and Mrs. William B. Richardson
Martha Ann Savage
Mr. and Mrs. Raoul Savoie
Mary Gamble Scherr, Jr.
Helen Schevill
Margaret Halsted Seamans
Mr. and Mrs. Mark Serrurier
Julius Shulman
Thelma Siegel
Sigma Phi Fraternity, Alpha Chapter
Earle Simpson
Mr. and Mrs. Allen O. Smith
Dr. Francis F. Spreitzer
Mrs. Eugene Strand

Grace Sutherland
Mr. and Mrs. Harlan Swift (Margaret Gamble)
Isabella Tabor
Francene Thomas
Neville Thompson
Mr. and Mrs. J. Eric Thorsen
Mr. and Mrs. Arch Tuthill
Mr. and Mrs. Alfred Ulan
Karl W. Vancil
Mary Kew van der Pas
Agnes Vanderkloot
Mr. and Mrs. W. J. van Rossem
Harriette Von Breton
Arthur Waugh
Mr. and Mrs. Stevens Weller
Mr. and Mrs. Alexander Whittle
Robert Mosley Webster Williams
Elizabeth Townsend Winckler
Richard Hage Winckler
Carleton Winslow
Mr. and Mrs. Kenneth Wormhoudt
Mr. and Mrs. James S. Wyatt, Jr.

Designed and produced by Adrian Wilson, San Francisco
with the assistance of Joyce Lancaster Wilson,
Aleta Jenks and Maria Poythress Epes.

Composed by Twin Typographers, Salt Lake City.

Printed by George Waters Photolithography, San Francisco.

Bound by Mountain States Bindery, Salt Lake City.

GREENE & GREENE

GREENE & GREENE

Furniture and Related Designs

RANDELL L. MAKINSON

with photographs by Marvin Rand
including eight pages of color photographs

Salt Lake City

To Marvin Rand

Published by
Gibbs Smith, Publisher
P.O. Box 667
Layton, Utah 84041

Printed and bound in the United States of America

Library of Congress Cataloging-in-Publication Data
Makinson, Randell L., 1932-
    Greene & Greene: furniture and related designs / by Randell L.
Makinson.
       p. cm.
    Originally published: Peregrine Smith, 1979.
    Includes bibliographical references and index.
    ISBN 0-87905-060-8 (hbk.) ; ISBN 0-87905-125-6 (pbk.)
    1. Greene & Greene. 2. Arts and crafts movement—California.
3. Furniture design—California—History—20th century.
4. Decorative arts—California—History—20th century. I. Title.
II. Title: Greene and Greene
NK2439.G76M35 1997
749.213—dc21   97-6061
                                                   CIP

New photo-documentation for this book was carried out
under a grant from the National Endowment for the Humanities
in Washington, D.C., a Federal Agency. Opinions in the
text are the author's and do not necessarily represent the view
of the Endowment.

Contents

Preface

This book is written as a companion volume to *Greene and Greene—Architecture as a Fine Art* and deals with the furniture and related designs of both the firm and of Charles Sumner Greene and Henry Mather Greene independently. As the research progressed over the years it became more and more clear that the quantity of the furniture and related designs was so great that it could not be dealt with properly if included with the discussion of the development of the Greenes' architecture. Furthermore, the furniture and related designs of Greene and Greene are an art form in themselves and require the focus which separate attention places upon the subject. The extraordinary quality of design and craftsmanship, the changing character of the work, and the great variety of subjects designed by the brothers is dealt with chronologically and reviews the flexibility and speed of the brothers' quest for designs which to them appropriately paralleled the developments within their architectural work.

The phrase, Greene and Greene furniture, has been used too broadly over the years to identify the work for which they are best known. However, that era of the Greenes' designs was preceded and followed with equally significant works representative of the evolution of their talents, opportunities, and their joint and independent philosophies. Closely related are the abilities of those master craftsmen who virtually became a part of the Greene and Greene family—artisans whose individual talents coupled with their respect and devotion for the brothers transformed their two-dimensional dreams into reality.

The separate chapters of the book are so organized to focus upon the influences on the brothers and their early furniture designs, the short period of exploration and developments leading to their very personal design vocabulary, the opportunities which made possible the full unfolding of that unique style, the later period of changing client tastes, and finally the later works of each of the brothers as independent creative artists.

Over the years little has been written or published on the furnishings of the Greenes, inasmuch as most of the work has remained in private ownership and not available for public viewing. The single ongoing opportunity for public awareness of the Greenes' furnishings is the David B. Gamble house built in 1908 and bequeathed in 1966 to the City of Pasadena in a joint agreement with the University of Southern California. Since that time the opportunity for public visitation to the Gamble house has furthered the singular identification of Greene and Greene furniture with simple elegant forms, exquisite craftsmanship and finish, and the rhythmic patterns of square ebony pegs in the expressed joinery detailing. Not until the major exhibition "Greene and Greene: The Architecture and Related Designs of Charles Sumner Greene and Henry Mather Greene: 1894-1934" held at the Los Angeles Municipal Art Gallery in 1977, organized jointly by the Los Angeles Municipal Art Gallery and the University of Southern California, was there an opportunity to see the vast amount of interior work by the Greenes. Prior to that time the treatment of Greene and Greene furnishings and designs has had only the scant attention of a few short articles and the master's thesis by furniture designer John Caldwell. Following the exhibition there has been growing interest in this specialized area of the Greenes' creative talents with a technical article presently in process by Alan Marks for *Fine Woodworking* magazine featuring the systematized vernacular of the Greenes' furniture designs as a first truly American furniture expression.

The research for this study has come primarily from documents in the Greene and Greene Library, The Gamble House; the Documents Collection, College of Environmental Design, University of California at Berkeley; Avery Architectural Library, Columbia University; from members of the Greene and Hall families, the present owners of the furnishings studied; and from the enriching experience of exploring the work itself.

There are many to whom I am indebted for their genuine assistance in the research and preparation of this study and their names are listed in the acknowledgements in the rear of this volume.

I am indebted most deeply to Marvin Rand whose photographic genius has documented this study since 1958 and whose patience, genuine interest, valuable analytical comment and personal generosity have been of major importance in the production of this book; to Professor Emmet L. Wemple whose continuing council since the beginning has been invaluable to me and to the subject; to his and David Tilton's creative designs of the Greene and Greene exhibition and catalogue; to Virginia Ernst Kazor and Doris Gertmenian all of whom comprised the team which produced the exhibition; and to the National Endowment for the Arts which joined with the Los Angeles Municipal Arts Department and the School of Architecture and Fine Arts, University of Southern California who provided special funding for the exhibition.

Portions of this research have been carried out under grants from the American Institute of Architects whose Rehmann Fellowship in 1956 allowed for the early study and the National Endowment for the Humanities whose grant allowed for the photo-documentation of Greene and Greene furniture and related designs, a project carried out in association with Marvin Rand under the auspices of the School of Architecture and Fine Arts, University of Southern California.

Special appreciation for coordinated early research and assistance goes to Professors Robert Judson Clark and Robert W. Winter, Esther McCoy and Reynor Banham; to Margaret Nixon for her invaluable editing of the manuscript; Richard Firmage for his coordination of the production of the book, and to publishers Gibbs and Catherine Smith.

This portion of my overall research on Greene and Greene has been associated with my work as Curator of The Gamble House, University of Southern California. In this association special appreciation is expressed to Zohrab Kaprielian, Executive Vice President, Dr. Paul Hadley, Vice President Academic Affairs, University of Southern California; former Deans, Ralph Knowles and A. Quincy Jones, of the School of Architecture and Fine Arts; to Virginia Bissinger, Dr. Clark McCartney, Helen Carrier and the members of the Docent Council of The Gamble House.

In addition, for their invaluable assistance in obtaining

drawings and archive photographs, Dr. Adolf Placzek, Carol Falcione, Professors Kenneth Cardwell, Stephen Tobriner, and to Diane Favro, John Graves, Jay Cantor, L. Morgan Yost, LuVerne LaMotte, Edna Dunn, Mr. and Mrs. R. Donald Hall, Robert Hall, Gregson and Chad Hall, and Edward Bosley III.

Very special appreciation to those who made possible the study of the furniture, those kind owners who opened their households for study and photography; the members of the Greene families whose assistance was essential— Isabelle and Alan McElwain, Sumner and Harriott Greene, Ruth and the late Henry Dart Greene; Nathaniel and Genevieve Greene, Gordon and Betty Greene, and Bettie Greene.

For varying and special reasons James N. Gamble and the heirs of Cecil and Louise Gamble for the sharing of the Gamble family home with us all; to Irene Wright, Winifred Staniford, and the invaluable support of my secretary Jane Unruh whose understanding and added assistance has made this publication possible; to my father, Ronald R. Chitwood, and Paula and Harold Stewart whose encouragement has been essential; and finally very personal thanks to Emmet L. Wemple and David L. Tilton for their careful attention to the design of this book.

Randell L. Makinson
Pasadena

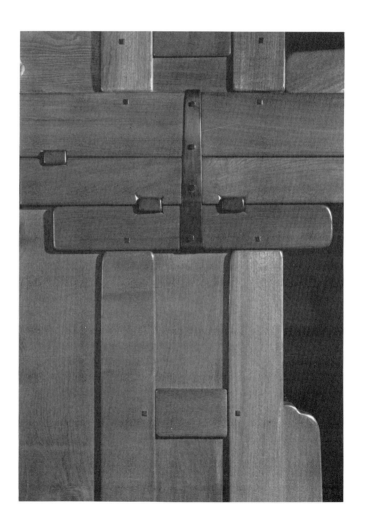

I

Influences and First Furniture Designs   1900-1904

Architects have always designed buildings, but before the latter half of the nineteenth century they had seldom so consciously and effectively related the scale of structure and the furniture to be placed within. The vigor and spirit of William Morris' philosophy and the developing Arts and Crafts Movement attracted vast numbers of individuals who had not previously been identified with the design of utilitarian objects. Homeowners and housewives were creating everything from stitchery to hammered copper pots. The times also witnessed the emergence of the architect as the designer and oftentimes maker of furniture. The Arts and Crafts Movement and the later Art Nouveau era emphasized the concepts of the artist's involvement with the full spectrum of design, be it interiors, furniture, carpets, everyday household items, or the visual and graphic arts. As a result, the fresh designs and superb craftsmanship based on Arts and Crafts principles — that design stemmed from function and form from the materials and tools used—effected the transition from the eclectic trappings of the Victorian era to the more homogeneous designs of the modern movement.

Among the Arts and Crafts Movement practitioners there were few as thoroughly and naturally devoted to its principles as California architects Greene and Greene. If composition and craftsmanship determine quality, then the Greenes were unsurpassed.

Although the major portion of the furniture and related designs were produced by the firm of Greene and Greene, Architects, these were primarily the expression of Charles Sumner Greene's creative imagination, encouraged by the support of his brother, Henry Mather Greene, and their close association with master craftsmen Peter and John Hall.

The Greenes achieved international recognition for their architectural vocabulary.[1] But the scope of their non-structural design has been largely overlooked. Even the phrase "Greene and Greene furniture" refers primarily to the furniture designed for their major residences—the ultimate bungalows — between 1907 and 1909, as these were the pieces which aroused the interest of photographers and writers. However, the Greenes' furniture and related designs spanned the period from 1900 to the mid-1930s and demonstrated their adaptability to change and the continuing development of their own philosophies and designs.

The first piece of furniture made by Charles Greene was a very simple dining table designed for his fiancée in 1900. The 48" square top was composed of geometric inlay patterns of scrap fruit woods, and cantilevered from a single straight square pedestal which flared at the base to give greater stability, and was attached with bolts and wing nuts to allow for easy and compact portability. This "wedding table" was significant not only for its direct design but also because it established Charles' early interest in the design and making of furnishings.

In the mid–1880s Charles had studied woodworking at the Manual Training High School in St. Louis. By the 1890s the Arts and Crafts Movement was in full swing. Yet this first piece of furniture did not appear until six years after the firm of Greene and Greene, Architects, had been established. Charles' delay in designing furnishings probably stemmed from the variety of his own interests; in letters to friends in Boston he often lamented the time taken up by the firm's practice which kept him from his pursuit of

---

1. In 1952 the brothers were presented with the coveted Citation from the national organization of The American Institute of Architects, at which time they were hailed as "Formulators of a New and Native Architecture."

Charles Sumner Greene, circa 1906.
Photograph courtesy of Los Angeles Public Library.

Henry Mather Greene, circa 1906.
Photograph courtesy of Los Angeles Public Library.

Right:
First furniture made by Charles Greene, designed for his fiance in 1900.
Marvin Rand photograph.

Below:

Breakfast room, George H. Barker house, Pasadena, 1902.
Photograph courtesy of Documents Collection,
College of Environmental Design, U.C.B.

The clean design of this dining table and its joinery suggest
early Greene and Greene design. However, the structure of the
chairs, the form of their backs and of the cross details, and
the curve of the legs of the server are out of character with
the Greenes' other work.

poetry, painting, and photography.[2] In addition, neither Charles nor Henry was apparently attracted by the flamboyance of the sinuous line found in much of the Art Nouveau work published in the *International Studio Magazine*. It was not until more ordered elements of that movement emerged that the Greenes' interest was aroused.

In the spring of 1901 Charles and his bride honeymooned in England and on the Continent. There is no record of his contact with the Arts and Crafts artists while he was abroad, but there is a clear change in the work of the firm in the two years after his return to California.

During his absence Henry had begun designs for a major estate for Senator George Huntington Barker in Pasadena, California. This grand design in a pseudo-Colonial Revival Style was for the firm a brief experiment with more historical forms; but, while the major portions of the interiors were developed along traditional lines, Charles finished several rooms in a more Arts and Crafts type character. The natural finished woods and straightforward furnishings of a study and secondary dining room presented a dramatic contrast to the elegant formality of the white painted formal spaces complemented with neo-classical furniture.

Some art historians see the furniture of the secondary dining room as evidence of early Greene and Greene designs. But although certain details of the table and server suggest this possibility, the chairs and overhead fixture cast considerable doubt on the theory.

At the turn of the century a principal means of communication and influence were the periodicals of the day. The *International Studio Magazine* was devoting much of its attention to the work of both recognized designers and unknown craftsmen. The Greenes' scrapbook contains clippings from the work of C.F.A. Voysey from the 1897 issues of the magazine as well as references to the work of Frank Lloyd Wright.[3] Although the scrapbook indicates the Greenes' early reading of individual issues of the magazine, Charles' personal library included a bound set of the *International Studio Magazine*. His notes in the bound volumes indicate that he pored over their contents throughout much of his life.

In the 1897 issue he made notations on the bronzes of the Flemish artist Constantin Meunier and entered into his scrapbook an illustration of a Voysey interior. His notations on another article entitled "Art in Gridirons" suggest a possible relationship between illustrations of German wrought iron and forms found repeatedly in the Greenes' later iron work. However, it is particularly interesting that he did not comment on an article which appeared in the same issue on Charles Rennie Mackintosh furniture.

Charles had undoubtedly seen in issues prior to 1900 other articles on the furniture designs of Mackintosh, M. H. Baillie Scott, J. Herbert McNair, C. R. Ashbee, Frank Brangwyn and others. And, beginning around 1900, articles began appearing on furniture designed along the lines that Gustav Stickley was to popularize which would later be identified as Mission or Craftsman furniture in the United States.

In 1901 in the published work of Josef Hoffmann in Vienna, more disciplined forms were emerging in the Art Nouveau Movement—highly ordered forms, based upon linear geometry, the repetition of the rectangle and the square, and a concern for the total unity of all parts of the design. While Hoffman was perhaps the most successful and influential of the Vienna Secessionists, the master of this philosophy was the Scotsman Mackintosh.

In that same year the *International Studio Magazine* was publishing the work of Peter Behrens with illustrations of rug and door designs which relate to forms seen in the Greenes' later work. Of equal importance in these issues was the scope of Arts and Crafts activity. The period was bursting with creative energy in all facets of design, architecture, silversmithing, stitchery, pottery, etc.

However, the publication which had the most dramatic impact on the Greenes was the first issue of Gustav Stickley's magazine *The Craftsman* which arrived in October 1901. That first issue must have exhilarated the Greenes for here was a man not only writing of a new Craftsman

---

2. Numerous letters by the brothers during the 1890s are housed in the Documents Collection, Greene and Greene Library, The Gamble House.

3. Greene and Greene Library.

Design by the Vienese architect, Josef Hoffmann, c. 1900.

Following several of his contemporaries at the turn of the century, Josef Hoffmann embraced the concept of total relation of his architecture and furnishings. Like those of Charles Rennie Mackintosh, the linearity and geometric repetition in his designs were a dramatic contrast with the more sinuous forms of the Art Nouveau movement.

philosophy in America but also producing furniture of the highest quality and workmanship. Of his new association Stickley wrote:

> The United Crafts endeavor to promote and to extend the principles established by [William] Morris, in both the artistic and socialistic sense...Present tendencies are toward a simplicity unknown in the past....The form of any object is made to express the structural idea directly, frankly, often almost with baldness.[4]

4. Excerpts from *The Craftsman*, Volume 1, no. 1, October 1901, pages i, 47.

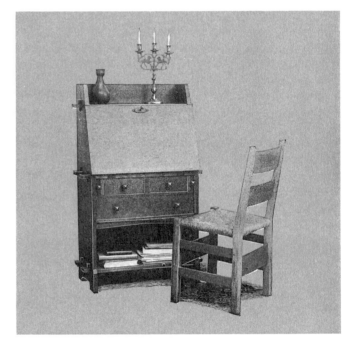

Illustration of Gustav Stickley's furniture from the first issue of his magazine *The Craftsman*.

The Greenes' chair design for the Jennie A. Reeve dining room and the desk for Adalaide Tichenor, both in 1904, show clearly the influence which the first issues of *The Craftsman* had upon their own designs.

Within a few months the Greenes furnished much of the James Culbertson house in Stickley's furniture, selecting the very pieces that had appeared in the first two issues of *The Craftsman*.

Stickley's influence upon the Greenes went far beyond the mere use of his "United Crafts" furniture, and can be clearly seen in the interiors and furniture designs of the Greenes' work between 1902 and 1904.[5]

5. Gustav Stickley later dropped the term "United Crafts" in deference to the identification "Craftsman" furniture with notice to his readers to look for his name associated—a reference to copies of his work by others including his own family.

View of living room, James A. Culbertson house, 1902. Photograph courtesy of Mrs. Edna Dunn.

Charles Greene's early interest in Oriental timber structure as expressed in the corbels of the bay window and in the ceiling detail is blended with the rigid linearity of Henry Greene's clear leaded glass window designs and Stickley's craftsman furniture.

17

Illustrations from the Greenes' scrapbook of their clippings from the series of articles by Will Bradley which appeared in the *Ladies Home Journal* between November 1901 and August 1902. Courtesy Greene and Greene Library.

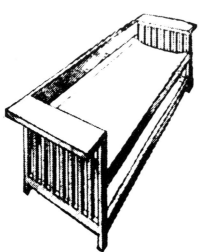

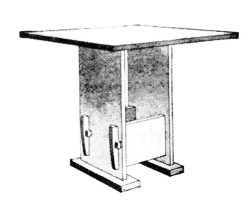

Meanwhile, the Turin Exhibition of Decorative Arts in 1902 was extensively covered by the *International Studio Magazine*. Notations in Charles' handwriting appear on many of the articles and illustrations of the exhibition and indicate his particular interest in the design of the interior furnishings.

Between November of 1901 and August 1902 a series of articles on interior and furniture design by Will Bradley appeared in the *Ladies Home Journal* which also promoted the ideals of the Arts and Crafts Movement. Bradley, unlike the Greenes, was interested in the sinuous line of Art Nouveau, although for him it appeared to be more of a stylistic decoration applied to the surface of designs having the straightforward integrity of Stickley furniture rather than the more flambouyant extravagances found in European Art Nouveau work. The Bradley articles must have touched a nerve in the Greenes for numerous illustrations from his series were carefully clipped and pasted into their scrapbook. Although the Greenes never adopted the Art Nouveau characteristics of Bradley's furniture, his ideas, combined with the stimulus from *The Craftsman,* are directly related to the changing character of their work.

As the Greenes were moving rapidly into the Arts and Crafts Movement, a series of articles by Harvey Ellis, beginning in *The Craftsman* in July of 1903, presented his concepts of the interrelationship of design, architecture and furnishings. While architecturally there was little similarity between the work of Ellis and the Greenes, his illustrations seem to have stimulated their own involvement with interior design and furnishings.

Of particular note is the Ellis illustration of a music room utilizing two-dimensional patterns of squares in wall surface detail. These, like Hoffmann's illustration, were more graphic than architectural and came off more as decoration. But the Greenes' treatment was functional, three-dimensional and a structural part of an overall design. The square and rectangular pegs which later became a signature of Greene designs were working parts of an articulated joinery which fit together not unlike a Chinese puzzle.

Thus, whereas the Greenes' exposure to some of the geometric directions of the Arts and Crafts Movement was through the periodicals of the day and to a more two-dimensional graphic pattern, their own response was closer to the three-dimensional designs of Charles Rennie Mackintosh. The Greenes' work of 1905 is more closely related to Mackintosh's wood detailing of the wall paneling for Queens Cross Church in 1897 than to any other structure. While there is no documentaion of any association or correspondence between Greene and Greene and Charles Rennie Mackintosh, their works suggest a natural identification between the two firms.

Woodshop and portion of rear of Charles Greene's home in Pasadena c. 1903, from the rear garden of the White sisters' house. Photograph courtesy Greene and Greene Library.

Living room of the home of Charles' sisters-in-law, Martha, Violet and Jane White, Pasadena, 1903. Photograph courtesy Documents Collection, College of Environmental Design, U.C.B.

To complement the White sisters' furnishings the Greenes designed the tea table (center), the built-in fireside bench, and appear to have made an attempt to shield the glare from the new electric lighting fixtures.

The first furniture designs for clients were for Charles' sisters-in-law, Martha, Violet and Jane White, whose house the Greenes had designed and built next to the house of Charles. In addition to the total development of the interior of the dining room, Charles designed a small table for the living room along the lines of Stickley's craftsman furniture. But, influenced as he was by Stickley's work, he added his own personal touch in the subtle variations in the lines of the border.

Charles wrote an article for *The Western Architect* in which he commented on the White sisters' house and revealed his accord with Arts and Crafts unified design principles:

The dining room is wainscotted in deep toned redwood to the height of doors, and hung with a few old prints.

There is a fireplace and on each side of it, a small china closet with doors paneled below and leaded above. The large window in front has a fine view of the mountains. A shelf over the fireplace and china closets holds several Japanese pieces of old Imari blue.

At the east end of the room there is a broad window ledge containing a little aquarium specially designed to accord with the room and its furniture of birch. This latter was treated to harmonize with redwood. The top of the table is finished to use without a cloth, and neither heat nor water will damage it. The rest of the furniture was designed to fit the room.[6]

6. "Bungalows—by Charles Sumner Greene, Architect," *The Western Architect*, Volume 12, No. 1, p. 4.

Living room tea table, White sisters' house, Pasadena, 1903. Marvin Rand photograph.

Though the designs of Gustav Stickley's ''Mission'' furniture strongly affected the Greenes' earliest works, Charles' personal variations were evident in the projections of the pegged joinery and in the line of two of the edges of the top of the tea table.

Wall lighting fixture, Josephine van Rossem
house No. 1, Pasadena, 1903.
Marvin Rand photograph.

Interior sketch, Mary R. Darling house, Claremont,
California, 1903.
Academy Architecture, 1903.

Charles' sketch for *Academy Architecture* magazine reveals
clearly the influence which *The Craftsman* magazine had upon
his own interior design concepts in 1903.

Next door, in the upstairs bedrooms of the Josephine
van Rossem house, the first lighting fixtures designed by
the firm featured several wall sconces of redwood blocks
which were detailed into the board and batt paneling.
Though extremely basic, these wall brackets were the be-
ginnings of a succession of varied lighting refinements over
the years incorporating leaded glass lanterns, tiffany glass,
favrile shades, and occasionally lighting shielded with a
folded fabric of silk pongee.

Charles' interior sketches for the Mary R. Darling house
published in *Academy Architecture,* 1903, II, reveal not only
his desire to control the design of the whole interior and
its furnishings, but also the influence which *The Craftsman*
had upon him at the time. The furniture designs and his
drawings for lamps, carpets, andirons, etc. all follow the
pattern of those either designed by Stickley or recom-
mended and advertised in *The Craftsman* as appropriate for
bungalow living. And, like the drawings of Hoffmann and
Ellis, Charles' sketches covered every aspect of the interior,
the built-in cabinetry, shelving, window seats, fabric designs, and picture frames, all harmonizing with the overall
architectural statement of the space.

Little if any of the furniture in the sketches for the Darling house was built, but the Greenes were already committed to the idea of including every facet of furnishings
in the design of interiors.

Early the following year, this commitment was demonstrated in the house for Jennie A. Reeve in Long Beach,
California. The Greenes designed the furniture, built-in
cabinetry, lighting, leaded stained glass and the detail in
the wet plaster of the friezes as well as the outside lighting,
fencing and landscaping—all of which related to the architectural character of the structure.

The first photographs illustrating the Greenes' full control of interiors were of the Reeve house. The dining room
photographs reveal the speed with which they combined
their personal artistic talent with their newly acquired
craftsman attitudes to produce a completed space, highly
organized and dominated by their own innovations. The
influence of Stickley remained, but already there were distinct differences.

Dining room, Jennie A. Reeve house,
Long Beach, California, 1904.
Photograph courtesy Documents Collection,
College of Environmental Design, U.C.B.

In 1904 Stickley's influence is dramatic in the
chair and dining table, but Charles' imagination
and creative flair are revealed in the combined gas
and electric wall lighting fixture, and in the design
of the ceiling lantern and leaded glass. His playful
watercolor details in the plaster frieze reveal the
relaxed confidence which he had so quickly
developed.

Living room inglenook, Jennie A. Reeve house,
1904. Photograph courtesy Documents Collection,
College of Environmental Design, U.C.B.

The Greenes' interior art flourished so rapidly
that the quality of cabinetwork detailing, craftsmanship and leaded glass work usually identified
with the major houses of later years was in fact
being practiced in 1904 as evidenced by the curio
cabinet of the living room inglenook.

Far left:
Bedroom bureau, Jennie A. Reeve
house, 1904.
Marvin Rand photograph.
Left:
Joinery detail of bedroom bureau.
Marvin Rand photograph.

The bold expression of mortise
and tenon joinery and projecting
pegs softened by gently rounding
the edges enriched the Greenes'
furniture designs, added an honest
decorative element, provided a
sensitive variation to the scale and
proportions of their designs and
ultimately became, in more refined
stages, a signature of their work.

Interior lantern, Jennie A. Reeve house, 1904.
Marvin Rand photograph.

The Greenes' early technique for gaining variation to the
leading design was to overlay the lead came between the glass
with sheet lead cut in the designed pattern and attached
with solder.

In the table and buffet design the wood pegging pro-
truded slightly and then was softened by gently rolling the
cut ends of the pegs. As a result, the joinery not only was
a more direct expression of the nature of the construction
but also produced a decorative rhythm and variation.
Simple as the expressed joinery was, it became one of the
key characteristics of the Greenes' entire structural philosophy in both their architecture and their furniture. They
also designed the china cabinet doors of leaded clear glass,
and wall lighting brackets with leaded glass lanterns—a
considerable refinement over the van Rossem wall lights
just a few months before—including a gas jet for use when
the new electric power failed.

Throughout the house hanging lanterns of leaded glass
were capped by broad copper hoods which hinted of the
Orient. The built-in seating in the fireplace inglenook of
the living room was to be repeated again and again in the
Greene interiors. A close inspection of the photograph of
this inglenook reveals a level of refinement in the glass
and cabinet detail which has not generally been attributed
to the Greenes until their work on the elaborate bungalows
several years later.

There is a sense of freshness and experiment in the Reeve house. This is suggested by the variety of techniques used in handling the leaded glass work. For the lighting fixtures, designs were cut out of sheet lead and laid over the major portions of the leaded glass. A different treatment of handling lead is found in the stained glass window at the foot of the stairway. Here there is a seeming conflict in the abstraction of the design. The upper part is a more traditional representation of a mountain-ocean scene complete with sea gulls over which runs an abstract vertical stylized plant pattern. In contrast, the bottom panels are considerably more abstract in their depiction of flower and stem and relate more closely to similar designs by Charles Rennie Mackintosh, Harvey Ellis and Elbert Hubbard. A third and more refined handling of leading is found in the clear glass of the curio cabinet in the living room which deals more lyrically with line and scale.

The chest of drawers in oak and cedar clearly demonstrates the brevity of Stickley's initial dominant influence on the Greenes' furniture design. Here the design demonstrates Charles' early training and his firm belief in the expression of the role of all component parts. Joinery components of mortise and tenon and cross pegging became decorative elements—so boldly honest as to be potentially clumsy were it not for their gentle shaping, scale and finish which transformed them into a form of sculpture. Even the drawer pulls and wooden keyhole plates were direct, but with a rhythm which adds interest and variation to the overall design. The contrast between this approach and the two-dimensional applied decorative features of many of their contemporaries distinguished the Greenes' work and accounts in part for their delay in responding to the flood of furniture designs by those enamoured with the ornateness of Art Nouveau designs.

Stained glass window at the stair landing, Jennie A. Reeve house. Marvin Rand photograph.

The versatility of Charles Greene's furniture and interior designs and his ability not only to adapt to change but, more importantly, to seek out and create change was dramatically illustrated in his work for Adelaide Tichenor, whose home was also built in Long Beach shortly after the Reeve house in 1904.

The Tichenor furniture marked a distinct change of direction, an end to the first era in the Greenes' furniture designs, and a real break with the influence of Gustav Stickley. Nearly the entire furnishings of the household were his to create or select. This was not an easy task. Charles believed in the value of inspired client participation and once wrote that "the intelligence of the owner as well as the ability of the architect and skill of the contractor limit the perfection of the result."[7] But Mrs. Tichenor challenged him constantly, as their correspondence shows, and forced him to stretch his creative imagination and talents to the fullest.

The Tichenor furniture was closely related to earlier designs. The crisp directness of form and the lack of applied decoration remains. The bold expression of the joinery was almost raw. What did change were the materials, design and spirit. Ash was the primary wood with oak used only for the doweling. Soft stains which disappeared when oiled were washed into the grains, leaving a very subtle tone to the coloration in the grain of the wood.

7. *Ibid.*

Bedroom bureau, Adelaide Tichenor house, Long Beach, California, 1904. Marvin Rand photograph.

In a refinement on the earlier design for the Reeve bureau, Charles made use of his interest in the Orient by incorporating the "lift" or abstract cloud forms in his design of the Tichenor bureau to soften the otherwise straight lines, thus giving a more graceful appearance.

What wrenched Charles from his earlier precedents and established a recognizable Greene and Greene style was his effort to blend subtly curved forms into an otherwise linear composition and, by combining an honest use of joinery giving interest and variation, arriving at a less harsh overall effect. He accomplished this with such finesse that there was no need for applied decoration.

The softened lines of these designs were derived from an interest in Oriental culture shared by both Charles and Mrs. Tichenor. For the first time he incorporated the "lift" into the movement of line—a form long used by the Oriental craftsman as an abstraction of the cloud form. In Charles' work the lift acknowledged his respect for the Oriental arts but at the same time incorporated the freshness which sprang from the spirit of personal expression in Southern California.

Over the years, a wide range of curvilinear forms became one of the major characteristics of the Greenes' architecture, furniture and leaded glass designs. The lift form as handled by both Charles and Henry Greene was distinct. The departure from the total use of the straight line removed the harsh architectural character often associated with furniture designed by architects and, instead, created pieces with a scale and appearance more humanly pleasing.

Charles' confidence in his own talents is evident in the playful way he wove decorative humor throughout the interior furnishings. Mrs. Tichenor's interest in the owl resulted in an abstracted silhouette in the design of the escutcheons for the door hardware, in the brass back panel of a bedroom washstand and in the leather panels of a large four panel screen.

In spite of the rapport and artistic respect shared by Mrs. Tichenor and the Greenes, the correspondence between them revealed very human responses to the progress of the work and the details of the designs. At times Mrs. Tichenor grew impatient. In a letter about the screen she wrote: "Can you leave your Pasadena customers long enough so that I may hope to have my house during my life time? Do you wish me to make a will telling who is to have the house if it is finished?"[8]

8. Correspondence of September 27, 1905. Courtesy Robert Judson Clark and the Documents Collection, College of Environmental Design, U.C.B.

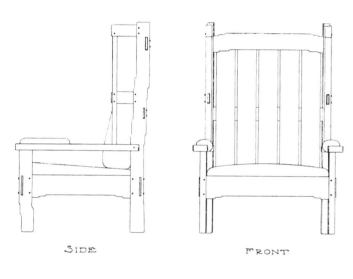

SIDE

FRONT

PLAN

BED ROOM CHAIR

TICHENOR HOUSE

Bedroom wingback chair, Adelaide Tichenor house, 1904. Drawing courtesy Documents Collection, College of Environmental Design, U.C.B.

This was the first of a series of designs for wingback chairs, each of which is handled quite differently, indicating Charles' fascination with wingback concepts.

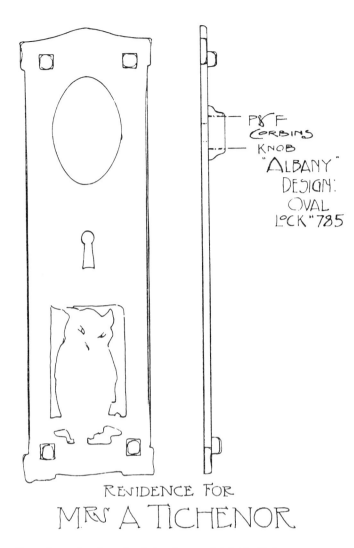

P & F
CORBINS
KNOB
"ALBANY"
DESIGN:
OVAL
LOCK #785

REVIDENCE FOR
MRS A TICHENOR

Escutcheon for door knob hardware, Adelaide Tichenor house, 1904.
Drawing courtesy of Documents Collection,
College of Environmental Design, U.C.B.

The incorporation of the owl motif in the door hardware and in other furnishings throughout the house reveals the humor of both client and architect.

The screen is one example of Charles' imagination. Here the mundane need for hinge hardware was handled by Charles in such a way as to become the most dominant feature of the entire composition, a characteristic to be repeated throughout his career. It directly expressed its function; yet the design went much further, combining function and aesthetics. The hinge is dominant and in its interlacings allowed for total flexibility in folding the parts of the screen in any direction. The detailing was far from being the easiest solution, but the end result suggested simplicity.

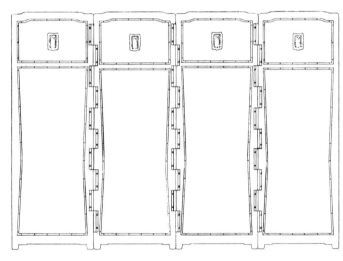

SCREEN WITH LEATHER PANELS.

Leather paneled screen, Adelaide Tichenor house, 1904.
Drawing courtesy Documents Collection,
College of Environmental Design, U.C.B.

The handling of the necessary hinging for the folding screen so that it gives the primary character and enrichment to the design, was a typical and sought-after characteristic of Greene design.

The piece of furniture in the Tichenor house which best expresses the refinement in furniture design from 1904 to 1907 is a dropfront desk. The drawing itself, a beautiful graphic composition, tells the whole story. The desk is straightforward, but far removed from the Stickley linearity. Soft sculptured forms weave into the side panels and project above as bookends. Butterfly cabinet joinery, the cleted door construction, carefully organized expressed brass screw heads, and the lift of the drawer pulls complement each other in an honest but decorative manner. Here there was no need for applied decoration. Even the vertical side elements which break up the flatness of the side panels are working parts of a concealed compartment in the rear of the desk.

The boldly decorative utilization of basic structural joinery is characteristic of all of the Tichenor furniture. It is also characteristic of the Greenes' overall philosophy and speaks for the disciplined hand which Henry Greene exercised upon the later work. Charles' imagination and love for intricate detail benefitted from this restraining influence to retain the direction of the early furniture designs.

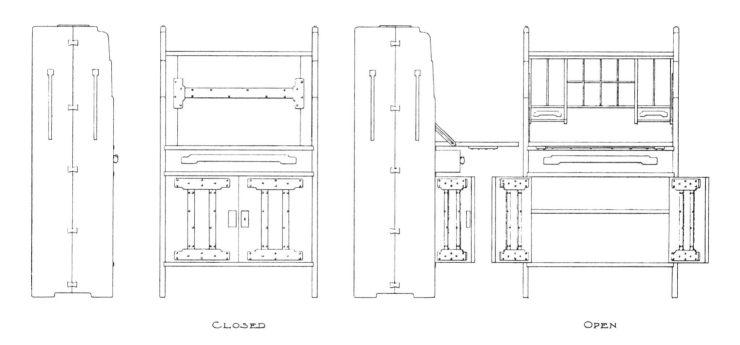

CLOSED   OPEN

DESK

Writing desk, Adelaide Tichenor house.
Drawing courtesy Documents Collection,
College of Environmental Design, U.C.B.

No ornament or furniture design better indicates the Greenes' break from the straight lines of Stickley's earlier influence. Use of curved lines, inlay joinery, and bold sculptural expression of the parts comprising the total design had now established a distinct Greene and Greene style.

Writing desk, Adelaide Tichenor house.
Marvin Rand photograph.

The Tichenor writing desk is a pivotal
piece of furniture representative of the
first era of a distinct Greene furniture style.

Above :
Stained and leaded glass, Adelaide Tichenor house.

Right:
Wall lighting fixture, Adelaide Tichenor house.
Marvin Rand photographs.

In one year's time the development of wall sconce designs
had progressed from the brusque ruggedness of those for the
first van Rossem house (1903) to this which added the
refinements of leaded Tiffany glass and fixtures integrally
related to motifs carried out in the interior and furnishings.

   In addition to the furniture, the Tichenor house exhibited
a maturing of lighting fixture designs and utilization of
stained glass leading techniques which gave Charles greater
options in his compositions. Thin sheet lead was cut out in
patterns desired and attached to the interior leaf of the lead
came between the pieces of stained glass. In so doing
Charles had full variation in the width of line and he used
this effectively to more freely express the vine patterns of
the dining room windows and the special composition of
seagulls in flight for the windows of the downstairs bedroom. Further, by carefully selecting pieces of Tiffany glass
with orange and blue combined, the silhouette of the sheet
lead overlay gave the feeling of the gulls in flight at sunset
over the ocean just outside. In composition, quality of glass,
and in the craftsmanship of fabrication, the stained glass

Copper wall clock, Adelaide
Tichenor house, 1904.
Marvin Rand photograph.

No element of the house
escaped Charles' and his
client's attention. The clock
adds further example of
the firm's concern for graphic
composition.

lanterns for the wall lighting fixtures represented a considerable refinement over those just a few months earlier for Jennie A. Reeve. Here too the "lift" softens the design which combines linear abstraction with curvilinear form within the same fixture.

One of the most unique elements within the house was a wall clock in hammered copper in which Charles worked with the forms of the numbers giving the overall design a free and playful character. Like the interiors, the Greenes fully handled the garden design and this more than the house and furnishings interpreted oriental influences more directly. Following an urgent request from Mrs. Tichenor, Charles made a special trip to the Louisiana Purchase Exposition in St. Louis to see the handling of woods which he liked very much and for the selection of interior furnishings. There his orders for the house included fabrics, pieces of Grueby pottery and some special tiles to be used in the interior detail.

Isolated examples of individual pieces of furniture carry even further the forthright structural character of Charles' work. The shelving and settle designed for the Arturo Bandini bungalow in 1903 were almost brutally straightforward. But a similar settle for Edgar W. Camp the following year shows a dramatic softening of the overall character. Here the arms were tapered and shaped to flare in response to their function and the joinery and the edges of the wood members were rolled. The lines of the bookshelving integrated into the wall paneling were likewise softened and sculpted.

In the short span of just two years, 1902–1904, the firm had entered into and become a significant part in the Arts and Crafts Movement in America. The Greenes were of course influenced by the publications of the day; but at the same time they were constantly exploring, developing, changing and refining their work and eagerly drawing from new clients the challenges which would drive them on to greater achievements.

In the two years following the Tichenor designs, the Greenes' continuing interest in Oriental art and their association with several highly gifted craftsmen would give added impetus to the variety and refinement of their furniture until they were producing art forms which established them among the foremost figures of the Arts and Crafts Movement in America.

Table lamp, Adelaide M. Tichenor house, 1904.
Courtesy of Documents Collection,
College of Environmental Design, UCB.

This lamp was the first of the few table lamps designed by the Greenes. The lamp shade depicts ocean scenes and is one of the rare designs where Greene and Greene reflect the popular forms of the Art Nouveau.

II

Developments in Design and Craftsmanship 1904-1907

In the early years Charles and Henry had considerable difficulty in finding craftsmen sufficiently skilled to meet their very high standards of workmanship. In the Pasadena area there were no cabinet shops equipped with the tools, machinery, and trained personnel to produce their custom designed furniture. It is not known where the Tichenor and other earlier pieces were actually built. In 1905, however, they became associated with the master woodscraftsmen Peter and John Hall and with the leaded glass artisan Emil Lange. It was the combined talents of these three men in collaboration with numerous other craftsmen whom the Greenes attracted which made possible the fine quality as well as the quantity of Greene and Greene furnishings during the next six years.

Peter and John Hall were born in Stockholm, Sweden—Peter in 1867 and John in 1864. By 1871 the Hall family had moved to Illinois and finally settled in Rock Falls. Neither Peter nor John had any formal training in woodworking; both were essentially self-taught craftsmen.

Peter came to Pasadena in 1886 and within a few years had won recognition as the best stair builder on the West Coast. Between 1889 and 1892 he worked in Seattle and Port Townsend, Washington. He then returned to Pasadena at the request of Charles Armstrong Roberts, a painting contractor, to do the stair and mantelwork for the large residence of Professor Thaddius Lowe. Here he met Roberts' daughter, Lida Alice, who rode down to the Lowe house every week with the payroll, and a little more than a year later they were married.

Meanwhile John Hall had followed his brother to the West Coast. His pencil sketches indicate his major role in the design and work on the woodcarving for the new courthouse in Port Townsend: the commission that had taken Peter north from Pasadena. John was a sensitive and somewhat retiring artist. In later years he preferred to work for his brother rather than to assume a leadership role. Nevertheless, his creative drive was as vigorous as that of Charles Greene and had been apparent at an early age. His first designs were dated 1880, when he was sixteen, and many of these were sketches for his carvings.

During the 1890s Peter and John Hall were employed by the Pasadena Manufacturing Company. In 1897 Peter held the position of bench hand and John that of carpenter. By 1899 John was foreman, doing additional carvings for work in Port Townsend as well as designing numerous houses on his own. In 1900 Peter was working on his own as a stair-builder; two years later he became a building contractor.[1]

Peter Hall met Charles and Henry Greene while he was engaged in the modifications for the first Dr. William T. Bolton house which had been designed by the Greenes. The three men developed a great respect for one another as artist craftsmen, and it has been generally assumed that Charles and Henry induced Peter Hall to build and equip his own shop in order to handle the specialized work then on the Greenes' drawing boards. On June 15, 1906, within a few months of meeting the Greenes, Peter Hall took out

1. Information on Peter and John Hall has been compiled from interviews with Leonard W. Collins, senior draftsman for Greene and Greene; with Mrs. Guy E. Hodgkins, Mr. and Mrs. R. Donald Hall, Mr. and Mrs. Robert Hall, Mr. and Mrs. Gary Hall, Gregson and Chad Hall, members of Peter Hall's family; and from members of the John Hall family.

a building permit for the construction of a one-story carpentry shop for himself to be located at 900 South Raymond Ave., Pasadena. Meanwhile, his first work for the Greenes was minor alterations to the Todd Ford house. This commission was immediately followed by the contract for the construction and furnishings for one of the Greenes' most important works, the Henry M. Robinson house.

While the Greenes were demanding more and more from woodcraftsmen, they were also attempting to refine the process of leading in Charles' stained glass designs. The limitation of the uniform dimension of the leading had prompted Charles to improvise by using cut sheet lead as an overlay in order to add greater variation in line width and form. As effective as this was, it lacked refinement when related to the Greenes' woodwork. Therefore, in their search for a master glass fabricator, the Greenes approached the firm of Sturdy-Lange.

Emil Lange had come from a Milwaukee brewing family and had worked for some years in the leaded glass shop of Louis Comfort Tiffany's Studios in New York. Tiffany was at that time the leading figure in the production of quality glass and in the development of new techniques in fabrication. It was in his shop that Lange learned new techniques and developed his skills. After he came to California and went into business with Harry Sturdy, Lange was reputed to have the best supply of Tiffany irridescent glass in Los Angeles. Later he became more widely known for the leading techniques which he developed in response to Charles Greene's search for improved means to effect his glass designs.

Little is known of Sturdy and there is no indication of any personal association between him and the Greenes. But Emil Lange was to become part of the Greene "family" of master craftsmen. Like Peter Hall, Lange's first major work for Greene and Greene was for the Henry M. Robinson house.

There were numerous other master craftsmen whose combined talents and respect for Charles and Henry Greene would make possible some of the finest examples of Arts and Crafts furniture in America. Among them, however, Peter and John Hall and Emil Lange stood out as the major support in the Greenes' quest for excellence.

Peter Hall circa 1910.
Photograph courtesy of Mr. and Mrs. Robert Donald Hall

John Hall circa 1920.
Photograph courtesy of Mr. and Mrs. Robert Donald Hall.

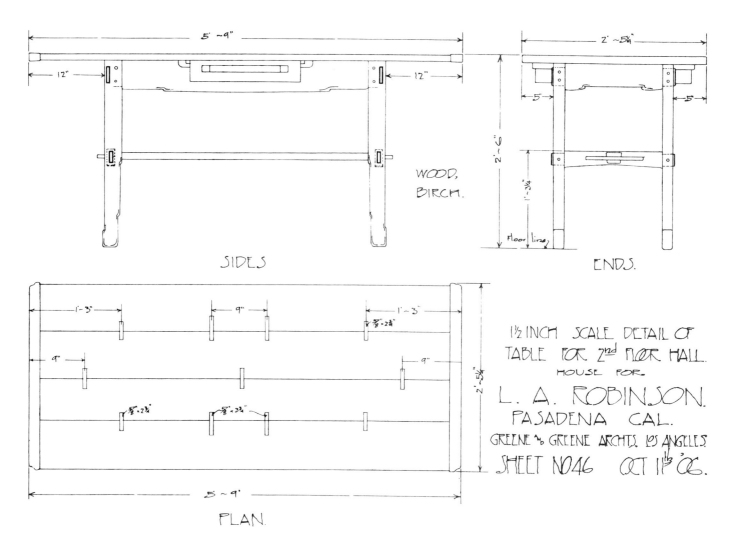

SIDES

ENDS.

WOOD, BIRCH.

PLAN.

1½ INCH SCALE DETAIL OF TABLE FOR 2ND FLOOR HALL. HOUSE FOR.
L. A. ROBINSON. PASADENA CAL.
GREENE & GREENE ARCHTS. LOS ANGELES
SHEET NO 46   OCT 11TH '06.

Drawing of table for second floor hall, Henry M. Robinson house, Pasadena, 1906.
Drawing courtesy Avery Architectural Library.

While this and other designs for the Robinson furniture related closely to the late period of the Greenes' early style, the living and dining room pieces introduced new directions and further refinements in detailing, materials and form.

Between the Tichenor house and furnishings of 1904 and the ultimate bungalows between 1907 and 1909, the most significant commission was the large home and furnishings for Henry M. Robinson begun in 1905. Here, as with their other wealthy clients, the Greenes were given ample creative opportunity, and Charles was able to continue refining his furniture and related designs. The Robinson furniture is a delicate blend of Charles' earlier ideas with the later refinements which broke completely with previous designs and set the stage for a distinct style.

Four designs in particular bear a close relationship to the furniture for Mrs. Tichenor a year earlier: a desk and library table for the den, the second-floor hall table of birch, and the entry hall seat of white cedar and oak. To some students of Greene and Greene furniture these pieces represent a closer tie to the philosophies of the Arts and Crafts Movement and are therefore held in higher regard than some of the later and more refined designs. Like the Reeve and Tichenor furniture, they possess a directness in form, joinery and materials identified with the more modest bungalow designs.

Entry hall shoe bench, 1906.
Courtesy of Documents Collection, College of Environmental Design, UCB.

Joinery of both the bench and the stairwell construction were carefully interrelated.

Library table for den, 1906.
Marvin Rand photograph.

The simple graceful lines of the den table elegantly bridge the two stylistic concepts within the Robinson furnishings.

Two important elements—materials and form—dramatically separated the living room and dining room pieces from all previous furniture by the firm. In both areas fine mahogany woods were used for the first time. Mahogany was used subsequently over a long period of time. Second, and just as important, was the carry-over from the Tichenor furniture of Charles' interest in Oriental forms. However, here he was strongly influenced by Chinese household furniture forms dating as far back as four centuries. This is particularly felt in the dining chairs and the living room couch. Moreover, Charles' fascination with Japanese temple structural joinery was demonstrated in the base of the Robinson dining table, the top of which became a form frequently used for dining tables for later clients. The Oriental influence was also suggested in the rest of the living room furniture.

Dining room armchair, 1906.
Marvin Rand photograph.

In a sudden and major departure from earlier concepts, the Robinson dining chairs took their forms almost directly from Chinese household furniture dating back as far as four centuries.

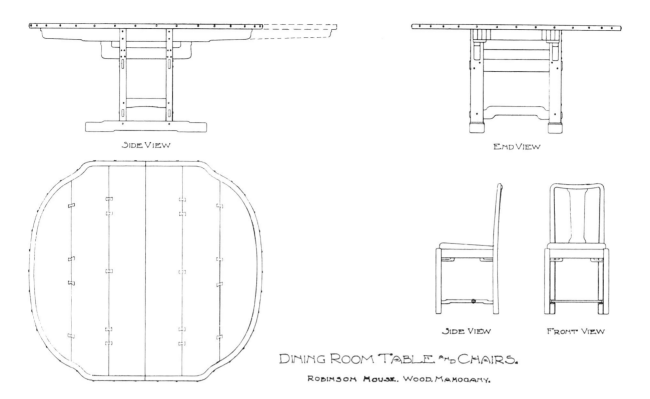

SIDE VIEW

END VIEW

SIDE VIEW FRONT VIEW

DINING ROOM TABLE and CHAIRS.

ROBINSON HOUSE. WOOD. MAHOGANY.

Drawing for dining table and chairs, 1906.
Drawing courtesy Documents Collection, College of Environmental Design, U.C.B.

Clean, simple lines of the table pedestal reflect the Greenes' regard for temple construction and at the same time provide for the stability necessary for extending the table to double its length without separating the supportive structure. The 'cloud lift' interpretation given to the form of the top of the table was repeated several times for other clients; however, in each instance the supporting bases were different.

Right:
Dining table, 1906.
Marvin Rand photograph.

Left:
Wall gas lighting fixture, 1906.
R. L. Makinson photograph.

Due to frequent breakdowns in power and as a carry-over of tradition gas lighting was often installed and detailed to blend with the electric lighting fixtures.

Clear leaded glass windows of upper level of entry hall, 1906. Whitland Locke photograph.

The Robinson house was also a testing ground for leaded stained glass, lighting fixtures, andirons, as well as the overall development of the house. Particularly interesting is the variation in these elements within the same structure. Some elements are far more sophisticated than others and yet all seem quite appropriate in their own places.

The den related far more to earlier and more rustic designs while the dining and living rooms reached new levels of refinement. The leaded glass compositions for the den suggest some of the glass designs of Frank Lloyd Wright which were sometimes carried out by Orlando Giannini. That Giannini might have been involved in the fabrication of the den windows of the Robinson house is not entirely out of the question for he was in Pasadena on commissions for other architects during that period. However, the glass work for the entry windows and for the major lighting fixtures has a distinctly different character and appears to have been the first work of Emil Lange for Greene and Greene.

The chandeliers and the major lighting fixtures of stained glass for the Robinson house marked a new era for the Greenes. Lighting design no longer dealt with the mere housing of the bulbs. It became a sculptured art form and had a major impact upon the character of the interior spaces. One of the most unusual features was the dining room chandelier which combined mosaic leaded irridescent glass with a highly sensitive and graceful mahogany framework. It was suspended from a more direct craftsman-era cedar ceiling plate of a fairly large size, and equipped with weights of boxes in mahogany with finger lap and ebony square peg joinery to allow the entire fixture to raise and lower by a system of suspended leather straps.[2] In the hands of one less sensitive than Charles Greene, such a complex concoction of forms and elements could have been disastrous. In his hands it became a beautiful and sensitive work of art.

2. The use of the square ebony peg identified with the Greenes' work appears first in the furniture for Dr. and Mrs. William T. Bolton and that for Mrs. Belle Barlow Bush in 1906. However, the shaping of the ebony pegs of the Robinson chandelier is representative of the refinement of 1907, suggesting that the interior furnishings for the Robinson house spread out over several years.

Den table lamp, circa 1906.
Marvin Rand photograph.

Fabric of silk pongee screens the
lighted open patterns of the red oak
shade which is supported by
metal arms joined and fastened
with specially cast triangular metal
lag screws.

Above :
View of living room looking into entry hall to the left with door to den to right, 1906.

Photograph courtesy Documents Collection, College of Environmental Design, U.C.B.

Oriental influences can be seen in the arm of the couch, the inset carvings of the bookcase and in the furnishings of the entry hall. Andirons, lighting and gas fixtures were a bold part of the enrichment of the space.

Left:
Living room desk, 1906.
Marvin Rand photograph.

Throughout the interior and exterior, the Robinson house provided the Greenes with the prospect of integrating all parts of the structure and the furnishings; and they took full advantage of this opportunity. They were so successful that other clients of substantial means were attracted to the firm.

Meanwhile clients of more modest means continued to request Charles' earlier furniture designs which were more appropriate for the smaller wooden bungalows. One of these clients was Josephine van Rossem for whom they had previously built two houses. In the third house for her—designed for her own occupancy—the furniture related more directly to the Tichenor designs, but at the same time exploited the bold expression of cleted door construction and repetitive use of exposed screws with such skill that the boldness of the design became graceful through the careful handling of scale and proportion.

Of major significance in the van Rossem design is the treatment of the paneling of the dining room. Here the Greenes used a repetitive rectangle in the detail of the vertical boarding and thus added a decorative element and a scale to the space. The repetitive geometry had a realistic three-dimensional quality consistent with the overall expression of joinery in the all wooden structure.

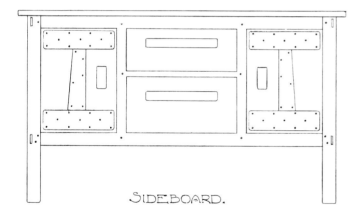

SIDEBOARD.

Dining room sideboard, Josephine van Rossem house No. 3, Pasadena, 1906.
Drawing courtesy Documents Collection, College of Environmental Design, U.C.B.

Raw screw fastenings and wooden structural cleats were treated so forcefully, yet carefully, that they gave character and individuality to this style of Greene designs.

Dining room, Josephine van Rossem house, 1906.
Photograph courtesy Mr. and Mrs. Walter J. van Rossem.

Deeply revealed detailing of the wall paneling of the van Rossem dining room is a classic example of three-dimensional character of the Greenes' geometric joinery, and has the feeling of the work of Charles Rennie Mackintosh in Queen's Cross Church, London.

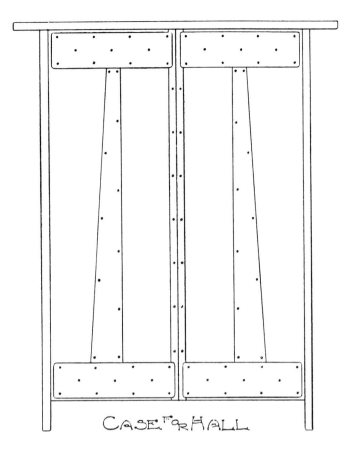

CASE for HALL

Hall case, Josephine van Rossem house, 1906.
Drawing courtesy Documents Collection,
College of Environmental Design, U.C.B.

In a similar modest manner, the sideboards for the John Bentz and Charles Willett bungalows is representative of the Greenes' ability to relate their furniture designs to other parts of their work.

During this period the Greenes extended their conception of total design to include exterior spaces as well as the interiors of their structures. They began to develop garden furniture and some elements of the streetscape. In the design for the gates of the Oaklawn subdivision, Charles had a chance to develop his interest in wrought iron, another area in which the firm developed compositions which soon became as identifiable as their architecture and furniture.

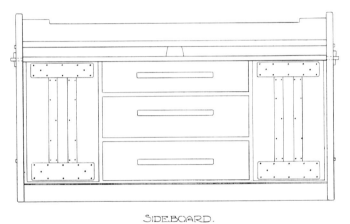

SIDEBOARD.

Sideboard, John C. Bentz house, Pasadena, 1906.
Drawing courtesy Documents Collection,
College of Environmental Design, U.C.B.

The simple and direct designs of the Bentz and Willett sideboards were typical examples of the furniture—separate or built-in—which the Greenes tastefully integrated into the design of so many of their bungalows large and small.

Wrought iron gates for Oaklawn
Portals, South Pasadena Realty and
Development Co., 1906.
Marvin Rand photograph.

Regardless of materials, the movement of line emanating from the
hand of Charles Greene produced
compositions of sculpture in the
most modest of utilitarian elements.

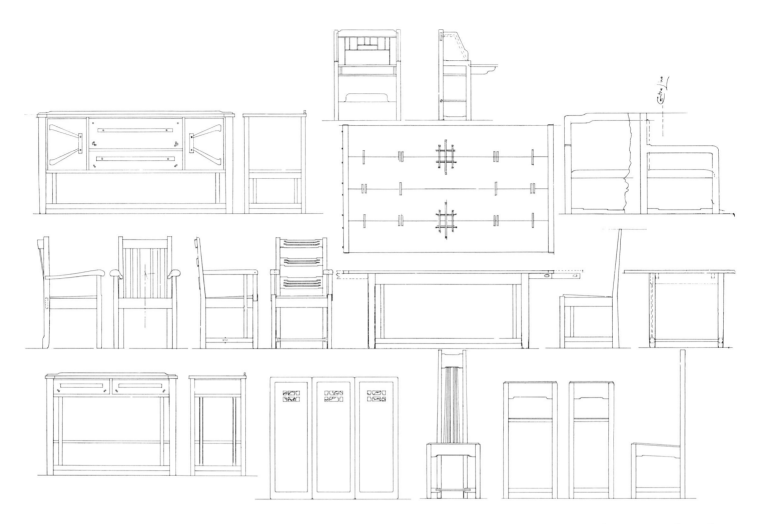

Preliminary sketches for furniture, Dr. and Mrs. William T. Bolton house, Pasadena, 1906.
Drawing courtesy Documents Collection, College of Environmental Design, U.C.B.

Dr. Bolton died unexpectedly before the house was completed. The dining room furniture was being made, completed and placed into the house. The balance of the designs as well as others were then commissioned and made for the first rental occupant of the house—Mrs. Belle Barlow Bush.

In July of 1906, shortly after work was started on the Robinson house and a month after Peter Hall took out the building permit for his carpentry shop, construction began on a second house for Dr. William T. Bolton. Both Dr. and Mrs. Bolton were enthusiastic about the Greenes' interior furnishings and consequently ordered many pieces of furniture for their living room, dining room, and entry hall. The Bolton designs demonstrated the rapid development of Charles' work with different materials, techniques, forms and detail and represented another major step toward a distinct Greene style. In some pieces the lift was again expressed, although more subtly now than in earlier years.

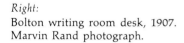

Bolton-Bush hall chair, 1907.
Photograph courtesy Greene and Greene Library.

Bolton dining room sideboard, 1907.
Photograph courtesy Documents Collection,
College of Environmental Design, U.C.B.

The Bolton sideboard appears to be the first fully developed use of the folded ribbon abstract inlay work which Charles later frequently utilized.

Right:
Bolton writing room desk, 1907.
Marvin Rand photograph.

In a bold effort to alleviate the usual weak support for the drop leaf desk, Charles projected the drawer and lower portion for the door to rest upon, and expressed the concept in the form of the front leg design.

47

Above left:
Bolton dining room chair, 1907.
Photograph courtesy Greene and Greene Library.

The less subtle handling of the lift form in the back detail is less effective in softening the strong linear quality of the back of the chair although Charles' gentle touch is clearly evident in the formation of the leg at the line of the seat.

Left:
Bolton dining room table, 1906.
Photograph courtesy Greene and Greene Library.

The carefully calculated proportioning of the secondary verticals of the leg and strut composition relate to similar details in the chairs and produce the unusual character of the Greenes' most linear dining table until Henry Greene's designs for Walter L. Richardson in 1927. Many elements of the Bolton furniture suggest that Henry may have worked closely with Charles on these designs.

Above :
Bolton dining room, 1907.
Photograph courtesy Documents Collection,
College of Environmental Design, U.C.B.

Crisp lines of the dining table and chairs are complemented
by the inlay detail of the sideboard and serving table, the
irridescent Tiffany glass patterns of the doors to the kitchen
pantry, and by the free flowing abstract paintings in the frieze.

As in the Robinson dining furniture, there was a relationship to Chinese household furniture. However, there was
a fresh and different quality about the Bolton designs in
relating the playful intensity of the folded ribbon inlay work
of the dining pieces with the severity of the repetitive vertical and horizontal structural lines. In addition, the Bolton
furniture appears to be Charles' first use of the square ebony
peg which was soon to become his trademark. But here the
ebony peg was less refined. The edges were not as sensitively rolled and the face was more flat than in latter interpretations. The juxtaposition of two pegs of varying proportion touching at a corner was used only in the Bolton
furniture. Nevertheless, with the exception of the library
table, there was still a strong tie to the linear qualities in
Stickley's designs, although these were softened. In the
tables for the entry hall the Oriental influence furnished
a graceful lightness in contrast to the robust solidity of the
dining pieces.

Bush clock, 1908.
Photograph courtesy Documents
Collection, College of Environ-
mental Design, U.C.B.

Typical of several pieces designed
especially for Mrs. Bush, the clock
was adorned with inlay work of
bees which were to be symbolic of
the initials for Belle Barlow Bush.

Bush library table, 1907.
Photograph courtesy Greene and
Greene Library.

Likely the first of the Greenes' gateleg drop leaf table designs, the
library table and other designs for
Bolton and Bush furniture represent
the first use of the square ebony
peg now identified with the furniture
designs of 1907-1911.

View of Bolton-Bush writing room, circa 1908.
Drawing courtesy Documents Collection, College of Environmental Design, U.C.B.

Charles' work for Mrs. Bush included picture frames and book-plates as well as designs for curtains which were appliqued by Mrs. Bush's niece.

Bolton-Bush entry hall table, 1907. Marvin Rand photograph.

One of the most sensitive and graceful of all Greene designs, this table is strongly related, like the Robinson dining chairs, to traditional Chinese household furniture designs.

Dr. Bolton died before the house was completed and only the furniture for the dining room was finished. Mrs. Bolton moved East and rented the house, complete with the dining room furniture, to Mrs. Belle Barlow Bush. Mrs. Bush had most of the remaining furniture made. Later she had Charles design several other pieces including several small curio cabinets, a clock, small tables, and picture frames. These designs were inlaid with small bees in ebony signifying the three letters of her names: Belle Barlow Bush. Most of the furniture was produced at the Peter Hall mill, but two of the curio cabinets were made by Mrs. Bush's nephew, Walter A. Gripton, who had a cabinet shop in Pasadena. His sister, Ethel Gripton, carried out Charles' abstract patterns for applique work on the living room curtains.[3]

The curio cabinets and the clock were designed in 1908. By this time the Greenes were deeply involved in the furnishings for their ultimate bungalows and consequently these pieces reflect the increasing refinements of their most notable work.

The last piece of furniture for Mrs. Bush was a large couch for the living room. This couch is vividly remembered by the family because it took four years to complete. This delay was undoubtedly caused by the extraordinary amount of furniture being produced by this time at the Peter Hall mill for the Greenes' clients.

Mrs. Bush, like several of the Greenes' other clients, became intimately involved with and excited about Charles' interest in the total design of interiors and furnishings. Her close association with the Greenes lasted for many years. Even after she moved to Boston in 1914 she had Charles design bookplates for herself and for at least one of her daughters.

3. Correspondence with Mrs. Leet Bissell and interviews with Mrs. W. Herbert Allen, daughters of Mrs. Belle Barlow Bush.

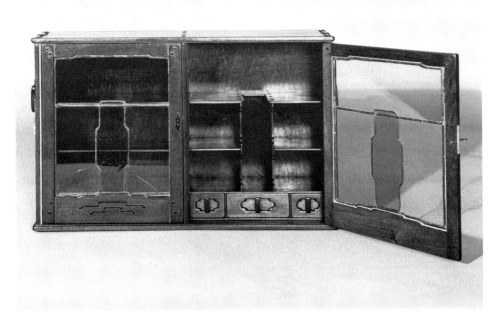

Bush curio cabinet, 1908. Marvin Rand photograph.

In August of 1908, Charles sent Mrs. Bush two designs for the small cabinet with variations of solid wood or glass doors of differing patterns. Her response called for the glass doors, and a request for special sizing of the interior shelving for a special keepsake, and left the final design completely to Charles' taste.

Far right:
Clear leaded glass window, James A. Culbertson house alterations, 1907. Marvin Rand photograph.

The abstract flowing line work for the stair landing windows added to the Culbertson house are the richest expression of Charles' flirtation with Art Nouveau forms.

Right:
Leading detail.
Marvin Rand photograph.

During the period between 1905 and 1907, the refinements in design and in techniques of wood craftsmanship paralleled the development in the quality of the leaded and stained glass work. The association with Emil Lange was reflected in some of the work for the Robinson and Bolton houses although the glass fabrication for the John Addison Cole house in 1907 was apparently the work of others.

Frequently the Greenes commissioned leaded stained glass work from the Judson Art Glass Studios located on the bluffs overlooking the Pasadena Arroyo, an area flourishing with artisans.[4] On these occasions Charles or Henry would go into the Judson Studios and work out the cartoons for the leading design along with Judson glass artists.[5]

---

4. The Judson Studios joined with many of these craftsmen forming the Arroyo Craftsmen, an organization devoted to the Arts and Crafts Movement. As active as the individual artists were, the periodical begun by the group—*The Arroyo Craftsman*—survived only one issue.

5. Interviews with Horace and Walter Judson.

Major alterations and additions to the James A. Culbertson house (1902) were begun in 1906. The entry hall was enlarged, the stairwell redeveloped, the dining room totally redeveloped in the space previously housing the kitchen and a new one-story service wing added off the corner of the house.

The most significant aspects of these modifications were the refinements in the designs and craftsmanship of the interiors of the entry and dining room. Intricately patterned carvings were done for the frieze in both spaces, and de-tailed paneling, lighting fixtures, leaded glass, ceiling relief detail, hardware, and carpet designs represented a preview of the work for the elaborate bungalows just on the horizon.

The Culbertson remodelings were the grand finale of the four year period during which the Greenes entered into the area of furniture design and evolved a style marked by originality and superb craftmanship. Their interior work had begun with the James Culbertson house and now the period of their developmental years closed with highly significant designs for that same client.

Carved wood panels for James A. Culbertson house alterations, 1907. Marvin Rand photograph.

Charles worked daily with the woodcarvers in Peter Hall's mill. He allowed the grain of the redwood to influence his design. Water color washes were gently used on the raw wood for subtle coloration of certain details and gold leaf applied to accent running motifs.

Entry hall after remodeling, James A. Culbertson house, 1907.
Julius Shulman photograph.

With the exception of the stained glass door (the screen and
furnishings of a later generation), this photograph exhibits the
fully redesigned entry hall work of 1906 and 1907, including
the redwood frieze carvings, the subtly patterned oak wall
paneling, lighting fixtures of Tiffany leaded stained glass and
the undulating ribbon detail framing the panels of the ceiling.

III

A Distinct Style 1907-1911

By 1907 the Greenes had developed a style in both their architecture and their furniture and a confidence in themselves which attracted more and more clients. The years of experimentation were behind them. The reputation of the firm was well established. They were now able to select those clients with the vision and the means to encourage the design of interior furnishings of the highest quality in both composition and craftsmanship.

So great was the amount of work coming in that Greene and Greene were now employing up to fifteen draftsmen. Several of these, headed by Leonard W. Collins, spent most of their time on furniture drawings. Peter Hall added space and equipment to his own shops in 1907 and 1908 and placed his brother in charge of the mill and the making of furniture. This was to have a decided impact upon Charles' designs. John Hall's long experience in cabinet making clearly distinguishes the work under his supervision. Charles' pencil sketches for furniture found among John Hall's papers indicate the close professional rapport between the two men. The first conceptual freehand drawings were carefully studied by both before final detailing and construction drawings were done.

This same rapport existed between Charles and many of the master craftsmen working in the mill on furniture, carving or lighting fixtures. David Swanson—a young master craftsman from Sweden who joined Peter Hall in 1908 and later became shop foreman—vividly remembered the Greenes. Henry, he said, rarely visited the mill as he was too busy on major construction and seeing to the operation of the offices. Charles was a totally different character. He came down to the mill every morning—put on a smock and worked right with each of the workmen. He had long flowing hair and would work with the tools himself while in the shops. The men had a great deal of respect for Charles and got along with him well as long as they did not differ with him—though extremely mild and soft-spoken, he was dominating and could induce clients to spend the money required to produce such fine and intricately fabricated furniture.[1]

The mill was far better equipped than most normally identified with the hand-crafted work of the Arts and Crafts Movement. Though some of Charles' earliest and late pieces of furniture were done by him by hand, the quantity and sophistication of the furniture between 1907 and 1916 required power tools and milling capabilities which were developed in the Hall mill specifically for the Greene and Greene work. Long under-floor shafts powered by gasoline engines generated the series of belts which would come through the floor to operate the various pieces of equipment along the line. On the job sites similar small gas-engined, belt-powered equipment allowed for considerable detail and finish work.

By now Charles had developed a system of forms and joinery which allowed him complete flexibility and yet retained a genuine continuity. So basic were his concepts that his system still enables young artisan craftsmen to compose contemporary and independent designs which nevertheless relate to the spirit of Greene designs.

1. Interviews by the author with Leonard W. Collins.

Interior of Peter Hall
Manufacturing Co.,
Pasadena, circa 1915.
Photograph courtesy Mr. and
Mrs. R. Donald Hall.

Long under-floor shafts run
by gas engines powered the belts
to operate the various pieces
of machinery.

Right:
Charles Greene preliminary
freehand sketch for Gamble
dressing table, 1908.
John Hall papers, courtesy of
Gregson Hall.

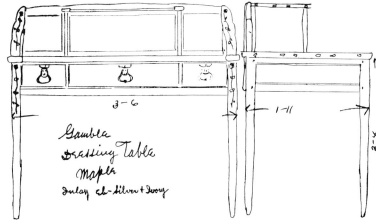

In principle, the system followed the same concepts underlying the Greenes' architecture: the total was composed of separate parts; the identity of those parts was openly expressed; the bringing together of two similar or dissimilar elements created a point of transition and the resolution of that transition often developed a totally independent third condition which both acknowledged the joining of elements and at the same time brought an enrichment to the total composition. In addition, the system of softly shaped square and rectangular ebony pegs added a playful latitude and decorative variable to the necessary task of fastening parts. In general, the ebony peg was a form of blind fastening; it covered a brass screw counter-sunk with washer into the square or rectangular hole. On occasion Charles' organization of the points of fastening were often complemented with additional pegs carrying out a rhythmic theme in the design.

Two surfaces were seldom brought together in the same

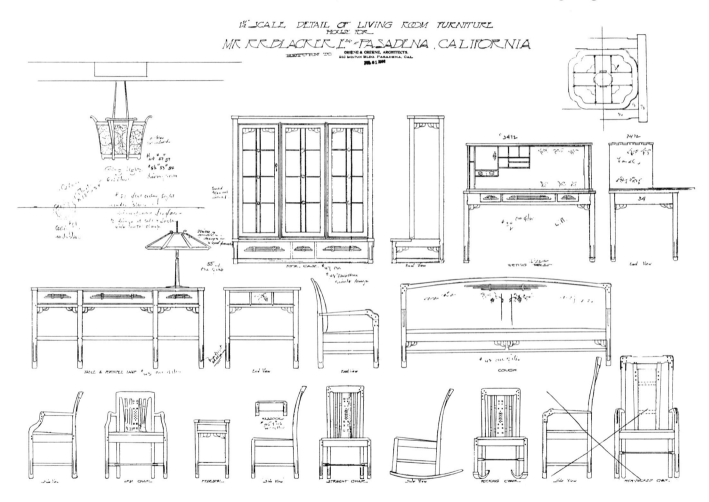

Preliminary drawing for living room furniture, Robert R. Blacker house, Pasadena, 1907.
Courtesy Greene and Greene Library.

plane. One member generally was recessed to allow the other to dominate. When necessary, as in table tops, joints were made flush with butterfly inlay joinery, and edge pieces with butt joints spliced with an edge exposed ebony spline cross-fastened by ebony pegs. Ends of wood were usually capped with a cross member and these were boldly detailed to express their attachment.

Because wood continues to expand and contract, the overall early concept was to so compose the parts of the design that such movement could take place without apparent change in the visual character of the finished product.

Woodcraftsman Alan Marks' observations in his article for *Fine Woodworking* magazine focuses on this particular concept:

Several aspects of their table construction deserve attention. The majority of Greene tabletops and desk tops are solid wood. Others were veneered but only when the design required it, such as those with simple marquetry or inlay.

View of living room, Blacker house.
Leroy Hulbert photograph, Courtesy Greene and Greene Library.

Except for the oriental carpets and the piano the entire development of the interior was attended by the Greenes.

Detail of living room cabinet.
Marvin Rand photograph.

The corner motif was carried throughout the living room furniture. Use of the "dancing" square ebony peg joinery became the Greenes' signature throughout the years 1907-1911.

Living room cabinet, Blacker house.
Marvin Rand photograph.

Living room table, Blacker house.
Marvin Rand photograph.

Fruitwood, copper and silver inlay
of living room table.
Marvin Rand photograph.

Entry hall shoe bench with cabinet
in seat, Blacker house.
Marvin Rand photograph.

61

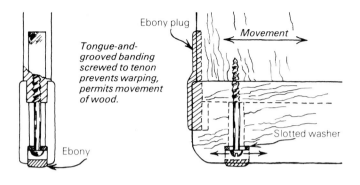

Detail of typical furniture joinery.
Drawing by Alan Marks, Courtesy *Fine Woodworking* magazine.

Others are edged with massive hexagonal or otherwise polygonal bandings. Of the rectangular, solid wood ones, all have banding tongue-and-grooved across the end grain to prevent warping. They are secured with screws, not glued. Expansion and contraction of the top is accommodated in a fully satisfactory way. Bandings were drilled with spaced, oversized holes for the screws. Rectangular mortises were chiseled to a depth of about 3/8 in. and fitted with slotted washers. Screws biting tightly into the tenon secure the banding and slide back and forth in their washers as humidity changes. The banding overlaps the tabletop and movement of the two pieces relative to each other is unnoticeable. Ebony plugs are glued into the tabletop, but float in special mortises in the bandings. [2]

Joinery was accentuated. Right angle corners were frequently composed with a finger lap joint and cross pegged with ebony. Mortise and tenon was utilized although not to the extent found in earlier furniture. The round peg yielded to the square. Handles were emphasized and often provided decoration. Leather became the major material for hinging screens and for hanging lighting fixtures. Occasionally, when desired by clients, inlay patterns were carried out with fruitwoods, silver, and semi-precious stones.

Although naturally there were differences between the designs for the various clients, the similarities were more obvious. Because of the larger budgets now available, the woods selected and frequently used included Honduras mahoganies of very fine grades, solid teakwood, ash, walnut, ebony, rosewood and maple. Unlike his later work, Charles, during this period, allowed the natural grain of the wood to provide enrichment and dealt with silhouette, form and joinery as dominant design determinants. Soft stains were rubbed repeatedly with boiled linseed oil and Japan dryer until the friction produced the heat necessary for the final finish. [3]

Detail of living room chair.
Marvin Rand photograph.

A continuous ebony spline joins the arm and leg members and is fastened with inset screws capped with ebony pegs. This technique was used throughout the Greenes' furniture of the period to avoid separation of joinery.

2. Marks, Alan. "Greene and Greene: A Study in Functional Design," *Fine Woodworking*, (September, 1978) p. 43.

3. Interview by the author with Mr. and Mrs. R. Donald Hall.

Living room writing desk, Blacker house.
Marvin Rand photograph.

The upper writing case is detailed with leather cushions which rest on the lower table and drawer unit.

Master bedroom chiffonier, Blacker house.
Photograph courtesy L. Morgan Yost.

This unusual design has a feeling for some of the work of Charles Rennie Mackintosh in the handling of the broad brimmed cap.

Entry hall cabinet, Blacker house.
Marvin Rand photographs.

Handles for the doors emerge from the abstract
pattern of the carvings.

Wall lighting fixture for downstairs bedroom
depicts an abstract composition of clouds and
flowers and stems in the stained glass. The
fixture relates in form and joinery to the wall
and ceiling trim detail.

Entry hall "Morris chair," Blacker house.
Marvin Rand photograph.

Below:
Adjustable back hardware repeated the square peg theme in the square lag screws and positioning locks.
Marvin Rand photograph.

The first of the furnishings for the ultimate bungalow clients were those for the Robert R. Blacker house in 1907. These were followed by the David B. Gamble and Freeman A. Ford houses in 1908, for the William R. Thorsen residence in 1909, and for the Charles M. Pratt house begun in 1910. However, there was considerable overlapping, and at times work was proceeding simultaneously on these jobs.

There were thematic variations between the various projects as well as within each home. Portions of the Blacker furniture exhibit greater hints of the Orient than is felt in other works. Even the very direct simple lines of the entry hall furniture in teakwood were touched with an Oriental influence at the base of the legs. The furniture for the dining, living and master bedroom was made with Honduras mahoganies and was enriched with varying amounts of inlay work of mother-of-pearl, silver, copper and fruitwoods.

Entry hall chandeliers in teakwood and Tiffany glass suspended by leather straps, Blacker house.
Marvin Rand photograph.

Ceiling fixture of downstairs bedroom library.
Marvin Rand photograph.

Dining room chandelier,
Blacker house.
Marvin Rand photograph.

The sculptural character of the
ceiling plate and the decorative
treatment of the leather hangers
overshadow the elegant simplicity
of the stained leaded glass light
box. Slivers of irridescent glass both
reflect and emit light from the
delicate slits in the wood side
panels. A companion fixture of
square proportions hangs in the
adjoining breakfast room.

Detail of exterior entry lantern in brass and leaded stained glass with hardware for copper downspout in background. Marvin Rand photograph.

The Gamble furniture was a more straightforward statement of the Greenes' systemized vocabulary. Inlay work or carvings were featured only in the bedroom pieces and a living room writing desk, and these related directly to elements within the room. For instance, the incised design in the silver beds which Charles designed for the guest bedroom echoed the silver inlay in the wooden pieces, and the Rookwood Pottery patterns were reflected in the master bedroom furniture.

Mr. and Mrs. David Gamble also called upon Charles to design furniture for Mrs. Gamble's maiden sister, Julia Huggins, who occupied a room in the Gamble house which had been especially designed for her. The furniture for Miss Huggins again possesses that remarkable straightforward, simple character of the early Greene furniture or the best of the later designs. Gone is elaborate decoration, and the beauty of the pieces results from the grain of wood and the superb scale and proportion of the design.

Living room table, chairs, and carpet, Gamble house. Marvin Rand photograph.

The Gamble table is one of the classic designs fully featuring the various elements of the Greenes' furniture vocabulary.

View of living room featuring a portion of the fireside
inglenook, piano and carpet design, Gamble house.
Marvin Rand photograph.

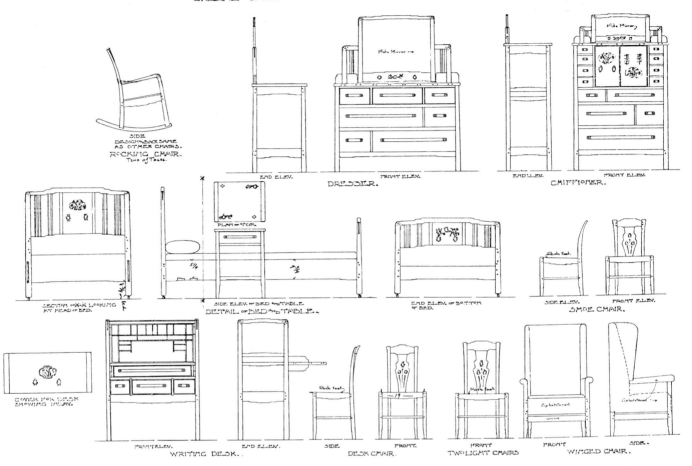

Preliminary designs for master bedroom furniture, David B.
Gamble house, Pasadena, 1908.
Drawing courtesy Greene and Greene Library.

With minor detail refinements, all furniture was made with
the exception of the overstuffed winged chair.

Bedroom window, Adelaide M. Tichenor house, 1904.

Living room carpet watercolor, David B. Gamble, 1908.
Courtesy of Documents Collection,
College of Environmental Design, UCB.

Right:
Entry door, Freeman A. Ford house, 1907.
Marvin Rand photographs.

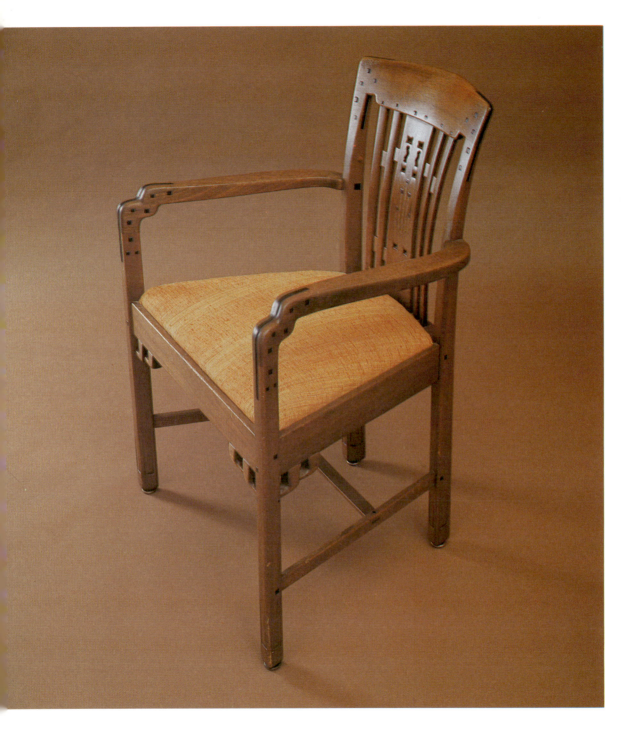

Living room arm chair,
Robert R. Blacker house,
1907.

Exterior lantern, Robert R. Blacker house, 1907.

Right:
Bathroom window, Robert R. Blacker house, 1907.
Marvin Rand photographs.

Interior window, David B. Gamble house, 1908.

Guest bedroom sconce, David B. Gamble house, 1908.

Facing page:
Entry hall, David B. Gamble house, 1908.
Marvin Rand photographs.

Above:
Game room armchair, Mortimer Fleishhacker house, 1923.

Above right:
Bathroom window, Freeman A. Ford house, 1907.

Right:
Dining room china case doors, Thomas Gould Jr. house, 1924.

Facing page:
Living room detail, William R. Thorsen house, 1909.
Marvin Rand photographs.

Interior wall lanterns, James Culbertson house, 1907.
Marvin Rand photograph.

Inlay work and proportioned drawer detail of master bedroom chiffonier, Gamble house.

Detail of inlay and joinery, master bedroom chiffonier, 1908.
Marvin Rand photographs.

Detail of carved redwood
living room frieze,
Gamble house.
Photograph courtesy
Documents Collection,
College of Environmental
Design, U.C.B.

Charles worked daily with
the carvers evolving
portions of the design from
the grain of the wood.
This photograph was taken
following installation
of the carving and prior to
the placement of the lock
wedges and metal
strapping.

Far left:
Living room rocker.

Left:
Living room armchair,
Gamble house.
Marvin Rand photographs.

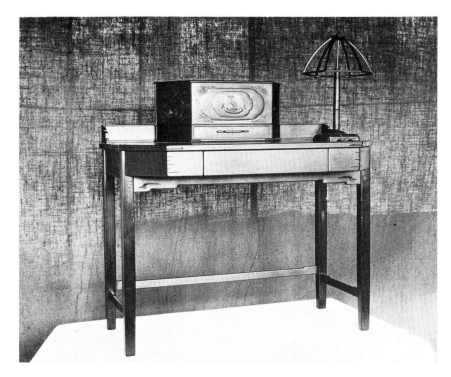

Detail of letter cabinet.
Photograph courtesy Documents Collection,
College of Environmental Design, U.C.B.

The Gamble family crest was incorporated into the carved front panel. Side door handles are part of the protruding tree trunk of the wood inlay work. Details are carried out in ebony and silver.

Above:
Living room writing desk, letter case and lamp frame.
Photograph courtesy Documents Collection, College of Environmental Design, U.C.B.

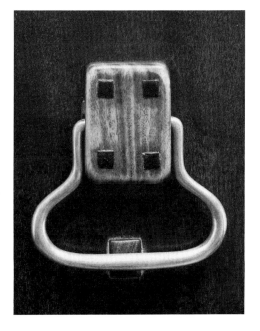

Gamble guest bedroom letter case detail.
Marvin Rand photograph.

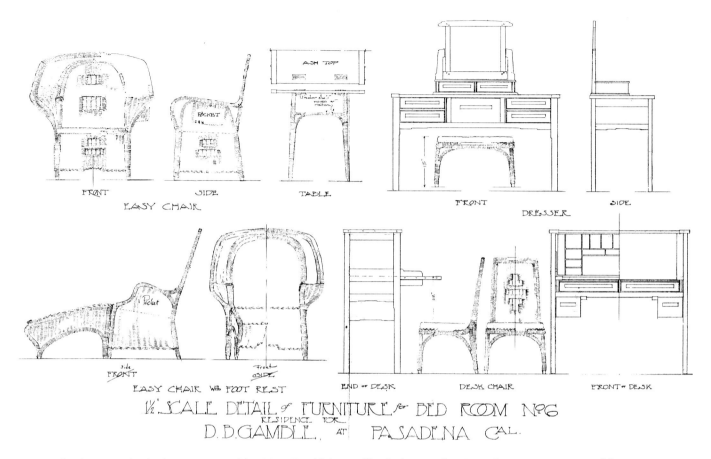

FRONT SIDE TABLE

EASY CHAIR

ASH TOP

FRONT SIDE

DRESSER

side
FRONT Front
aSIDE

EASY CHAIR with FOOT REST

END of DESK DESK CHAIR FRONT of DESK

1½" SCALE DETAIL of FURNITURE for BED ROOM №6
RESIDENCE FOR
D.B.GAMBLE, AT PASADENA CAL.

Designs for furniture for bedroom occupied by Mrs. Gamble's sister, Julia Huggins.
Drawing courtesy Documents Collection,
College of Environmental Design, U.C.B.

Charles' rattan furniture designs were rare and here were gracefully related to the wooden furniture of ash by combining the ash top table on a support of rattan and utilizing a rattan stool and chair for the dresser and desk. The stain coloring the rattan was also rubbed into the soft woods of the ash pieces, thus adding to the subtle harmony of the overall combinations.

View of living room of the Freeman A. Ford house looking into entry hall. Photograph: *Architectural Record*, December, 1913.

Following several variations with winged chairs for previous clients, the Ford chair is the classic. It was a direct and natural product of the articulated system of furniture construction that had emerged by 1908. In spite of its apparent massive scale and rigid geometry it blended well with the lighter pieces of furniture in the large and boldly detailed living room.

One of Charles' most unusual designs was the wingback chair for the Freeman A. Fords in 1908. Previously he had experimented with wingback chairs for Mrs. Tichenor in 1904, for Mrs. Bush in 1906 and for the Gamble bedroom in 1908—the latter a fully overstuffed version. But for Freeman A. Ford, the wingback chair was developed primarily in wood in a linear and planar composition. Instead of appearing clumsy, this chair had both charm and distinction and at the same time blended easily into the lighter furnishings of the living room. The rest of the furniture was equally charming and revealed Charles' romance with form. In the backs of the dining chairs the splats have a feeling for American Indian design, and the ebony pegs are more irregularly shaped and canted as if to prove that absolute order was something to be defied.

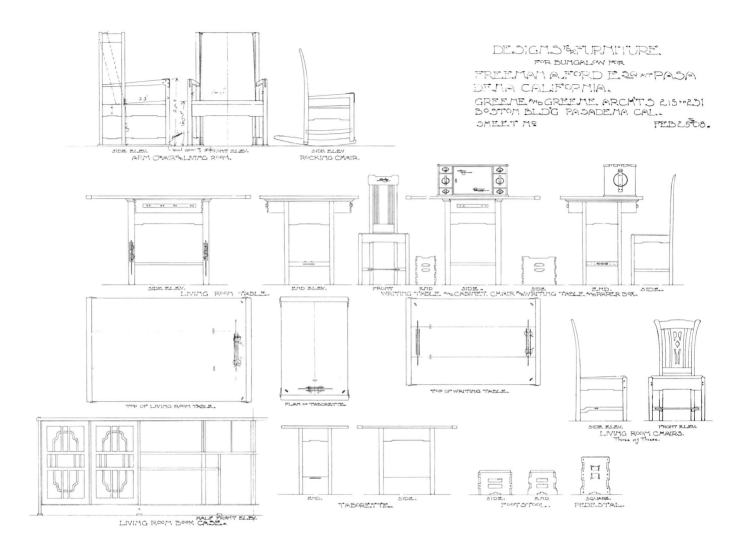

Preliminary designs for living room furniture for the Freeman
A. Ford house, Pasadena, 1908.
Drawing courtesy Greene and Greene Library.

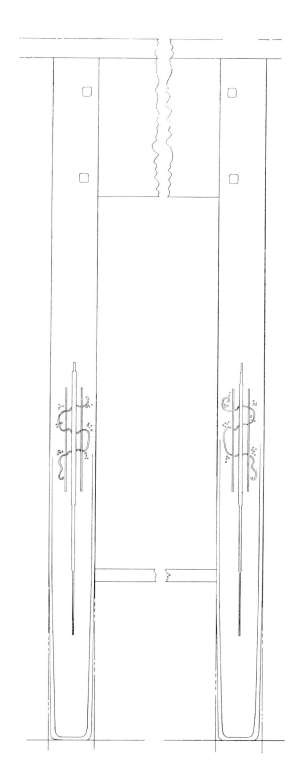

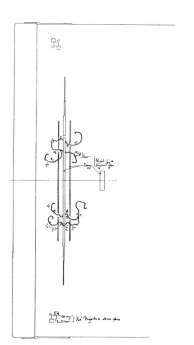

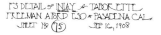

I'S DETAIL of INLAY of TABORETTE
FREEMAN A FORD E:O of PASADENA CAL.
SHEET № ⑮   SEP 16, 1908

Detail of inlay of fruitwood, ebony
and silver for taborette, Ford house.
Drawing courtesy Documents
Collection, College of Environmental Design, U.C.B.

Letter case for living room table, Ford house.
Photograph courtesy Greene and Greene Library.

Nearly the whole of the Greenes' detail system is expressed in this
piece: the finger lap joint, square ebony peg, variations of handle
treatment, silver piano hinging, ebony key and keyhole escutcheon,
abstracted cloud and vine inlay work, and the use of leather to protect
the table top from scratches.

Leaded glass and joinery detail of entry to dining room door,
Ford house.
Marvin Rand photograph.

Dining room wall lantern.
Marvin Rand photograph.

Hall ceiling lantern in metal and irridescent glass, Ford house.
Whitland Locke photograph.

The square peg motif was translated into the head detail for lag screws and metal fasteners.

Inlay detail of the dining room sideboard related to a similar design in the dining table top.
Marvin Rand photograph.

Right:
Preliminary sketches for portion of dining room furniture, William R. Thorsen house, Berkeley, California, 1909.
Drawing courtesy Documents Collection, College of Environmental Design, U.C.B.

Peter Hall sent craftsmen from his shops in Pasadena to Berkeley where the furniture was made in the basement "Jolly Room" of the Thorsen house.

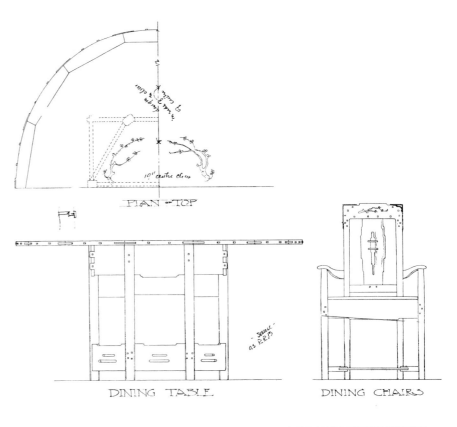

PLAN · TOP

DINING TABLE   DINING CHAIRS

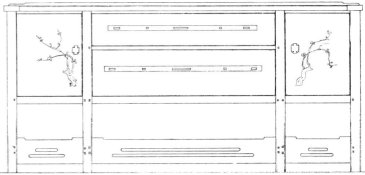

Although fewer in number, the designs for William R. Thorsen are some of the most classical and elegant of Charles' work. The sideboard and server in the dining room are masterpieces in scale and proportion. The handling of the lift in these pieces transcends the Oriental influence and becomes a new and fresh expression of Charles' artistry.

Dining room serving table.

Classic proportions and the further refinement of the oriental cloud motif give the overall design a simplicity which is as contemporary today as it was startling in 1910.

Below right:
Dining table, Thorsen house.

Below left:
View of dining host chair illustrating the unusual twist in the arm design, a concept used frequently in Greene furniture.
Marvin Rand photographs.

90

Above right:
One of two ceiling lanterns of the dining room.

Above left:
Entry hall lantern, Thorsen house.

Detail of firescreen.
Marvin Rand photographs.

The floral and folded ribbon design in the firescreen appeared repeatedly in many variations in Charles' designs after 1910.

View of living room, Thorsen house.
Marvin Rand photograph.

Wrought iron gate to side gardens, Thorsen
house.
Marvin Rand photograph.

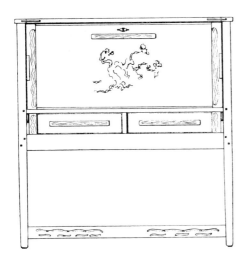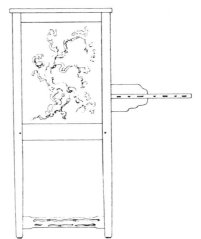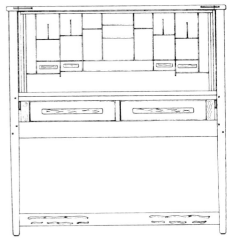

FRONT CLOSED.   SIDE.   FRONT OPEN.

DESK.

SILVER WIRE INLAY ON HANDLES.
PERFORATIONS ON LOWER RAILS.

Above:
Finished drawing for living room desk, Pratt house.
Drawing courtesy Documents Collection,
College of Environmental Design, U.C.B.

Left:
Detail of ebony key and keyhole escutcheon, silver inlay of
dropfront handle and fruitwood tree inlay of door of Pratt
living room desk.
Marvin Rand photograph.

The Charles M. Pratt furniture also had its own individual qualities. There were similar details and uses of the lift, but the heights of the ladderbacks of the chairs and rockers was unusual and pleasing. There is considerable wood inlay in the front and side panels of the desk and silver inlay in the handles of the library table. But in spite of the power and coloration of these inlays, the handling is subordinate to the overall forms and adds more of a textural effect which, in the case of the drop-front desk, compensates for its large scale.

Left:
View of end of living room, Charles M.
Pratt house, Ojai, California, 1909.
Marvin Rand photograph.

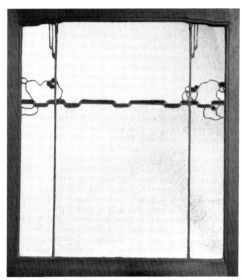

Above:
Clear leaded glass sliding door of living
room bookcase, Pratt house.
Marvin Rand photograph.

In a beautifully restrained and quiet composition, the leading design combines both
the linear and sinuous line work identified
with the Greenes' art.

Pratt house living room desk photographed
in the Peter Hall mill.
Photograph courtesy Greene and Greene
Library.

Far left:
Octagonal living room table, Pratt house.

Left:
Frame of classic ladder-back rocking chair, Pratt house. Photographs courtesy Greene and Greene Library.

Detail of living room timber joinery and lantern, Pratt house.
Marvin Rand photograph.

Capitalizing on the difficult, the Greenes were at their best when confronted with the bringing together of numerous seemingly unrelated elements.

Above:
One of several living room leather armchairs, Pratt house.

Dining room chandelier
of mahogany and Tiffany
irridescent glass detailed
with bits of jade.
Marvin Rand photographs.

97

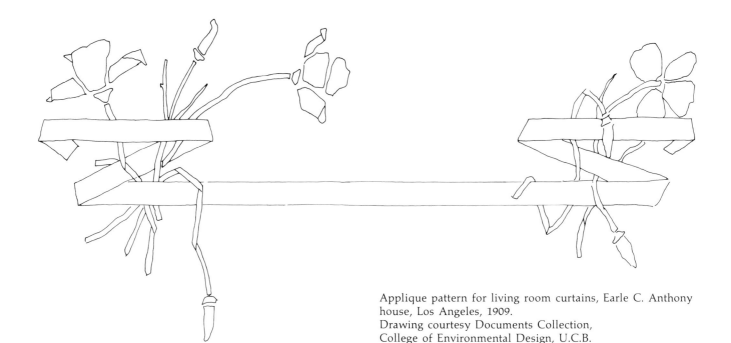

Applique pattern for living room curtains, Earle C. Anthony
house, Los Angeles, 1909.
Drawing courtesy Documents Collection,
College of Environmental Design, U.C.B.

The dining tables as well as the library tables generally
exhibited both a refinement of earlier concepts as well as
variations. For the Blacker house the table was stationary
and made larger by the placement of a related breakfast
table at the end, whereas the Gamble and Pratt tables followed the earlier form of the Robinson table and concentrated on the elaborate cantilever structure to permit the
addition of leaves without the separation of the base. The
base of the Gamble dining room table was so carefully proportioned, detailed and finished that it became a piece of
wood sculpture. Successful as the Gamble table was, however, there was a directness in the functional bare bone
structure of the Pratt and Robinson table bases which would
be more highly respected by the structural purist.

As Charles' confidence in his own abilities and creative
drive increased, he was able to convince his clients that he
should design more and more of their interior furnishings.
For the ultimate bungalows he was including in his work
leaded stained glass, lighting fixtures, carpets, hardware,
fireplace tools, garden pottery, curtains, fabrics, bookplates,
and other household items as well as landscape designs.

Dining room table, David B. Gamble house, 1908.
Marvin Rand photograph.

By 1907 Emil Lange and Charles Greene had developed techniques for leaded glass fabrication which produced the effects that Charles had long been seeking. Their method allowed for greater variation in the breadth of the leading. Standard lead came was used between each piece of cut glass and the design soldered together. Sheet lead was then cut as an overlay in the pattern and dimension required. The leaf of the lead came from one side was then cut off, solder applied to the back of the sheet lead then attached to the heart of the came by heat from a medium

Detail of leading technique which Charles Greene and Emil Lange developed to provide greater variation and texture in the leaded glass designs.
Marvin Rand photograph.

heated soldering iron. Solder was then floated onto the entire surface of the sheet lead pattern and a copper finish achieved by chemical treatment with bluestone. To achieve the textured surface of the leading—as in the entry doors of the Gamble house—the solder was floated onto the surface of the sheet lead in individual drops giving variation in size and form when hardened. When one side of the glass was thus finished, it was turned over, the leaf of the lead came similarly removed and the process repeated in identical manner. At the same time similar processes for varying leading techniques were developed simultaneously in the east with no apparent connection with the experiments being done by the Greenes and Emil Lange. Others would follow quickly but this method of glass fabrication was so costly that its use was rare by others, particularly in residential work where it was used so effectively by Greene and Greene.[4]

Charles added a further subtlety to the best of Louis Tiffany's glass variations by laminating two, three and even four layers of glass in order to achieve the soft variations in colors to suit his particular taste. Techniques began with those used by the Tiffany Studios in New York with whom

4. Interviews with glass artisan Claus Willenberg who worked at one time in the Sturdy-Lange art glass studios in Los Angeles.

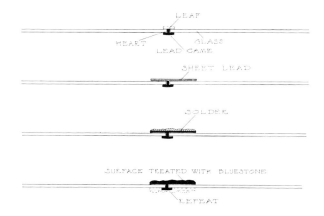

A diagram of the technique used to provide the wide range of line value and texture to the Greenes' leaded glass work.

Above :
14″ high bronze andirons,
Thorsen house.
Photograph courtesy Documents
Collection, College of
Environmental Design, U.C.B.

Living room lantern and plaster relief,
Blacker house.

Lily pad motifs echoing the pond
of the garden were carried out in
the overhead stained glass lanterns
and in relief in the plaster ceiling
which was treated with an overlay
of gold leaf.

Lange had formerly been associated. Each piece of glass was wrapped with copper foil, attached one to the other with solder and molten lead, and then soft lead placed over the joints. In special instances the finished product would be acid-etched as in the veins of the leaves in the doorway of the Gamble house.

In the lighting fixtures, Charles' designs were carried out with Tiffany glass and fabricated by Lange. The glass panels were then placed into wooden or metal frames which were either affixed to the wall or hung from the ceiling with leather straps or metal rods. It is obvious that Charles took great delight in the variety and scope of lighting and was constantly searching for new ways to work with the recently developed electric technology.

In a few instances Charles was given the opportunity to design carpets, the most noteworthy of which was for the

David B. Gamble house in 1908. His watercolors for this carpet exhibit a remarkable quality of abstract composition for the times. Records are incomplete but suggest that the carpets were woven in Austria from Charles' watercolor sketches.[5] However, when they arrived in Pasadena, Charles was so dissatisfied with one of the dye colors woven into the pattern that he engaged the Iran Company in Los Angeles to unweave the one color and reweave it to his exact specifications—a job which took several weeks.

Charles was also developing the hardware for some of the ultimate bungalows. In many instances this involved

5. One letter in the Greene archives suggests that the carpets were made in England. However, Sidney Gamble, who was 18 years of age at the time the carpets were made, recalled their being woven in Austria. Notations on invoices from the Iran Company in Los Angeles refer to the 'German rugs.'

not only the metal straps for the fastening of the great timbers both inside and outside the structure, but also included andirons for fireplaces, the fireplace fenders, tools and electric switch plates. These items were manufactured by several firms in the Los Angeles area, including in 1911 the Pacific Ornamental Iron Works and by 1914 the Art Metal Company of Los Angeles. Dates of invoices from these two firms for work for the William R. Thorsen house indicate the length of time between the construction of the houses and the initial furniture and the design and production of the related designs of interior furnishings.

Charles' enthusiasm was infectious. Consequently, some of his clients encouraged him to design applique work for various fabrics used in curtains and bedspreads. The stitchery would then be carried out by the ladies and elder daughters of the families involved.

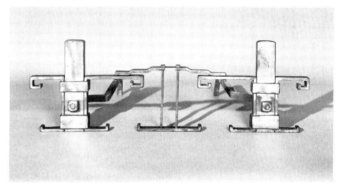

Andirons designed for Mrs. Belle Barlow Bush were made also for Peter Hall's home, circa 1910.

Peter Hall was intrigued by this innovative design which allowed for the central portion of the andiron to adjust to varying widths of the firebox by the placement of the end drop into any of several square holes in the longer arm of each andiron.

Left:
Loft lantern, Freeman A. Ford house, 1907.
Marvin Rand photographs.

The Greenes' control of the landscaping prompted Charles to design outside furniture for the terraces and the garden as well as garden pots. The pottery was produced by the Gladding-McBean Company in Lincoln, California; although in later years Charles worked with a pottery manufacturer in the San Jose area, where he actually painted the glaze patterns himself.

Glazed ceramic garden urn for the Pratt house and also utilized in the gardens of the James A. Culbertson house. Marvin Rand photograph.

During this period Charles designed a handsome large cabinet for his own office to house his fine collection of architectural drawings and publications. He was also engaged to do the interior lighting and leaded glass windows for the Earle C. Anthony residence of 1909. These windows represent some of the best stained glass window designs of his entire career.

By 1909 Charles was exhausted by the pressure of work and, consequently, he and his family visited England for a year where he relaxed, associated with writers and artists, painted in watercolors, and associated with the noted etcher, Sherbourne.[6] The fact that Charles was able to leave the practice at such a demanding and critical time is evidence of his confidence in his brother Henry, Peter and John Hall, and Emil Lange. Excerpts from an important letter from Peter Hall to Charles Greene dated August 9, 1909, are revealing:

> The Berkeley job is progressing nicely, the brick work is turning out beautifully. We have the frame up ready for shakes and I think it looks very well. We get along very nicely with Mr. Thorsen....

And in another paragraph:

> The pianos are under way and we will make at least one case from the drawing you left us. I think they will turn out very well.
>
> The Gamble House is ready to be accepted and the furniture about completed. Everything looks very well. I am well pleased with it. It will be all ready for Mr. Gamble when he arrives. The Blacker furniture is well under way

6. Interview with Charles' eldest son Nathaniel Patrickson Greene.

and is working out beautifully. It will be all ready when he arrives except the finishing which cannot be done until the inlaying is done. I forgot to mention that Mr. Blacker's electric fixtures are all done and hung and they look very well.

I have been spending most of my time lately at Berkeley. We are doing some work at Mr. Culbertsons, changing the stairway, but will not be able to finish it until you return as Mr. Culbertson wants you to design the work.

In reference to other work in the Greene office, Hall went on to write: "Your brother is getting along nicely; the work is moving along well ... he has submitted several new plans and he has had bids on them, but has not gone ahead. We have figured on four different plans since you left, competition on all...." [7]

When Charles returned from England in late 1909 nearly his entire energies were focused on the interior furnishings for the ultimate bungalows. But in his own mind he felt that by this time he had done about all he could do with wood. He was also anxious to spend more time in writing, painting and other artistic endeavors.[8] It is not surprising then that he withdrew somewhat from the ordinary architectural work in the office and turned his attention to the few major commissions which offered special challenges.

Fewer and fewer opportunities came to him over the next decade, and as his own interests shifted away from the architectural practice in Pasadena, so too did the direction of his interior furnishings. Yet between 1907 and 1910 Greene and Greene had produced some of the finest furniture in America emanating from the Arts and Crafts Movement.

7. Courtesy Documents Collection, College of Environmental Design, U.C.B.
8. Interviews by the author with Nathaniel P. Greene.

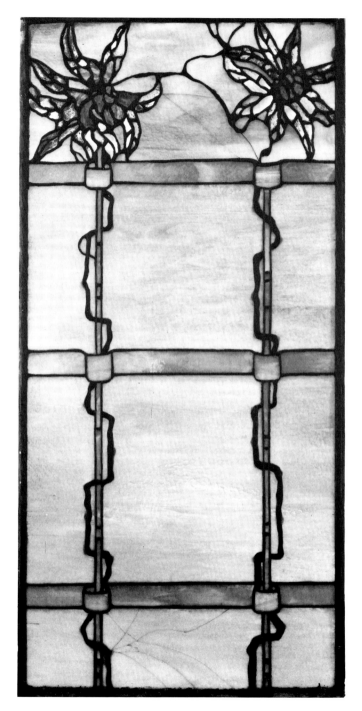

Right:
Stained glass window, Earle C. Anthony house, 1909.
Marvin Rand photograph.

The window composition represents typical forms used in the Greenes' designs during the years of their most noted works.

IV

Changing Attitudes and New Directions   1911-1916

The last major commission authorizing Greene and Greene to design the total interior and furnishings was for the elaborate residence for Cordelia A. Culbertson and her two maiden sisters. They were the only clients after 1910 who had both the interest and the means to give Charles the artistic and economic freedom he demanded.

In the preceding four years the Greenes had been spoiled by the seemingly unlimited budgets provided by wealthy clients. After Charles' return from England several large residences had been designed for various clients, but they had gone no further than the drawing boards, primarily because of the high costs involved. Then, too, public tastes were changing, turning away from natural woods and leaning towards what would soon be identified as Spanish Colonial Revival. Charles himself was seeking out new materials and new forms. The scope and the unusual site of the Culbertson house was an exciting challenge, and the confidence which the three sisters had in him promised a close and satisfying working relationship.

Although the basic lines of the Culbertson furniture had the same forthright character of Charles' earlier designs, the tastes of the three ladies combined with Charles' own interest in inlay work led to distinct differences between this furniture and all others designed by the firm. Brocaded fabrics were used in upholstery, extensive etching was done in the clear glass of various cabinet pieces, and the most decorative element is to be found in the inlay work of the furniture for the entry hall.

In the latter part of 1912, the Culbertson sisters sent Charles to New York to select some furnishings in addition to those he had designed, as well as various fabrics, lighting fixtures, and other accessories for the interiors. He purchased many items for the Culbertsons and also various wall fabrics for his own house.

In an article which Charles wrote for the *Pacific Coast Architect* in March of 1914, his discussion of the furniture and interiors indicated a deep concern for the designs and furnishings of the historical past.

He wrote:

The furniture of the hall consists of two tall back chairs of very dark crotch mahogany, inlaid with koa, lilac roots and vermillion. The design is a delicate band with twining wild roses. There is a large case or wardrobe of the corresponding design and material. Also two smaller tables at each side of the opening to the living-room. The floor covering is Bohemian hand-tufted rugs in shades of blue, with a touch of soft dull gold after a Chinese pattern. The same is in the living-room.

The living-room furniture is of the same material, but slightly different design from the hall. The chairs and two couches are covered with silk brocade, black and gold, after an old Queen Anne pattern, in imitation of the Chinese. The walls of both rooms are covered with linen velour specially designed for hangings. The color of this and the woodwork is something near cafe au lait, but being changeable, it harmonizes well with the rugs and tones with the dull gold. There is a large desk table with a dull black marble top, delicately gold-veined. There is a bookcase and a secretary, both with glass doors. A cut design of roses suggests the inlay design of the hall pieces. There is a very delicate inlay of golden in color. In the photographic reproductions the color scale has been somewhat disarranged. Some harsh lines and contrasts that are not to be seen in the original, show disagreeably.

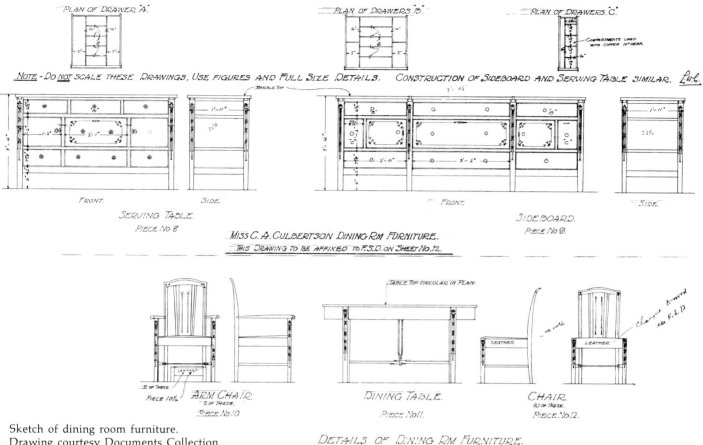

Sketch of dining room furniture.
Drawing courtesy Documents Collection,
College of Environmental Design, U.C.B.

Of the furniture in the dining room, Charles went on to write:

> This furniture is of mahogany, but light and warmer than that of the hall and living-room. The center table is round and has simple ribbon inlay in the top, which is meant to hold a small centerpiece and vase of flowers when not in use. The serving table and sideboard have tops of numidian marble, to match the panel in the mantel. The carved inlay is of oak knots, representing reeds and lotus flowers.[1]

Further in the article he discussed the various pieces of furniture which he selected rather than designed for other aspects of the house, some of which included Queen Anne carved walnut chairs and settees, Queen Anne lacquered chairs, secretary, and other pieces of the same period. He discussed the guest room furniture, which is a lacquered set; it has not yet been determined whether these pieces were designed by him or whether he selected them on his trip to New York. In the final paragraph of the article he stated very clearly that the furniture and fittings of the Culbertson house were either selected or designed and executed by the architects.

1. "Culbertson Residence, Pasadena, Cal.," *Pacific Coast Architect*, (March 1914), pp. 10, 11.

105

Living room desk case and chairs,
Cordelia A. Culbertson house, Pasadena, 1911.
Photograph courtesy Documents Collection,
College of Environmental Design, U.C.B.

Although the photograph is dominated by the brocade print of the chair upholstery, the desk case has the basic directness usually identified with the work of Charles Greene. The large scale of the piece is gently softened by his masterful sculptured detail in the corners and legs and by the playful cut glass detail of the bookshelving doors.

Entry hall armoire and highback armchair. Photograph courtesy Documents Collection, College of Environmental Design, U.C.B.

Charles' personal interest in inlay and carving was given creative opportunity by the three maiden Culbertson sisters, and he exercised his imagination to the fullest.

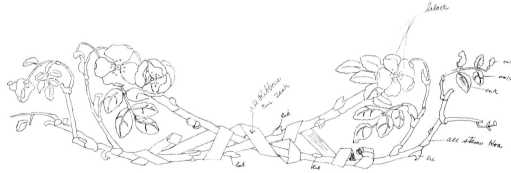

Typical detail of inlay work.
Drawing courtesy Documents Collection,
College of Envirnmental Design, U.C.B.

The careful selection of inlay woods included oak, vermillion, maple of differing colors, knurled white oak, mahogany, ebony, lignumvitae, and light colored teak.

View of dining room.
Photograph courtesy Greene and Greene Library.

Early drawings for the dining room furnishings included wall sconces, a central chandelier, and a center vase for the table—all designed to relate to the furniture. The final design featured antique lighting fixtures with molded plaster ceiling relief.

Detail of sideboard.
Marvin Rand photograph.

Marble matching the fireplace of the dining room capped the serving table and sideboard and related to the subtle colorations of the inlay detail and carved ebony drawer pulls.

Detail of wrought iron stair railing leading to the Italianate
pond of the elaborate lower gardens.
Marvin Rand photograph.

One of two identical lanterns which grace the steps at
the sidewalk.
Marvin Rand photograph.

The heavy carved copper and marble bases were designed
to complement the antique lanterns which matched those used
elsewhere in the house and on the terraces.

Charles was so completely involved in the structure and interior furnishings of the Culbertson house that he had no time to concern himself with other work in the office between 1910 and 1913. As a result Henry took almost the entire responsibility for a commission for Mrs. Parker A. Earle for an apartment house called Herkimer Arms.

The importance of the Earle apartments to the Greene story is the amount of built-in and mass-produced furniture which Henry designed and which was made by the Peter Hall mills. In addition to the built-in furniture, Henry's sense of the curious and his concern for saving space led to a combination of overlapping uses of space within each small apartment. As the living room was also the bedroom, he placed a raised closet to the right of the entry and up two stairs. This allowed for the bed to slide out from underneath the closet. When the bed was not in use, a sliding panel could be pulled out from the wall and used as a desk. He demonstrated this same ingenuity in other aspects of the interiors of these small apartments. Each apartment had a complement of small tables, bedroom bureaus and a very

Gate leg table, Earle apartments.
Marvin Rand photographs.

The design for the gate leg table operation was unusually simple.

simple, well-designed drop-leaf circular table, all of which were mass-produced. This was the only occasion when Greene and Greene designs were made in multiple quantities. The leg structure of the drop-leaf table was so basic and fundamental that a number of furniture makers have wondered why such a direct, straightforward system for a gateleg table had not been developed by others much earlier.

Henry was also responsible for the electric lighting for the residence of Mr. and Mrs. Henry A. Ware, who wanted certain traditional English designs followed in the interiors. The major problem confronting Henry was the fact that because of poor eyesight Mrs. Ware was bothered by electric lighting fixtures. His solution was to provide indirect lighting by means of a graceful and simple wooden light trough surrounding the entire living room. Moreover, the sculptural character of the fixture and the simplicity of the way with which he joined the various lengths of the light trough demonstrate his direct but sensitive approach to the solving of awkward problems.

Parker A. Earle apartments, Pasadena, 1911.
Marvin Rand photograph.

Built-in shelving with pull-out desk encloses the raised closet under which the full-size bed is stored when not in use.

Indirect lighting detail, Henry A. Ware house, Pasadena, 1913.
Marvin Rand photograph.

Sideboard, 1913, Charles S. Greene house, Pasadena.
Marvin Rand photograph.

In marked contrast to Charles' designs for clients after 1910, the unadorned simplicity of the furniture for his own home related to the firm's early designs and draws its primary beauty from the richness of scale and proportion.

In late 1911 Charles designed one of the first pieces of the more refined furniture for his own home—a rosewood writing desk. Late in 1912 he designed additional pieces, including chairs, writing tables, dining table, sideboard, and a particularly interesting corner china cabinet, all of which were made at the Peter Hall mill. What was most interesting about the furniture for his own home was the dramatic simplicity in contrast to the elaborately decorative work being done at the same time for the Culbertson sisters. Perhaps Charles' deference to his clients explains the variance of designs from one client to another while the simplicity of his own furniture suggests that he himself preferred to live with more direct and simpler pieces of furniture. It is also possible that the simplicity of his own furniture was influenced as much by cost as by taste. At the same time some of his designs for later clients indicate his fascination with intricate inlay work and complex floral compositions in folded ribbon patterns worked into soft plaster.

Between 1907 and 1909 Charles developed a signature which he would woodburn into the underside or sometimes even on the exposed portion of his furniture. The family of Mrs. Belle Barlow Bush clearly recalled that some time after the furniture had been delivered, Charles came by one day with his tools and woodburned his signature into each of the pieces he had designed for the Bush household.[2]

On May 27, 1912 Charles filed an application with the United States Patent Office for registration of a trademark.

It was about this time that Charles Greene dropped the name Charles and began to go by his middle name alone until he moved to Carmel where his stationery and signature became C. Sumner Greene.

Corner china case, Charles S. Greene house.
Marvin Rand photograph.

2. Correspondence with Mrs. Beatrice Barlow Bissell.

113

To all whom it may concern:

Be it known that I, SUMNER GREENE, a citizen of the United States of America, residing at Pasadena, county of Los Angeles, State of California, and doing business at 215–232 Boston Building, in said city, have adopted and used the trade-mark shown in the accompanying drawing, being my fac-simile signature, no claim being made to the words " His True Mark," for furniture, in Class No. 32, Furniture and upholstery, as follows: chairs, tables, stands, commodes, lounges, davenports, sofas, bedsteads, dress-

His
Sumner
True
Greene
Mark

ers, looking-glass frames, sideboards, book-cases, desks, hat-racks, cabinets, stools, benches, piano-cases, piano benches and stools.

The trade-mark has been continuously used in my business since November 30, 1910.

The trade-mark is applied or affixed to the goods, or to the packages containing the same, by branding on some portion of each article with a red hot metal brand, and is my signature.

SUMNER GREENE.

Trade-mark document for furniture and upholstery,
February 3, 1914.
Courtesy Greene and Greene Library.

Woodburned into visible areas of the furniture, this signature was utilized inconsistently and for a very short period of time.

The one other major commission between 1911 and 1915 on which Charles was working was the large residence and estate of Mr. and Mrs. Mortimer Fleishhacker in Woodside, California. No furniture was initially designed for this house, but the association with the Fleishhackers did result in designs for alterations to the Fleishhacker residence in San Francisco. Designs were begun in 1914 and were carried on for several years. Although some of the designs for the San Francisco house were never carried out, particularly those for the furniture, the drawings indicate a similar ornate character to the furniture as that for the Culbertson sisters in 1911. This concern for complex ornament, folded patterns and historical motifs was not only evident in the furniture designs but also in wall lighting sconces, moldings and plaster reliefs. Similar to the interiors for the Culbertson sisters, the design sketches are very elaborate and included swagged draperies of heavy fabrics with bold valances and a total conceptual development of the entire interior space. Charles was obviously eager to do the entire job; however, only portions of it were carried out.

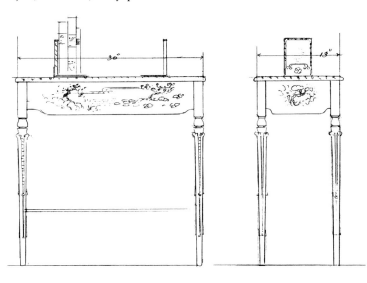

Sketches for furniture project for Fleishhacker
San Francisco house.
Drawing courtesy Documents Collection,
College of Environmental Design, U.C.B.

Charles harmonizes the plasticity of his intricate plaster relief designs with the detail carvings and shaping of the furniture in wood.

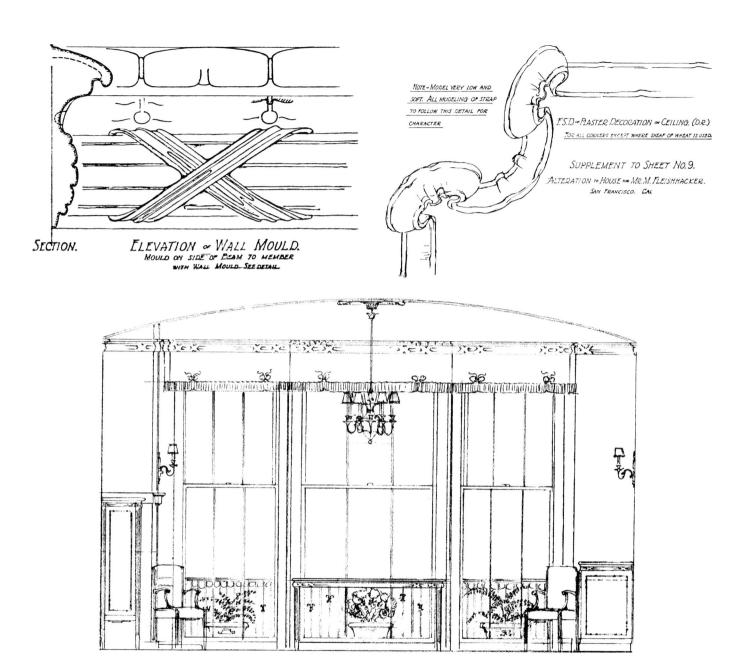

SECTION.

ELEVATION of WALL MOULD.
MOULD on SIDE of BEAM TO MEMBER
WITH WALL MOULD SEE DETAIL

NOTE - MODEL VERY LOW AND
SOFT. ALL MODELING OF STRAP
TO FOLLOW THIS DETAIL FOR
CHARACTER

F.S.D. of PLASTER DECORATION on CEILING. (D.R.)
FOR ALL CORNERS EXCEPT WHERE SHEAF OF WHEAT IS USED

SUPPLEMENT TO SHEET No. 9.
ALTERATION TO HOUSE FOR MR. M. FLEISHHACKER.
SAN FRANCISCO. CAL.

Preliminary sketch for interior remodeling, Mortimer
Fleishhacker house, (designed by others), San Francisco, 1915.
Drawings courtesy Documents Collection,
College of Environmental Design, U.C.B.

The architectural work was carried on for several years in
plaster relief designs and cut glass windows. The furniture
was never made; however, its design sketches are very similar
to the armchair which Charles later made for the game room
for the Fleishhacker home in 1923.

115

Shortly before Charles decided to move his family to Carmel, Mr. Gamble and the residents along Westmoreland Place had been plagued with tourist busses driving along their private street. As a result they commissioned the Greenes to close one end of Westmoreland Place and to design and place signs at both ends indicating that Westmoreland Place was a private and not a through street and that it was not accessible to company bus tours. The end result was a beautiful composition of boulder piers at Rosemont, formerly Lester Avenue, and the furnishing of Westmoreland Place with wrought iron gates with the same movement and grace as the wrought iron work in the Earle C. Anthony Auto Showroom of 1911 and in the gates to the portals of Oaklawn done in 1906. The signs on Westmoreland Place exhibited a playful but serious typeface selection and were suspended from a wooden structure which related to the two Greene and Greene houses nearby—the Gamble house and John Addison Cole house. At the same time, in developing the open end of Westmoreland Place, Charles had divided the entrance and exit around a majestic deodar tree. In later letters to Henry he expressed a great disappointment that the lines of the street were not adhered to in the actual construction by Mr. Gamble and the other residents.[3]

As less and less work came into the office after 1911, Charles grew more and more attracted to the life-style of the people around Carmel—the painters, writers, poets and photographers with whom he enjoyed associating. During his visits to the Fleishhacker job site in Woodside, he had visited Carmel several times and eventually on June 2, 1916 he and his family moved there. This date marks the beginning of the end of an era for the Greenes, although the actual dissolution of the firm did not take place until 1922.

Charles and Henry continued their great respect and affection for each other, but they recognized that their individual desires were diverging and leading down different paths. Though there would be occasions where the brothers worked together on new projects for previous clients, the years of semi-practice and semi-retirement for Greene and Greene is now a story of each of the brothers independent of the other.

3. Correspondence from Charles Greene to Henry Greene in April 1917.

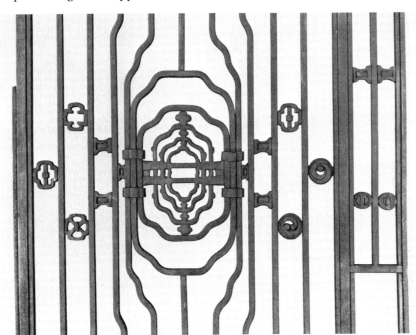

Left:
Elevator detail of wrought iron work,
Earle C. Anthony Automobile Showroom,
Los Angeles, 1911.
Marvin Rand photograph.

Similar designs were utilized in the balcony railings, stairway housing, and entrance doors and canopy.

Gates and portals of Westmoreland Place, Pasadena, 1916.
Marvin Rand photograph.

The Tanner Livery Company would frequently bring tours
through Westmoreland Place in open vehicles and drivers
would extoll the virtues of Pasadena living over megaphones.
The distractions eventually prompted David Gamble and the
other residents to engage the Greenes to close off one end
of the private street to through traffic and to place signs at the
entrance indicating the street was private property.

V

C. Sumner Greene — The Later Years   1916-1934

After Charles Greene moved to Carmel his work on interiors and furnishings was commissioned primarily by former clients or new owners of the large residences completed in earlier years. At the time of the move Charles was completing work on a significant lamp design for the Culbertsons, and was deeply involved with the work for Mr. and Mrs. Mortimer Fleishhacker in San Francisco. Correspondence in December of 1916 indicated that eleven men were working on the job at that time.[1] While this did not involve furniture it did involve a great deal of detailed work on the molded and carved plaster relief in the interior of the space and in the marble carvings for mantels and other details.

Early in 1917 Charles first heard from Henry that the Culbertson sisters were considering the sale of their house. It was purchased on April 29, 1917 by Mrs. Dudley P. Allen. She was so impressed by Charles' designs of the interiors and furnishings of the house that within a week she had travelled up to Pebble Beach to discuss with him the design of further furnishings. According to Charles' correspondence, Mrs. Allen ordered sketches for a screen and two mirrors for the dining room, marble jardinieres for the hall, another lamp for the living room, and a piano case for the garden room. Over the years both Charles and Henry Greene developed a good working relationship with her, and she highly valued the subtleties of Charles' workmanship. Although there would be a great deal of work with Mrs. Allen within the next decade, at times there were difficulties in communication and misunderstandings about

deliveries and costs, many of which were created by Charles. As early as July 5, 1917, just a few weeks after meeting Mrs. Allen, Charles wrote:

> I have been waiting for word from Mrs. Allen, but as I have not heard I think she must be away. If you think it necessary, I will come down even if I don't hear from her. It is such a job to get figures on her work at a distance. Everybody is afraid of it or me. I am out of patience with people who must have figures as if they would make the work any cheaper. However, I hope she will let me do the work; it would be a great help to me just now.

In another letter to the office in Pasadena, Charles wrote on June 27:

> If Mrs. Allen would only decide to do something, I could come down there and help Hal out, but otherwise it is so expensive.

With reference to Charles' writing that was in process in Carmel at the time, he writes further:

> My story has been sadly neglected lately since I commenced Mrs. Allen's furniture drawings, but just now they are off my hands for a few days until John Hall can figure some of it. I won't have much respite though.[2]

1. Correspondence from C. Sumner Greene to his father in December, 1916. Courtesy of Robert Judson Clark and Documents Collection, College of Environmental Design, U.C.B.

2. Excerpts of Charles Greene's correspondence, courtesy Robert Judson Clark.

By September, however, all problems had been resolved and Charles was moving ahead on the furniture designs for Mrs. Allen. These included an attachable round top as well as a rectangular top which could be attached to the dining table designed earlier for the Culbertson sisters. The attachments for the alternate additional tops were so intricate that Charles even designed the hardware used to install and stabilize them. By September 10 John Hall had been authorized to do the more expensive table top. Work proceeded swiftly and some of the items, such as the mirrors for the dining room, were delivered to Mrs. Allen as early as October.

In 1908 Mrs. Allen remarried and became Mrs. Frances F. Prentiss, and it was under this name that the house was frequently published over the years. Charles did numerous drawings for dining room screens and the piano lamp which she had ordered. The drawings for the lamp indicate his concern for the most minute detail in the forming of the cast bronze of the bases and reveal a sophistication and concern for form which was very much akin to the graceful designs of Louis Comfort Tiffany for his lamp bases. The full-size detail drawings for the dining room screen exhibit a similar sophistication and concern for detail. Although there were numerous preliminary sketches of various designs for the piano, none of them were carried through to a final design, and the piano probably was never made.

Charles' account books indicate that he continued work-

C. Sumner Greene, 1934.
Photograph by Henry Greene,
courtesy Greene and Greene Library.

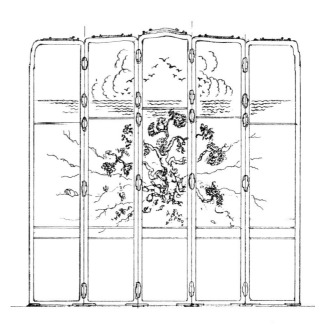

Folding screen for dining room, (Cordelia Culbertson home) for Mrs. Dudley P. Allen (later Mrs. Francis F. Prentiss), 1917. Drawing courtesy Documents Collection, College of Environmental Design, U.C.B.

119

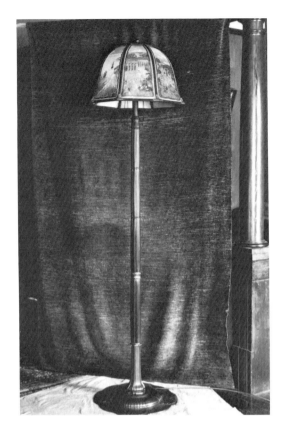

Above:
Table lamp for the Culbertson sisters, 1916.

Shortly before the sale of the house to Mrs. Dudley P. Allen in April, 1917, the Culbertson sisters commissioned Charles to design a table lamp for the living room which combined an antique oriental urn with fixture design and shade paintings by Charles.

Above left, left:
Piano lamp for living room for Mrs. Dudley P. Allen, 1917.
Photographs courtesy Documents Collection, College of Environmental Design, U.C.B.

Shade and base details were designed to coordinate with the lamp done for the Culbertson sisters the previous year.

120

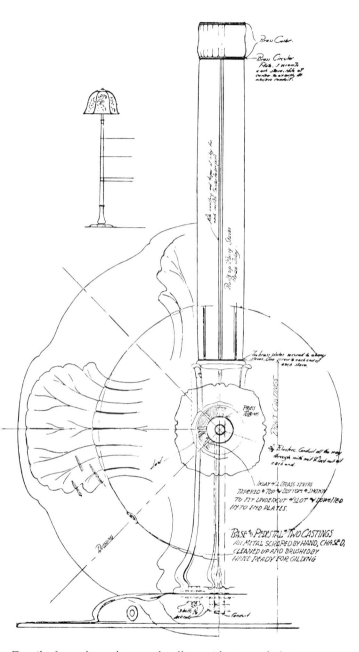

Detail of cast brass base and collars with stem of ebony
staves with brass inlay for Allen piano lamp.
Drawing courtesy Documents Collection,
College of Environmental Design, U.C.B.

ing for Mrs. Prentiss through 1920. Accounts for April 1919
and February 1920 indicate payments of as much as $3000
for panels. The nature of these panels and where they were
placed is unknown as these do not appear to be the carved
and painted plaques made for the dining room some seven
years later. The 1920 entries record expenses for a trip to
Los Angeles in connection with the Prentiss furniture, although the pieces of furniture were not identified. It is quite
possible that there was a break in the relationship between
Charles and Mrs. Prentiss around 1920, for the records
show that Henry Greene was designing furniture for Mrs.
Prentiss in 1925, and it was not until 1926 that Charles again
became actively involved in further work for Mrs. Prentiss.

In 1917, about the time he started on the initial work for
Mrs. Prentiss, Charles was also commissioned by Mr. and
Mrs. Henry M. Robinson to add several pieces to their
earlier furniture. This also included the enclosure of a side
porch for a game room. The wooden carvings in the paneling of this room reflected the sculptural character of the
plaster relief resembling that done for the Fleishhacker's
San Francisco house the year before. The following year
the Robinsons commissioned a tea table and lamp which
was very similar to the design of a floor lamp developed as
the piano lamp for Mrs. Prentiss.

Detail of carved marble mantel, D. L. James house.
Marvin Rand photograph.

The marble carvings were done in San Francisco and relate
to other wooden patterns which Charles carved.

In addition to work for former clients, Charles was
deeply involved in work on the D.L. James house in Carmel
Highlands. In a letter of September 22, 1921 discussing an
adjustment of architectural fees, there is a reference to furniture and fixtures on the same 6 percent basis. Drawings
indicate Charles' eagerness to design the furniture for the
James house. One such drawing was for a white oak desk
somewhat similar to his previous work, but showing considerably more sculptural carving in the wood. This marks
a departure from Charles' previous furniture as here he
was emphasizing carved form rather than the natural grain
of the wood or the inlaid patterns. According to their son,
Daniel, the Jameses felt that Charles' furniture was much
too light for their taste. They preferred more massive antiques in the house and subsequently selected seventeenth
century Italian and English pieces.[3]

In 1923 Charles began work on his own studio in Carmel.
Here the carvings for the timbers of the living room, various
beams for door openings, the carved doors and a large
bookcase designed for the studio demonstrate the continuing strength and versatility of his creative imagination.

3. Interviews with Daniel and Lilith James.

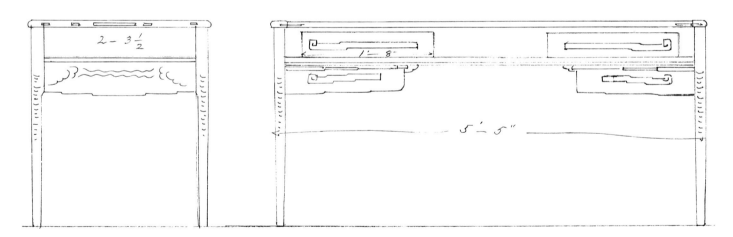

Sketch for proposed furniture for D. L. James house,
Carmel Highlands, 1918-1923.
Drawing courtesy Documents Collection,
College of Environmental Design, U.C.B.

The design of white oak was too light in scale for Mr. and
Mrs. James who eventually furnished the house in European
antique pieces.

Elaborately carved entry door,
C. Sumner Greene studio,
Carmel-by-the-sea, 1923.
Marvin Rand photograph.

The carved exterior of the solid
teakwood door is an interesting
contrast with the elegant linear
simplicity of the inside face.

Interior of C. Sumner Greene's studio showing the large bookcase designed for his office
in the Boston Building in Pasadena during the era of the work on the elaborate bungalows.
Roy Flamm photograph.

Detail of bookcase.
Marvin Rand photograph.

The carvings in wood are again representative of Charles' preoccupation with the plasticity of his designs in plaster relief for the Fleishhackers, Jameses, and in his own studio.

Bookcase designed and built by Charles for his Carmel studio in the mid-1920s. Marvin Rand photograph.

Built of inexpensive low grade woods, Charles painted the surface which he treated and rubbed as though working with a lacquer finish.

Interior of the small office in Charles' Carmel studio.
Roy Flamm photograph.

Three distinct eras of Charles Greene's designs are represented here: the very early Stickley-influenced plain oak filing cabinet which Charles built in 1903 in the shop behind his Pasadena home; the mahogany cabinet to the left relating to the furniture from the elaborate bungalow years (1907-1911); and the sculptured treatment of forms and space of his later studies.

Entry hall of the Carmel studio.
Roy Flamm photograph.

Detail of French door between entry and main room of Carmel studio.
Marvin Rand photograph.

This excellent door was never completed and still exhibits the sequence of Charles' wood carving from pencil and chalk initial ideas to the nearly completed carving.

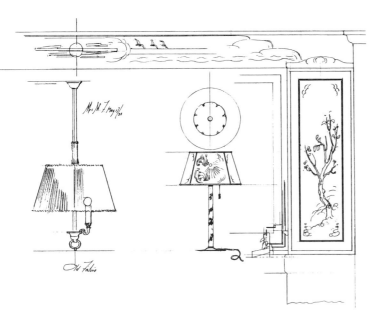

Sketch of proposals for the Fleishhacker game room.
Drawing courtesy Documents Collection,
College of Environmental Design, U.C.B.

Forms in this drawing for the frieze are more typical of the
finished carvings; however, the cabinet door sketch is less
contrived here. The chandelier and table lamp were never
constructed.

Right:
Corner of game room interior added to Mortimer Fleishhacker.
house, Woodside, California, 1923.
Marvin Rand photograph.

The linearity of the French doors relates the converted open
porch space to the character of the original design of the
house in 1911. Charles' interest in stylistic abstraction in his
carvings dominates the interiors in the many cabinet doors,
wooden friezes, furniture, and in the patterns pressed into
the soft plaster of the walls and ceiling.

In 1923 Mr. and Mrs. Mortimer Fleishhacker again called
on Charles, this time to enclose a side porch of their residence at Woodside as a game room. The commission was
quickly accepted for Charles was not only in need of work,
but still eager to do further work on the Fleishhacker house
at Woodside and to design furniture for that house. The
game room was fully crafted by Charles; it was the only
room in the house developed in natural woods, and it was
the first time in over two decades that he actually had an
opportunity to make client's furniture himself. He had
developed a woodshop next to his studio in Carmel. The

combination of the carvings for the paneling, the doors to cabinets, the game table, four chairs and arm chair took over two years to complete. The similarity in the design for the furniture of this game room and the proposed sketches for the furniture for the D. L. James house was an indication of Charles' determination to carry out his new ideas regarding the sculptural quality of carvings in the furniture of the early twenties.

In addition to the paneling and furniture, Charles' designs made it necessary for him to make the instruments with which he tooled the leather of the upholstery and the leather top of the game table which were then accented with color and leather glaze. The Fleishhacker game room furniture is a good example of the major role which John Hall played in the detail and construction of furniture. Without John Hall's expertise and without the proper equipment of the mill the joinery of the furniture for the Fleishhackers was less sophisticated. Such devices as a simple metal clip screwed to the top and the edge of the table were utilized in the Fleishhacker furniture in the same manner as in the very early furniture designed for the Adelaide Tichenor house in 1904.

Table and chairs for Fleishhacker game room photographed in Charles' Carmel studio.
Photograph courtesy Greene and Greene Library.

In 1925 Charles made the acquaintance of Martin Flavin, a prominent writer associated with MGM Studios. Flavin had recently had a large home designed by another architect built on Spindrift Road below Carmel Highlands overlooking the rocky coast of the Pacific Ocean. Over the years he engaged Charles in numerous projects which he later described as giving the home all of the fine character that it possessed.[4] The initial work for Flavin involved the design of a table in 1925. Between 1925 and 1930 Charles' work for Flavin consisted primarily of architectural projects, but in 1930 drawings were begun for a special private library which Flavin would use for his writing. The interior was entirely of redwood. Charles himself carved all of the panels and installed the paneling, the bookshelves and the ceiling. He designed a desk and a chair for the room as well as moveable hanging hammered copper reading light fixtures, and special lighting fixtures with handles which hung on the wall and could be lifted from their mounts and carried along the shelves to aid in the search of a particular book. Charles' carvings for Martin Flavin also included the major door between the living room and the new library, a significant large redwood relief over the fireplace mantel in the living room, and the mantel supports.

4. Correspondence to the author.

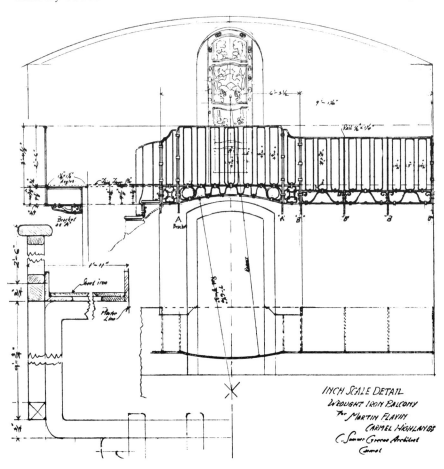

Drawing courtesy Documents Collection, College of Environmental Design, U.C.B.

View from living room into library, Martin Flavin house, Carmel Highlands, 1931. Marvin Rand photograph.

Detail of moveable hammered copper hand lamp in the Flavin library.
Marvin Rand photograph.

One of three swinging reading lamps in the Flavin library.
Marvin Rand photograph.

Tooled leather bedroom screen for Mrs. Francis F. (Allen) Prentiss, 1926.
Photograph courtesy Greene and Greene Library.

Carved marble entry urns for Mrs. Francis F. Prentiss, 1927.
Marvin Rand photograph.

Early in 1927 Charles again was doing a considerable amount of work for Mrs. Prentiss. There had also been some work in 1926 related to another elaborate screen for Mrs. Prentiss' bedroom. However, one of the major projects which ultimately became a point of controversy between Charles and Mrs. Prentiss was the request for a series of nine carved and colored panels to be placed around the dining room. To Mrs. Prentiss the dining room seemed unfinished and upon her request Charles prepared sketches which were shipped to Mrs. Prentiss on February 9, 1927. The extent of the work for Mrs. Prentiss in 1927 and the variety of Charles' involvement is best understood through the reading of the correspondence between Charles and his brother Henry. In a letter dated June 9, 1927, Henry wrote:

> I have just received a short letter from Mrs. Prentiss in which she says if you would have the tea table, the screen, the lights for the entry hall, and the ornaments for the front entrance completed, she might give you a little lee-way on some of the panels for the dining room, but that she would not want to have to wait until the end of the season for them...she surely has made all concessions, and it is now up to you to stick with the things and get them out for her and avoid any further disappointment to her.

On December 14 Henry wrote:

> I believe if you can get those ornaments for the front entrances here and get the three panels for the dining room here and hung, she will feel all right.

Henry to Charles on January 27, 1928:

> Mrs. Prentiss called me on the telephone just a few moments ago and asked me to write to you not to do anything more on the panels you are making for the dining room. She says, quite frankly, she does not like them. She says they are not at all what she expected—she thought that you would do something that would just blend in with the walls, but these three panels that you have hung look spotty and disturb the harmony that she felt in the room before. She rather criticizes you for not letting her know costs and doing something so she would understand a little better what was to be done before doing it. I do not know what is wrong unless it is your method of doing things.

130

On January 9, 1928 Mrs. Prentiss received a bill for the amount of $1,551.30 from the marble carver for his work in making the two marble vases to stand beside the front entrance. In response to the bill, she wrote to Charles on February 9, 1928 as follows:

I need not say, perhaps, that I am rather astonished at the size of the bill for the two jars. It really had never occurred to me that they would reach such a sum, and though, of course, I did not ask you for an estimate, or you, perhaps, said you could not give one, I should have requested it before carrying on with the work. However, that is completed and they must necessarily stand. I think they are very attractive, but I must say that if I have you do any future work for me, I must request an estimate of the cost because everything that has been done recently has been a good bit beyond my expectations.

With regard to the plaques in the dining room I am still of the opinion that they are not an asset, but are rather a detraction from the beauty of the room. I cannot visualize them with the color eliminated as ornamental, and I think that we shall just have to eliminate them entirely. They are so utterly different from what I had expected that I do not see how I can use them in any part of my house, and I think that I shall have to return them to you expecting that you can use them elsewhere. If it seems just to you that I should pay for the cost of material, I will be glad to do so. Otherwise it seems to me that you may have to, perhaps, stand the loss.

Charles responded to Mrs. Prentiss on February 15:

Thank you for your check for $1,916.75 in full for urns at front entrance 1188 Hillcrest Avenue.

I am both sorry and pained to know that you are dissatisfied with the cost of this year's work. Speaking of estimates, it seems to me that you do not know or have forgotten that your house and all in it were completed without an estimate and exceeded all expectation.

But your fine discriminating sense singled it out from many others. Won't you believe that this was the reason? It seems plain to me.

There is nothing reckless or extravagant about the work. No artist can figure original work for only one set of objects, even the factory can't; but the factory multiplies sets so that the original cost is only a fraction of the cost of each set sold.

If you had come to me to build the house, but had limited me to an estimate, 1188 Hillcrest could never have existed. Business, I admit must run upon business lines, but this is not business, this art of helping to make living pleasurable and beautiful beyond the merely useful.

As for the plaques, I think you have forgotten your encouraging letter of February 28, 1927, in which you gave me the order for the nine plaques...do you think it fair or business-like to simply reject them? It is far from my

Three preliminary sketches for nine proposed panels for the dining room for Mrs. Prentiss, 1926.
Drawings courtesy Greene and Greene Library.

intent to force anything on you that you do not like, but with changed and softened colors you would get the effect of restfullness that you expect. This I am not only willing but anxious to do. I am sorry that I forgot at the time your particular feeling for color, but I have already given the reason.

Please remember that I have tried to fill your order for these plaques in good faith and have spent months of my time on them.

Mrs. Prentiss replied in March, 1928:

I have thought long and carefully concerning the matters in your recent letter and while you are quite right about my words of approval of your designs for the panels in the dining room, I have to confess that the panels have not quite come up to my expectation.

As I have studied them, I just cannot see them in any altered shape or color in that room, and as the room is so perfect without them I think that we shall have to let the matter drop and I shall let you send the bill to me for those ones completed. I may be able to find a place down in the loggia for them.

On March 26, 1928 Charles wrote to Henry:

I have settled with Mrs. Prentiss and she says the three plaques are to go in the loggia. I am thoroughly disappointed, but it can't be helped. I feel that the plaques are as good as anything I have ever done and the dining room will always seem unfinished to me.

...If I thought they were defective or were not up to the standard of my work I would not have charged a cent for them. Well! That's that, and I suppose that it is the last I shall hear from her, but I think she is not malicious in the least and the things may win her back when she sees them long enough. I should never have overlooked her taste for color if they had not hurried me to the point of desperation.

In spite of the disagreements there was a genuine close relationship between Mrs. Prentiss and the Greenes, and the letter from Henry to Charles of February 11, 1929 is illustrative of that attitude. Henry wrote:

I have seen Mrs. Prentiss once or twice since she returned to Pasadena on January 15, and the first time I was out I was in her bedroom and she remarked that she loved the screens you made for her.

...She liked the style of the screen, but did not like the style of the panels. I knew that you would be interested to hear this.

In the upper left-hand corner of the letter Charles' notation indicates his persistence. It states: "Answer February 19, 1929, ask Mrs. P. to let me recolor plaques."[5]

Other works demanding Charles' attention in 1928 and 1929 involved the design of a fountain for Mr. and Mrs. Robert Blacker for their home in Pasadena, and sketches for bookcases in the entry hall, although these were never completed. Also, as part of the development of the grounds and water gardens for the Mortimer Fleishhackers, Charles was directly involved in the design of many of the garden pots and more than two hundred urns which were made by the Garden City Pottery in San Jose. Charles was continually visiting the potter and painted the patterned glaze on the pots himself.

5. Correspondence related to Mrs. Prentiss courtesy of Robert Judson Clark and Greene and Greene Library.

Fountain for rear garden, Robert R. Blacker house, Pasadena, 1928.

Marvin Rand photograph.

Above:
Ceramic garden pot for Mortimer
Fleishhacker estate, Woodside, 1928.

Right:
Stone urn for water gardens, Mortimer
Fleishhacker estate, 1927.
Marvin Rand photographs.

Charles' artistic enthusiasm and lack of proper communication with clients created a similar series of misunderstandings with Mrs. Thomas Verner Moore who had commissioned a small stool for her son. Mrs. Moore had been making the cover for the seat herself and wrote to Charles on April 11, 1930:

> I have been hoping to hear from you about when the stool is to be ready. The work I was doing is ready to send. I should like to have the stool ready to give my son on Mother's Day.... I like to give my son a little remembrance that day...the price will be all right, so you don't need to let me know how much the cost is before you have it done.

However, after the stool was delivered, she wrote to Charles on December 29:

> When I saw you in Carmel I thought you were to make a very plain, but strong stool. I thought that it was to be of oak which would suit the furniture in my son's den. I told you it was a piece of his mother's work to be used in his den, so he could enjoy sitting in front of the fire for a smoke. As I said to you when I saw the beautiful work on it, that it was far too elaborate for the purpose it was to be used for. Then if the price you mentioned is correct, I was so astonished when you told me. That is prohibitive. I could not pay the amount you said. So I don't know that I can do anything else but send it back.
>
> P.S. Of course there is no use sending a seat without my work on it so please let me have the bill for the work done on that.[6]

Following further correspondence the stool was returned and kept in Charles' own possession.

Shortly thereafter Charles was commissioned by Mrs. Willis Walker to design a three-panel teakwood screen for her home. This screen was elaborately carved, but was not accepted by Mrs. Walker, probably because of its cost. That too remained in Charles' home the balance of his life.

6. Correspondence courtesy of Robert Judson Clark and Documents Collection, College of Environmental Design, U.C.B.

C. Sumner Greene with folding carved teakwood screen designed and made by him for Mrs. Willis Walker, 1934.
R. L. Makinson photograph.

134

Detail of one of the nine carved panels of the Walker screen. Marvin Rand photograph.

Stool for Mrs. Thomas Verner Moore, 1930. Marvin Rand photograph.

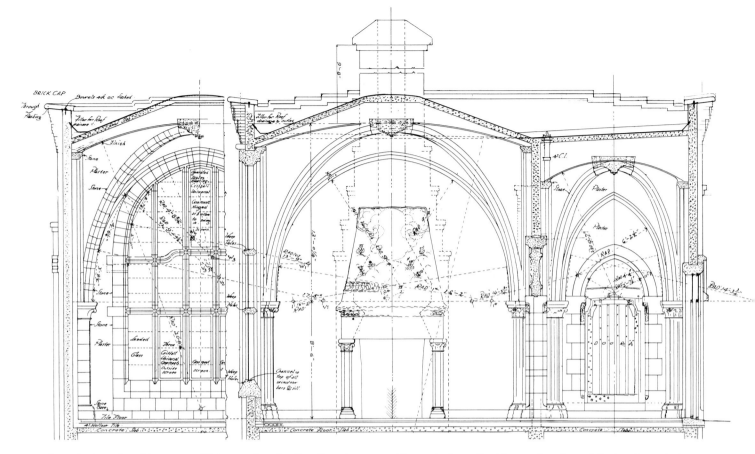

Late design of gothic room addition project for San Francisco home of Mr. and Mrs. Mortimer Fleishhacker, 1929-1932. Drawing courtesy Documents Collection, College of Environmental Design, U.C.B.

Elements from the Greenes' early architectural vocabulary and Charles' later sculptural period are intermixed in this attempted gothic design.

In the late 1920s and through 1930 and 1931 Mr. and Mrs. Mortimer Fleishhacker engaged Charles to make an addition to their San Francisco residence. This has become known as the Gothic room project and in Charles' own words presented the greatest challenge and was the hardest work he ever attempted in his life. Creation was becoming more difficult. Numerous sketches were done, many drawings carried well into refined stages, and the total development of the interiors attempted.

In early 1930 letters to Henry discussed the working drawings for the Gothic room. In November there was a reference to the plans being done. However, a letter from Charles in December indicates that they were still un-

finished. In February of 1931 Charles wrote that he was seeing daylight on the plans for the Gothic room. In June of 1931 he was taking estimates for the stonework, the woodwork, and the wrought iron for the vaulting. By mid-August Charles wrote to Henry that "some of our earlier schemes for the Gothic room have looked as hopeless as this, but between us, I expect, we will find a way out."[7]

Unfortunately, the project, in spite of the countless hours of planning, never entered construction. That is particularly unfortunate inasmuch as some of the drawings reveal a very sensitive weaving together of traditional Gothic forms

7. *Ibid.*

and recognizable characteristics of earlier Greene and Greene work. These were so carefully woven together that the end product would certainly have been one of the most unusual spaces ever created by either of the brothers.

The last few pieces of furniture Charles Greene produced by his own hands were made in the 1930s and included the stool for Mrs. Moore, the very handsome screen for Mrs. Walker, and a small table for his son, Thomas Gordon Greene and his wife. Possibly the last work was an incompleted cabinet for his wife, Alice, in which he playfully designed and carved various forms of animal life.

From the first to the last of Charles Greene's furniture designs, the basic form of the piece was of primary importance. The variation and detail of decorative elements depended upon his particular feelings at the time, his judgment of the client's wishes, and the particular era in which he was working. His personal fascination with carving revealed itself most often when he had plenty of time on his hands. It is, nevertheless, significant that the designs for his own home represent some of the purest, most direct, beautifully scaled and proportioned compositions of his entire career. The versatility, imagination, craftsmanship, and sensitivity which Charles brought to his furniture, his lighting fixtures, leaded glass designs, metal work, and all facets of the joinery, hinging, and mechanical apparatus were all given his undivided attention and all retain that certain continuity of spirit which distinguishes the furniture and related designs of Charles Sumner Greene.

Detail of one of four carved panels of a cabinet never completed for Charles' wife, Alice, circa 1934.
Roy Flamm photograph.

VI

Henry Mather Greene — The Later Years   1916-1930

Henry Greene's interest in the design of furniture and related designs began at the same time as Charles' when both were introduced to and embraced the principles of the Arts and Crafts Movement around 1902 and 1903. The demands of the firm, the necessity to administer the business of the office, the supervision of the work, and the coordination of the vast amount of activity engaged in by the firm, made it impossible for Henry to fully pursue his interests in designing furniture. It seems clear, though, when studying the furniture designs emanating from the firm between 1903 and 1906 that Henry's association is more clearly felt than with the furniture and interior designs after 1906.

During the period of the construction of the ultimate bungalows and their full complement of furniture and related designs, Henry, Peter Hall, John Hall and Emil Lange were completely immersed in the execution of the work while Charles was concentrating all his energies on the designs. The first of Henry Greene's furniture designs is a rough sketch for a round dining table and chairs for his own home. Only the chairs were made. However, it is most likely related to the period shortly following the Tichenor house of 1904 and preceding the refinements of the furniture following 1906. The design reflects Gustav Stickley's designs, although the lift form was already apparent.

The first of Henry's furniture designs made for clients appears to be in the period of the designs for Mrs. Belle Barlow Bush. There were two tables, one of which was similar in design to certain pieces for Mrs. Bush. On the back of a photograph of one of these tables, Charles noted that the table was designed by "Hal." There is no further identification as for whom the table was designed, and Henry's family has no recollection of such a table, although they believe that Henry had designed such items as bookshelves and built-in cabinets in his own home in Pasadena.[1]

Aside from furniture, there are several instances, particularly of skylight design and window design, which bear the decided imprint of Henry Greene's compositional abilities. Henry's sense of order and discipline was more likely to result in direct designs generally composed of straight lines arranged in vertical and horizontal compositions. This was exhibited in the 1902 windows for the living room of the James Culbertson house, and particularly well-handled in the direct and graceful glass compositions of the skylights for the residences for William W. Spinks and Dr. S. S. Crow in 1909.

Despite the disciplined nature of Henry's compositions, there was a playful sense in some of his designs—as in the china cabinets for the dining room and in the book cabinets for the living room of the Annie Blacker house of 1912. Henry's designs reflect the methodical, systematic order with which he conducted his entire life. He was somewhat of an amateur inventor; he was challenged by unusual situations and by the need for new technology. He was often brilliant in solving problems, as in the lighting system for Mr. and Mrs. Henry A. Ware discussed earlier.

---

1. Interviews by the author with Henry Dart Greene, Isabelle Greene McElwain and William Sumner Greene.

In 1915 Henry designed several pieces of furniture for an addition for the house of Dr. R. P. McReynolds. However, there is no record that this furniture was ever made.

In 1918, after Charles had moved to Carmel, Henry was involved in the addition to a structure designed by others for Mr. John Whitworth in Altadena. In the course of this job, he designed several pieces of furniture, bathroom cabinets, and wall lighting fixtures for the bedroom wing. These designs suggested earlier forms utilized in the Greenes' designs combined with a feeling for some of the characteristics related to the popular Spanish Colonial Revival.

Henry Mather Greene, 1924.
Photograph courtesy Greene and Greene Library.

Leaded clear glass china case doors, Annie Blacker house, Pasadena, 1912.
R. L. Makinson photograph.

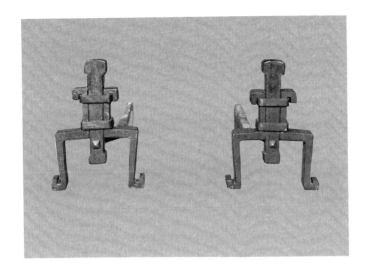

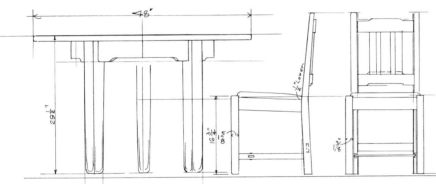

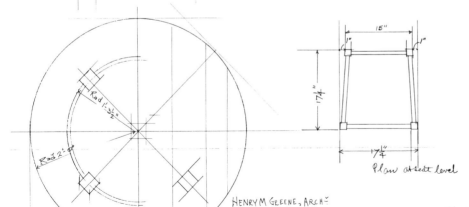

HENRY M GREENE, ARCH⁻
DINING TABLE & CHAIRS
Scale 1 IN = 1 FT

Plan at seat level

Above left:
Andirons, Henry M. Greene house, Pasadena, 1904. Marvin Rand photograph.

Above right:
Table designed by Henry for unknown client, circa, 1907.
Photograph courtesy Greene and Greene Library.

The design has characteristics similar to furniture for Mrs. Belle Barlow Bush.

Sketch by Henry Greene of dining room furniture intended for his own home.
Drawing courtesy Greene and Greene Library.

Tile inlay detail over den fireplace, Annie Blacker house, 1912. R. L. Makinson photograph.

Living room window, Annie Blacker house.

Henry's design for the living room windows breaks from the rigid linearity of the dining case glass, although the playful variations are almost mathematical in their progression.

Skylight in upper hall, William W. Spinks house, Pasadena, 1909. Marvin Rand photograph.

The linear geometrical design was typical of Henry Greene's compositions and here evolved from the natural expression of the structural framework.

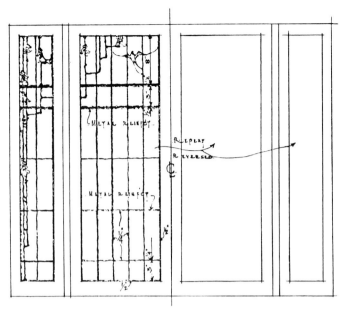

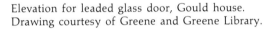

Elevation for leaded glass door, Gould house.
Drawing courtesy of Greene and Greene Library.

Even the nervous line of the leading in the drawing exhibits
Henry's desire to soften and bring a more lyrical character into
this leaded glass pattern accented by the free forms of birds
in flight. Designs such as this exhibit the sensitivity and
breadth of Henry's talents.

Wall lighting fixture for
John Whitworth, Altadena, 1918.
Marvin Rand photograph.

Combined here are forms from
typical Greene fixtures of the
wooden bungalow era with
details and variations characteristic
of the then popular Spanish
Colonial Revival.

Below:
Wrought iron railing, Kate A.
Kelley house, Los Angeles, 1924.
Marvin Rand photograph.

In the 1920s Henry was able to pursue many of his interests in interior and furniture design. One of the first of
these was in 1924 for the residence for Mr. and Mrs.
Thomas Gould, Jr. for whom he designed an interior mirror
for the landing of the stairwell, and clear leaded glass for
the china cabinet where he was able to blend the lyrical
movement of birds in flight with the regimented linear
composition of the window. Soon afterwards the leaded
glass for the windows for Mrs. Kate A. Kelly in Hollywood
moved further from the straight line toward a more free
and lyrical composition.

In spite of the long association between Mrs. Prentiss
and Charles Greene, it was Henry whom she commissioned
in 1925 for the designs for various pieces of bedroom furniture: a chair, a chaise lounge, a rocking chair for a drawing

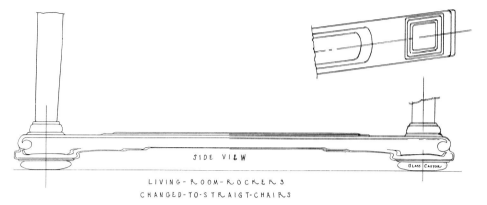

SIDE VIEW

GLASS CASTOR

LIVING-ROOM-ROCKERS
CHANGED-TO-STRAIGT-CHAIRS

Henry's concept to convert the living room rocking chairs designed for the Culbertson sisters to straight chairs for Mrs. Prentiss, 1925.

The sensitivity of the shaping of the wood stretcher of this design and the draftsmanship of this drawing by Henry are testimony of his multifaceted talents.

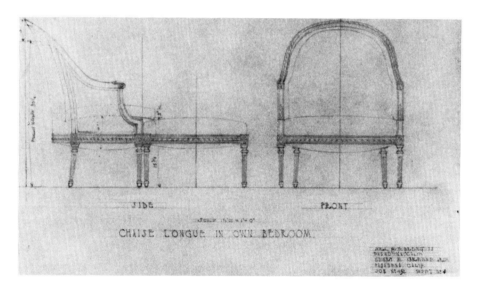

SIDE   FRONT

CHAISE LONGUE IN OWN BEDROOM

Sketch of proposed bedroom chaise lounge for Mrs. Francis F. Prentiss, 1925. Drawing courtesy Avery Architectural Library.

Tradition returns in the style of this chair; yet Henry has drawn the spirit of the wood detailing from the earlier furniture in the house designed by Charles.

Left:
Stained glass window, Kate A. Kelley house, Los Angeles, 1924.
Marvin Rand photograph.

143

room, and designs to change the living room rockers to straight chairs. I assume that these rockers had been part of Charles' earlier designs, although there is no documentation for this assumption. While the details for the bedroom chair and the chaise lounge seemed inspired by historical furniture styles, the designs for the rocking chair for the drawing room bridged the traditional style with the furniture which Charles had designed earlier for Mrs. Prentiss. Henry's studies for converting the living room rockers to straight chairs clearly indicated his ability to handle the sensitive scale and movement of lines so often

identified solely with Charles Greene's designs. The drawing for the new base of the rocker was so sensitively proportioned, and the curvature of the line and the forming of the wood so gracefully handled that it might have come from the hands of Charles, although the quality of the drawing, the pencil work, and the lettering identify it definitely as the work of Henry Greene.

Another project was the design of an executive office for the Pacific Southwest Trust and Savings Bank in Pasadena in 1926. Apparently Henry was engaged to develop the office, complete with the wall paneling, furniture, and car-

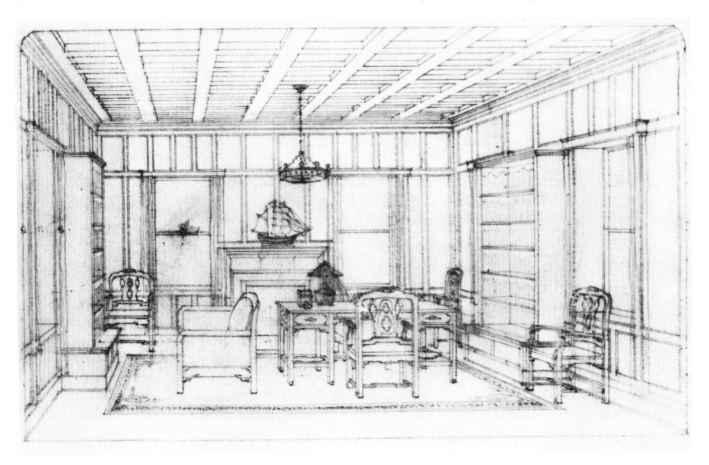

Sketch for project for an executive office, Pacific Southwest Trust and Savings Bank, Pasadena, 1926.
Drawing courtesy Avery Architectural Library.

Henry's furniture here appears related to designs for the elaborate bungalows of 1907-1911, to Charles' proposals for the D. L. James furniture, while also being influenced by oriental chair designs.

144

peting. This is the only indication that Henry was ever involved with carpet design. The furniture, however, was the most elaborate of Henry's designs. It departed from his normal linear austerity and became quite sculptural, much more like the furniture which Charles was designing for the ultimate bungalows between 1907 and 1910. There was an Oriental flavor to the desk, the chairs and the couch. Again, several schemes were carried no further than initial sketches, and apparently this too never went beyond the drawing boards. What is important, however, is the evidence of Henry's ability to adapt to differing situations and in so doing to handle his designs with a sensitivity for scale, proportion and line.

Following his second moving of the Jennie A. Reeve house (1904) in Long Beach, Dr. V. Ray Townsend turned again to Henry Greene in 1927 to resite the structure and fully develop the gardens including walks, fencing, gates and lighting. Townsend was so devoted to the design of the house that he commissioned further pieces of furniture which Henry designed to relate to and be used with the original furniture which was still in the house. Though there were differences in detail and subtleties of form representative of years of refinement and experience, Henry's new pieces had a contemporary quality which drew from the basic straightforward character more typical of the brothers' earliest furniture designs.

Small table for Dr. V. Ray Townsend, 1927.
One of several tables designed to complement Dr. Townsend's furniture which had been made for the Jennie A. Reeve house in 1904.

Living room table for Dr. V. Ray Townsend, 1927.
Marvin Rand photographs.

145

In 1929 Henry received one of his last and most important commissions, a residence in Porterville for Walter L. Richardson, to be built of adobe blocks made by the men on the ranch from materials from the soil. Here his concerns involved not only the design of the building, but the hardware (which was forged right on the site by the ranch hands) as well as some portions of the lighting fixtures. Most significant was the design of a walnut dining table in 1930. The purity of line and scale of proportion makes it one of the finest pieces of furniture ever designed by either of the brothers. If Henry Greene had designed no other

Detail of door knocker and hinges wrought and hammered by the ranch hands from Henry's designs, 1929.
Marvin Rand photograph.

piece of furniture than this, the Richardson dining table would be ample testimony to the creative talent which he brought to the design of furniture. Its structure is direct, it is softened by recognizable characteristics identifying it with earlier works of the firm, it is light in scale, and reaches to the future. Structurally inventive, Henry composed a system of drop-leaves at each end which when not in use folded under and were kept in place by the notch in the end of the stretchers used to support the leaves when lifted into place to extend each end of the table.

> Henry Greene gets credit for some straightforward solutions to table extension problems in the dining table from the Richardson house. Leaves folding beneath the table, out of the way, are no innovation, but two details deserve attention. His supporting sliders do double duty as notched holders for the tucked-under leaves. The ganged hinges are oriented to reveal only the round barrel when the leaf is folded under. The hinge barrels would obstruct the action of the sliders, unless one cleverly formed the sliders to drop down slightly to clear the hinge barrel as they pull out, then come up to provide support. A short notch cut in the top of the slider provides clearance during the last inch or so of its extension, when it comes up to full supporting level.[2]

When folded under, the rectangular flush wooden pegs which were a part of the wooden joinery were sufficient decoration in themselves. Beyond the simple, straightforward fastenings of the structure there is no applied decoration. The purity of scale, line, and the grain of the wood are sufficient.

It is ironic that about the same time that Henry was designing such a progressive piece of furniture he would write to Charles that he was concerned with the coldness and lack of beauty that he saw in the machine-made products of the modern age.[3] While he was a wood craftsman at heart, his sense of order and direct response to situations made him, more than Charles, an architect on the eve of the Modern Movement.

2. Marks, Alan. "Greene and Greene: A Study in Functional Design," *Fine Woodworking,* (September, 1978) p. 43-44.

3. Correspondence between Henry Greene and Charles' wife Alice, courtesy of Robert Judson Clark.

Dining table for the Walter L. Richardson house, 1930.
Marvin Rand photograph.

The engineering for the folding end leaves of this table
exhibits an inventive spirit which is only matched by the
simple elegance of the extraordinarily progressive design.

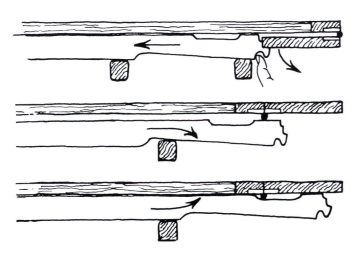

Detail of folded leaf of Richardson dining table.
Marvin Rand photograph.

Left:
Illustrations showing engineering concept behind folded
table leaf construction and support.
Drawing by Alan Marks, Courtesy *Fine Woodworking* magazine.

147

The close association that Charles and Henry had for many years might tend to make it difficult for many to determine the component parts of their combined efforts. Throughout the years, whether the work dealt with the architecture, interiors, furniture, or related designs, mutual respect and high regard made possible the production of some of the finest examples of the Arts and Crafts Movement in America. Apart from the architecture produced by the firm of Greene and Greene, there is little question that Charles Greene's genius created furniture and related designs which clearly represent high achievements of the Arts and Crafts Movement in the United States. At the same time, the product of that imagination would not have been possible in the quantity, quality and craftsmanship were it not for the close association and invaluable support of his brother Henry, the master craftsmen John and Peter Hall, Emil Lange, and the many fine artisans who worked so closely with Greene and Greene.

Wall lighting fixture for Richardson ranch house, 1929.
Marvin Rand photograph.

Entry door interior detail and hardware, Walter L. Richardson house, Porterville, 1929. Marvin Rand photograph.

In typical fashion Henry utilized the brusqueness of the plank and bolted construction to advantage—giving an appropriate rugged character and proper scale to blend with the bold adobe and stone structure of the ranchhouse.

EPILOG

I think C. Sumner Greene's work beautiful; among the best there is in this country. Like [Frank] Lloyd Wright the spell of Japan is on him, he feels the beauty and makes magic out of the horizontal line, but there is in his work more tenderness, more subtlety, more self effacement than in Wright's work. It is more refined and has more repose. Perhaps it loses in strength, perhaps it is California that speaks rather than Illinois, anyway as work it is, so far as the interiors go, more sympathetic to me....

He [C. Sumner Greene] took us to his workshops where they were making, without exception, the best and most characteristic furniture I have seen in this country. There were beautiful cabinets and chairs of walnut and lignum-vitae, exquisite dowling and pegging, and in all a supreme feeling for the material, quite up to the best of our English craftsmanship, Spooner, the Barnslys, Lutyens, Lethaby. I have not felt so at home in any workshop on this side of the Atlantic—(but we have forgotten the Atlantic, here it is the Pacific!). Here things were really alive—and the "Arts and Crafts" that all the others were screaming and hustling about, are here actually being produced by a young architect, this quiet, dreamy, nervous, tenacious little man, fighting single-handed until recently against tremendous odds.[4]

Charles Robert Ashbee — 1909
Chipping Campden, England

4. Excerpt courtesy Professor Robert W. Winter.

C. Sumner Greene and Henry Mather Greene photographed
on the rocky coastline below Carmel, circa 1950.
Cole Weston photograph.

Selected Bibliography

Caldwell, John Wallace. "A Graphic and Historical Inquiry into the Furniture of Charles and Henry Greene." M. A. Thesis, Department of Fine Arts, Los Angeles State College of Applied Arts and Sciences, Los Angeles, 1964.

Clark, Robert Judson (ed.) *The Arts and Crafts Movement in America 1876-1916.* Princeton: Princeton University Press, 1972.

Current, William R. and Karen. *Greene and Greene: Architects in the Residential Style.* Fort Worth: Amon Carter Museum, 1974.

(Greene, Charles Sumner). "Cordelia Culbertson Residence." *Pacific Coast Architect,* (March, 1914) pp. 10-11.

Hanks, David A. "The Arts and Crafts Movement in America, 1876-1916." *Antiques,* Vol. CIV, No. 2 , August 1973, p. 225.

Kazor, Virginia Ernst (ed.) *Greene and Greene: The Architecture and Related Designs of Charles Sumner Greene and Henry Mather Greene: 1894-1934.* Los Angeles: Los Angeles Municipal Arts Department and University of Southern California, 1977.

Makinson, Randell L. "Greene and Greene," Chapter III; McCoy, Esther, *Five California Architects.* New York: Reinhold, 1960.

_____ . "Greene and Greene: The Gamble House," The *Prairie School Review,* (Fourth Quarter, 1968), pp. 4-26.

_____ . "Special Report—Greene and Greene," with photography by Yasahiro Ishimoto. Osaka: Kakenaka Komutin Co., Ltd., *Approach,* (Spring, 1975), pp. 10-29, ff.

_____ . *Greene and Greene: Architecture As A Fine Art.* Salt Lake City: Peregrine Smith Inc., 1977.

Marks, Alan. "Greene and Greene: A Study in Functional Design." *Fine Woodworking.* (September, 1978) No. 12, pp. 40-45.

Roper, James H. "Greene & Greene," with photography by Marvin Rand. Little Rock: Bracy House, *American Preservation,* (April-May 1978), pp. 42-60.

Tracy, Berry B. (ed.) and Johnson, Marilynn. *19th Century America: Furniture And Other Decorative Arts,* New York: The Metroplitan Museum of Art, 1970.

White, C. H. "Teakwood for Interior Decoration," *Architect and Engineer,* (March, 1911), pp. 94-97.

Winter, Robert W. "American Sheaves from C.R.A." *Journal of the Society of Architectural Historians,* (December, 1971), pp. 317-322.

Index

Acknowledgements

In addition to those persons identified in the Preface, appreciation is extended to the following for their varying roles and contributions during the research for this book.

Eleanor Bush Allen
Richard and Wendy Anderson
Jerry Barclay
Mrs. B. E. Behrends
Beatrice Bush Bissell
Edward Blacker
Robert Blacker
George and Marilyn Brumder
Mr. and Mrs. John Caldwell
Leonard W. Collins
Marjorie Townsend Conley
William Cross

Harley and Jennie Culbert
Philip DeBolske
Donald and Marie Duffy
Paul Duffy
Flavia Flavin Edgren
Mrs. Guy L. Embree
Phillip J. Enquist
Mr. and Mrs. Conrad Escalante
Mr. and Mrs. George E. Farrand
Roy Flamm
Martin Flavin
Sean Flavin
Mrs. Mortimer Fleishhacker
Mortimer Fleishhacker, Jr.
Arthur Froelich
Fuller Theological Seminary
Mr. and Mrs. David G. Gamble

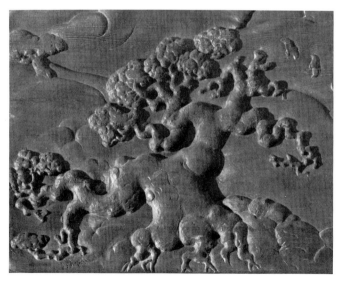

Mr. and Mrs. Edwin C. Gamble
Mrs. Sidney D. Gamble
Sidney D. Gamble
Constantine Gertmenian
Mrs. Penelope P. Gilde
Hank Gilpin
Mr. and Mrs. Douglas Goodan
Thomas Gould, Jr.
Isabelle Greene
Mr. and Mrs. Phillip Greene
Mr. and Mrs. Gary Hall
Nadine Hall
Dr. Robert Heebner
Max and Margery Hill
Mrs. Alice Hall Hodgkins
Huntington Library
Mr. and Mrs. Henry Hutchins

Dr. Hart and Patricia Isaacs
Mrs. Laura Ware Isham
Daniel and Lilith James
Mrs. John Bentz Jeffers
Eugene and Virginia Ernst Kazor
Rozene Kerry Lawrence
Mr. and Mrs. Robert Liefeldt
Richard Liu
Whitland Locke
Dr. C. Burke and Patricia Maino
Marie Marcus
James and Janeen Marrin
Margaret Meriwether
Elizabeth Gamble Messler
Dr. and Mrs. Joseph D. Messler
Kinzie and Irene Miller
Steven H. Milleron

160

Mrs. Mary C. Moore
Mr. and Mrs. Hartati Murdaya
Janice Nissen
Pacific Oaks College
Dr. Robert and Ruth Peck
Mr. and Mrs. David Pendell
Penny Penha
Mrs. Howard W. Porter
Daniel and Dorothy Power
Edvin and Margene Remund
James and Cynthia Richardson
William B. and Marjorie Richardson
Raoul and Patricia Savoie
Mary Gamble Sherr, Jr.
Julius Shulman
Sigma Phi Fraternity, Alpha Chapter
Scott Sinclair

Carleton and Betty Solloway
Mr. and Mrs. Frank Springer
Dr. Francis F. Spreitzer
Harlan and Margaret Gamble Swift
Philip and Rea Taylor
J. Eric and Elsa Thorsen
Mr. and Mrs. Arch Tuthill
Mr. and Mrs. Walter J. van Rossem
Karl W. Vancil
Dr. Robert Wark
Meg Wemple
Alexander and Edna Whittle
Mr. and Mrs. Harold Whittle
Mr. and Mrs. Orland Wilcox
Claus Willenberg
Richard H. and Elizabeth Townsend Winckler
Walter and Marilyn Hodgkins (Hall) Zaiss

Designed and produced by David L. Tilton
of Emmet L. Wemple and Associates,
Landscape Architects, Los Angeles
with the assistance of Laurie Burruss.